THE PRICE
OF THE
PAST

CLIFFORD G. GADDY

THE PRICE
OF THE
PAST

*Russia's Struggle
with the Legacy
of a
Militarized Economy*

BROOKINGS INSTITUTION PRESS
WASHINGTON, D.C.

Copyright © 1996
THE BROOKINGS INSTITUTION
1775 Massachusetts Avenue, N.W., Washington, D.C. 20036

All rights reserved

Library of Congress Cataloging-in-Publication Data

Gaddy, Clifford G.
  The price of the past: Russia's struggle with the legacy of a
militarized economy / Clifford G. Gaddy.
    p.   cm.
  Includes bibliographical references and index.
  ISBN 0-8157-3016-0
  1. Economic conversion—Russia (Federation). 2. Defense
industries—Russia (Federation). 3. Russia (Federation)—Economic
policy—1991–   . I. Title.
HC79.D4G33 1996
338.974—dc20   96-9966
                                                                          CIP

9 8 7 6 5 4 3 2 1

The paper used in this publication meets the minimum requirements of the
American National Standard for Information Services—Permanence of Paper for
Printed Library Materials, ANSI Z39.48-1984.

Typeset in Bembo

Composition by Harlowe Typography, Inc.
Cottage City, Maryland

Maps by Parrot Graphics
Stillwater, Minnesota

Printed by R. R. Donnelley and Sons Co.
Harrisonburg, Virginia

Foreword

Nothing causes the memory of old troubles to fade like the pressing immediacy of new ones. The evolution of popular consciousness during the monumental (and ongoing) Russian revolution is a case in point. In January 1992, in an effort to undo the damage caused by more than sixty years of misallocation of economic resources, Russia embarked on a program of radical market economic reform. But since then, public discussion has increasingly shifted from *why* it was deemed necessary to reform the economy—that is, from what was wrong with policy during those sixty years—to the perceived failures of the reform and the pain that Russians currently feel so acutely.

This book by Clifford Gaddy, a research associate in the Foreign Policy Studies program at Brookings, is an attempt to refocus attention on the link between current problems and past mistakes in one area of reform that is of vital concern not only to Russians but to the entire world: demilitarization of the Russian economy. Using statistics, findings from his own on-site observations, and basic economic reasoning, Gaddy shows how badly distorted the Soviet economy had become. This distortion was the result of a policy that subordinated the entire economy of the former Soviet Union to the overarching goal of competing militarily with an adversary that, in economic terms, was several times its size. He stresses that under the old Soviet system these distortions were not and could not be fully realized by either policymakers or the public. It is the continuing failure to completely understand the real price of the past Soviet policy of hypermilitarization, Gaddy argues, that makes it so easy for many in Russia today to talk about reversing some of the reform measures and restoring the status of defense industry.

Gaddy concludes that, regardless of its political future, Russia cannot escape the legacy of its Soviet-era hypermilitarization. How it deals with that legacy will be critical. Any attempt to ignore the costs of past mistakes—or worse, to consciously conceal them—will merely perpetuate their consequences and allow them to eat away even more at the heart of the Russian economy at precisely the point when Russia most needs to marshal all its resources to advance the welfare of its citizens.

The Brookings Institution gratefully acknowledges the financial support provided for this project by the John D. and Catherine T. MacArthur Foundation and the Carnegie Corporation of New York. Research related to the study was also conducted under projects sponsored by the National Council for Soviet and East European Research (NCSEER) and the Tokyo Club Foundation for Global Studies.

The views expressed in this book are solely those of the author and should not be ascribed to organizations whose assistance is acknowledged, or to the trustees, officers, or other staff members of the Brookings Institution.

MICHAEL H. ARMACOST
President

May 1996
Washington, D.C.

Acknowledgments

As this book makes clear, the topic of Russian defense industry and militarization is one replete with spurious data, false descriptions, unreliable interpretation, and outright mythology. To the extent that I have been able to overcome the limitations of information and analysis, I am indebted to many people—both those who assisted me in obtaining information (either directly, by providing data, or indirectly, by affording access to people and places in Russia) and those who helped interpret that information.

Hard statistics in particular have been and remain a precious commodity. Separately and independently, Andrew Aldrin, Michael Bradshaw, and David Colton provided me with unique sets of data. These turned out to be critical for my ability to form a statistical picture of Russia's defense industry, thereby allowing me to draw my own conclusions about its size, location, and impact on the rest of the economy. Those data on defense industry were complemented by many other types of statistical information about Russian regions and cities from various sources. Vladimir Treml was particularly generous in sharing statistics not otherwise available. I also would like to thank Misha Belkindas and Timothy Heleniak for their assistance.

In Russia, I obtained important information about the local economy in defense-industry regions from various government officials in many cities. I am especially grateful to the staff of the local statistics offices and employment centers in Perm, Chelyabinsk, and Izhevsk. In each of these places, there were individuals who considered my research important enough to merit going out of their way to give me statistics that ordinarily never make it to Moscow, much less to the West. I appreciate both their effort and their data, but I also value the opportunity I had to meet with them as fellow scholars, more than as bureaucrats.

Over a period of several years, research on this book has taken me to many enterprises, institutes, and government offices in several cities in Russia. Unfortunately, space does not permit me to mention most of the people whom I met. But I would like to expressly thank those individuals and institutions who officially hosted me and who provided accommodations and access. These included:

—In Moscow, the Institute of Economic Forecasting and its deputy director, Viktor Ivanter; and Anatoly Arkhipov, scientific secretary of the Institute of Economics.

—In Perm, the Perm Scientific Research Technological Institute (PNITI), Aleksandr Malafeyev, director of the institute, and Vadim Postanogov, its scientific secretary.

—In Chelyabinsk, Governor Vadim Solov"yev, Chelyabinsk City Mayor Vyacheslav Tarasov, and former city council members Sergei Mukharkin and Anatoly Grashchenkov.

—In Saratov, the enterprises of Tantal and SEPO and their respective general directors, Georgy Umnov and Valentin Pavlyukov.

—In Izhevsk, Jerald Cohn and his associates, Valery Shevtsov and Gregory Sundstrom, as well as directors Igor Valyakhmetov and Sergei Fomichev.

I would also like to thank the Kostroma Agricultural Academy for repeated opportunities to use the academy as a base for research into a region and a part of Russian society that, although almost totally lacking in defense industry, may have been one that was most adversely affected by the militarization of the economy. The first vice-chancellor of the academy, Anatoly Volkov, and Professor Eduard Lozhkin offered their own penetrating insights of developments in their country, both past and present. They also introduced me to many others who worked in agriculture, business, and local government.

Inside Russia, the person who has played the most important role for me in this project has been Anatoly Gur"yev. As the deputy mayor of Perm for economic affairs, he generously hosted me on numerous occasions. He also spared no effort in giving me the fullest and, I believe, the most objective picture possible on the problems and Perm's potential as it grapples with the legacy of having been one of the most heavily militarized large cities in Russia. To Anatoly, and all the members of his extended family in both Perm and Chelyabinsk, thanks.

In nearly all of my trips to Russia, and no matter what the ultimate destination, I benefited from the hospitality and assistance of Svetlana Bakastova and Vyacheslav Nekrasov in Moscow.

On trips to Russian defense-industrial centers, I have had the privilege not only of making return visits at different times of the year, but also of traveling with various Western colleagues. My first trip to Chelyabinsk was with Jim Leitzel and Michael Alexeev. Our joint research into informal economic activity, new private business, and the labor market in the economic transition provided an important context for my research on defense enterprises. A visit to Saratov in the company of Kathryn Hendley introduced me to new aspects of that city. Both before and after that visit, her repeated and lengthy stays in Saratov and her unique work with the Saratov

Aviation Plant have made it possible for me to have nearly continuous updates on the situation in the city and that key defense enterprise. More important, Kathryn's unparalleled experience in Russian industrial enterprises, both defense and civilian, and her expertise on questions of corporate governance and the legal system offered a vital "reality check" for my own observations.

I am grateful to Laurent Murawiec for many thought-provoking observations during our visit to Perm in 1994. In particular, our discussions on the nature of the defense-industrial city stimulated me to much deeper work on that issue.

Two projects under the auspices of the U.S. National Academy of Sciences (NAS) not only gave me the opportunity to make my first contacts in two important defense-industry regions at an early stage of my research but also to share the wisdom and insights of the knowledgeable American businessmen and scholars who also participated in the projects. An NAS delegation to Perm in late 1991 headed by Major General William Burns opened important doors at a time when that formerly closed city was just opening up to foreign visitors. A second NAS project, chaired by G. William Miller, was centered in Saratov.

The research results of many Russian scholars have been of great importance. Three in particular deserve mention. Sergei Belanovsky offered me some of his firsthand interview material from defense enterprises back in the Soviet era. Leonid Kosals and Yevgeny Kuznetsov shared their insights and information on numerous occasions both in Russia and abroad.

Outside Russia, conferences and workshops sponsored by the International Institute for Applied Systems Analysis (IIASA) in Vienna, the RAND Corporation, and Stanford University's Center for International Security and Arms Control (CISAC) provided welcome opportunities to interact with government officials and directors of Russian enterprises and research institutes and Western and Russian scholars.

Michael O'Hanlon, Jim Leitzel, Kevin O'Prey, Jerry Paner, Gertrude Schroeder, John Steinbruner, Vladimir Treml, and an anonymous reviewer read all or parts of drafts of this work. All of these people offered valuable and insightful critiques, comments, and suggestions. To the extent that I was able to follow their recommendations, the result has been a better book. To the extent that I could not, I apologize.

I am especially indebted to John Steinbruner for comments and constant encouragement for this project, not only on the topic in general but also for my particular approach to it.

Much of the information and the arguments presented here were presented in more academic form to students of the course I taught for three semesters at Georgetown University's Department of Economics and the

Center for Eurasian, Russian and East European Studies (CERES). My thanks to the CERES director, Harley Balzer, for support in developing a course on this topic.

During his time at Brookings and after, Kevin O'Prey collegially shared his own data, information, and insights, for all of which I am grateful. Most important, he was always willing to listen to and critique an argument or a theory about why things were as they seemed to be. Having his expertise readily available to me has been invaluable.

Finally, I would like to offer a special thanks to Kerstin Gaddy for her great support and patience during research that often took me away from home for weeks at a time, and for her detailed, insightful, and encouraging comments on the written results.

Completion of this study depended crucially on the contributions of many Brookings staff members, but most of all on the work of Melanie Allen, my research assistant. In addition to being responsible for sifting through the many and varied sources of written information relevant to this topic, she also developed, maintained, and managed the statistical database that incorporated data from many disparate sources, and she performed the statistical analyses used in the book. Melanie also prepared the glossary of Russian terms and the "Who's Who" directory. She supervised the work of interns, including Patricia Steffy, Alison Ney, Maureen Hanlon, Rene Brun, Tad Johnson, and Mary Szczesniak, whose contributions are also gratefully acknowledged.

The final manuscript was ably and patiently edited by Stephanie Selice and its factual content verified by Andrew Solomon and Patrick McDonald. A special thanks to Andrew Solomon for shepherding the manuscript through all the various phases of preparation.

Administrative assistance was provided at various times by Caroline Pecquet, Elisa Barsoum, Stacey Seaman, and Pat Fowlkes.

All of these individuals have my thanks for their contributions to this book. Few will agree with everything that I have written. None bear any responsibility for what they, or others, may consider errors and misjudgments.

Clifford Gaddy

Contents

Figures

Chapter 1

Shedding the Burden

F or nearly sixty years, the Soviet Union had the most militarized large economy the world has ever seen. By all quantitative measures—the volume of arms produced and the physical and human dimensions of the industrial apparatus used to produce them—the Soviet military-industrial establishment was unmatched. But militarization was more than merely a question of the size of one particular sector of the economy. It was a process that affected the very nature of the system in both its political and economic dimensions.

It is hard to imagine that the Soviet system could have persisted politically for as long as it did without the element of militarization. Continual references to a military threat from without, intensified immensely by the campaigns of glorification of sacrifice and patriotism surrounding the victory in World War II, played a major role in creating and perpetuating the climate of secrecy and control that was necessary to justify unquestioning acceptance of Communist rule. But it may have been in the economic sphere that militarization had its deepest effects. It helped legitimize some of the key features of the Soviet economic system. On the macroeconomic level, these included rigid centralized allocation of resources into priority sectors and economic isolation from the rest of the world. At the individual and household levels, militarization provided support for measures to restrict free choice in almost every aspect of people's personal lives—from where they lived and worked to what and how much they ate and wore.

All of this has now changed. Post-Soviet Russia has removed nearly all of the Communist era's restrictions on individuals. It is drastically reducing its military-industrial sector. In fact, by some quantitative measures, one could say that the country has already demilitarized. Russian arms factories today produce only a small fraction of the weapons they did five years ago, when they still formed part of the Soviet military-industrial complex. The number of people working on the military production lines has plummeted: Official Russian figures claim that two out of every three workers who were in weapons production in Russia in 1985 were no longer employed in arms manufacturing by 1995. Is militarization of the economy

1

therefore an issue of the past for Russia? Unfortunately, the answer is no. Apart from the question of the reliability of some statistics on current Russian arms production and employment—which will be examined later in this book—there is a more fundamental issue about Russia's economic demilitarization, and that is the price of the past. The cost that militarization imposed on the Russian economy represents one of the biggest continuing burdens that today's and tomorrow's Russia—regardless of the nature, extent, and speed of reform—will have to bear. One of the main purposes of this book is to try to uncover what those enduring costs of militarization are. Knowing how much of the burden carries forward to the present and future, and in what specific ways, is of vital importance to Russians as they make critical choices about future economic and social policy. I hope that such knowledge will also give those of us on the outside a better appreciation of the magnitude of the task that Russia is now undertaking—both what it has already accomplished and what lies ahead.

The Costs of Militarization

One of the most significant consequences of market reform in Russia has been to make the concept of cost explicit to every Russian citizen. Literally day by day, it is more obvious to people throughout society—whether producers or consumers, taxpayers or government bureaucrats—that every economic activity has costs as well as benefits.

The new awareness of cost has, however, been a mixed blessing for reform. On the one hand, when benefits have to be weighed against costs, society gains, because resources are being used more wisely. On the other hand, cost itself is something negative. And because it is only under market reform that the costs have become evident, many Russians blame the new economic system for having created those costs in the first place. That is, people frequently ignore the fact that many of the "new" costs were actually incurred under the old system, although they remained repressed at the time. This sort of misunderstanding is particularly widespread with respect to the defense burden. It is still difficult for many Russians to see that the apparent costs of demilitarization today actually result from the failure to account for the long-overdue costs of militarization of their economy in the past.

It is not surprising that it is so hard to recognize the extent of the lingering costs of militarization and the legacy they leave. As I stress throughout this book, under the political and economic system of the USSR, there was no way to accurately measure these costs. This is not to say that Soviet policymakers were unaware that the military had costs for the economy. On the contrary; throughout Soviet history, the issue of defense spending was at the heart of civilian-military relations. But it was never more than a vague debate in the sense of guns-versus-butter. More detailed discussions by Soviet leaders on the trade-offs between civilian and military spending or the burden imposed by the military on the economy as a whole were simply not possible.

The failure to measure the costs was due in part to secrecy and to the sanctity of military issues that prevailed in the Soviet Union. Because of the fundamental belief that it was immoral and unpatriotic to question the absolute priority of defense of the motherland, the very idea of calculating the costs of such defense was implicitly suspect. As a result, much of the data relating to defense industry were not even collected, and when they were, they were not shared with civilian planners and policymakers. The lower in the hierarchy of economic administration one went, the more acute the problem became. To take only one example, local government officials in the Soviet Union did not even know the true manpower situation in their own regions. Data on the labor force in large sectors of the defense industries were collected separately from those in the rest of the local economy. These data were reported not to the local officials, but to the Moscow officials responsible for control of the military-industrial complex. They were then added on to the aggregate labor figures for the region after the fact, but the data never figured in the local subtotals for industrial sectors (machine-building, chemicals, and the like) or for regions and cities.

When such key data are withheld, the ability of analysts and policymakers to know what is really happening in the economy is severely impaired. But a second and more fundamental reason for the failure to measure the costs of militarization in the Soviet Union was the very nature of the economic system. A competitive free-market system inevitably brings costs into the open. The plurality of agents with their individual rights over property (and their rights to acquire those property rights) and differing interests as to what should be done with the property makes cost more explicit. Whether they are buyers or sellers of resources, agents have to weigh the competing alternative uses of those resources. The competitive market ensures that there is a standard against which every economic activity is judged: the so-called opportunity cost, or the sacrifice of alternatives forgone when the activity is pursued. In such an economy, even military goods ultimately have to be subjected to that test. Of course, costs can and are concealed in market economies too. For a certain time, they may be actively repressed, or even simply ignored. But this cannot continue indefinitely, because the very activity of attempting to conceal costs is itself not without cost. In the case of the Soviet system, where there was no competitive market, people (including the leadership) had no standards against which they could compare and therefore no way to measure cost. This logic suggests that even a moderately marketized system could not have permitted the type and the degree of militarization that characterized the Soviet Union to persist for so long.

By the same token, the emergence of a market economy in post-Soviet Russia has been of monumental importance for the nation's defense sector. Today there is no doubt that the opportunity costs of defense spending are being taken into account in Russia. The country has demilitarized in unprecedented fashion—not simply because of the end of the cold war or because of attempts by democrats and market reformers to reduce the political weight of the defense-industrial complex. These have been important; but the main reason for Russia's demilitarization is that market prices have revealed that the nation cannot afford anything like the defense establishment it once had. In this sense, market reform has made the decision to demilitarize an easy one. A much more difficult task is that of dealing with the costs of the past. If market prices indicate that today's Russia cannot afford the defense burden it once bore, this implies that, in an important sense, yesterday's Soviet Russia could also ill afford that burden. To the extent that it had appeared able to, this must have been because other significant economic needs were being ignored. These neglected needs are a major part of the debt to the past that today's Russia has inherited.

The Elusive Peace Dividend

To speak at all of the costs of demilitarization may seem ironic. Things were supposed to turn out quite differently. In the early days of the post–cold war period, it was common in both East and West to hear the term *peace dividend*. The idea was that the big cuts in defense spending that were now possible would bring a bonus to the economy, because the resources—human and physical—that had been used to produce arms could instead be used to produce civilian goods. The size of the peace dividend could be calculated fairly precisely: one could simply add the amount of reduced defense spending to the overall total of nondefense goods and services in the economy. It was as if a large "defense tax" had been levied on the economy, and that tax had then been repealed.

But this presents a highly simplified notion of the defense burden. If it is one that ever had any relevance to an economy such as America's, it has little at all to Russia's economy. Because the Russian economy had been militarized without regard to cost, the effect was fundamentally different. In no country is militarization merely a straight levy on the aggregate amount of goods and services produced by the national economy. Obviously, if something is being extracted from the "normal," nondefense economy, it is not tanks and missiles; and, of course, they cannot be returned to it. But what is being extracted? Is it what is used to make the tanks and missiles—steel, rubber, copper, aluminum, the labor of welders, machinists, engineers, and scientists? Are they what can be returned to the civilian economy? What, precisely, would they then be used for? What if the size and structure of the civilian economy itself had been distorted by the defense build-up?

These questions are all relevant to the Russian economy today. Russia was militarized as a command economy; it is being demilitarized as a market economy. Because the process of marketization still has far to go, no one knows yet what will be "normal" for the Russian economy. Consequently, it is not at all clear how many, not to mention which, of all the resources being released in the process of demilitarization have a "normal" use. Take the example of a basic commodity such as steel, used in enormous quantities for military-industrial purposes. To produce that steel, ore deposits were mined and energy resources developed. Metallurgical engineers were trained, and geologists were educated. Cities were built, citizens induced to move there, farms set up to feed those people, and railroad track laid to bring goods and people in and out.

Even in a market economy, defense-industrial activity profoundly affects the structure of the economy. The increased demand for steel for use in defense production will affect price levels throughout the economy, causing firms and individuals to adjust their behavior in countless ways. The greater the size of the military sector, the more powerful the economic effects on the entire economy. And yet, to the extent that the process of procurement of defense goods is competitive and market prices are being paid for defense goods and services, the costs of military production are somehow being accounted for. Although the citizenry may hold and express different opinions on what the country needs for defense, it at least has a basis for knowing what the cost will be.

But in the Soviet system, everything was quite different. The production of huge amounts of steel and other commodities for military uses occurred under conditions in which it was neither possible nor permissible to think about cost. No one had tested whether the marshaling of human and physical resources to produce the steel made economic sense. No competing proposals for the use of steel were entertained. Steel production itself did not have to be compared to other economic activities. Many alternative uses of the resources that had gone into steel production were, in fact, ruled out altogether. No one examined whether the means expended to develop the steel mill could have been better employed to build a bank, a stock market, a shopping mall, or a housing development.

Moreover, eliminating alternatives from consideration at one economic level affected many other decisions at other levels, including those of ordinary citizens. The person who chose to become a metallurgical engineer or a foundry worker had never weighed his or her opportunities and preferences to become a stockbroker, bank clerk, or architect of single-family homes. As a result, the labor of metallurgical engineers and foundry workers was cheaper in the Union of Soviet Socialist Republics (USSR) than it otherwise would have been. This was not only because their wages were controlled but because people who otherwise might have preferred to be stockbrokers or bank officers or architects did not have those options. Similarly, many of the other inputs into the steel industry were artificially cheap because real choices could not be made. The same is true of a large share of everything that went into the defense-industrial complex. Today, the artificiality of much of the apparent wealth and resources embodied in that sector of the economy is being revealed precisely because costs—opportunity costs—are being acknowledged.

The "Conversion" Question

Finally, a few words on a term frequently associated with industrial demilitarization, "defense conversion"—that is, redirection of military production resources to nondefense ends. To what extent is conversion a serious alternative for Russian defense industry? The preceding discussion of demilitarization under market reform should suggest an answer.

If conversion is the simple substitution of civilian production for defense-industrial activity, Russia had its best chance of success during the Soviet era. A totalitarian, planned economy is ideally suited for conversion, just as it is ideally suited for wartime mobilization, and for the same reason: It can allocate resources at will, without regard for the free choices of the agents in the economy (that is, without regard for costs). But if conversion is not merely any reallocation of resources from military to nondefense uses but instead to ends that meet market criteria, then the situation is very different. A Communist Russia might have seemed able to reallocate resources with greater ease than today's Russia can. But, measured by the market, the economic results would likely have been quite negative.

Conversion by fiat would be a risky undertaking in any country, if only because its success is essentially dependent on the ability of government bureaucrats to accurately predict the behavior of the free market. In practice, it is often worse than that: The individuals responsible for devising ideas for conversion tend to give little consideration to the market at all. Typically, conversion programs are built on the premise that because the nation's current defense-industrial sector has a certain quantity of human and physical resources, configured in a particular manner, one necessarily starts there and asks, what else (besides arms) can all this be used for? But when choice of products is dictated primarily by available technology rather than by market demand, the result will likely be poor. Only by a huge stroke of luck will one of these configurations of resources and organization in a defense plant somewhere turn out to be close to optimal for producing a product for which there is demand. Although this may occasionally happen, in the overwhelming majority of cases conversion—at least as defined in this rather narrow sense—is not an efficient means of reallocation of the nation's resources.

For Russia, a "top-down" approach to conversion is made particularly complex by the immaturity of its market economy. The answer to the question of how to convert resources from military to civilian uses cannot be given without taking into account the market economy into which the resources are to be integrated. It is, after all, the market that will define what a resource is. But because the market itself is not developed in Russia, its verdict on what has value and what does not has yet to be delivered. For Russia, the first priority is not to preserve and protect the illusory value of assets embodied in its oversize defense-industrial sector, but to develop the market economy that gives those assets value.

In the end, even in Russia, market prices will be a powerful force to ensure that only that which is worth converting is converted. How much that is exactly is impossible to predict. But it will undoubtedly be only a small fraction of what many people perceive now to be the "resources" of the defense-industrial complex. Conversion, then, is likely to encompass only a minute part of what used to be the Russian military-industrial complex. The interesting question is what happens to the rest: the people, the cities, even the plants and the managers. Where will they be, who will they be, and what will they be doing? These are the questions this book is intended to help answer.

Outline of the Book

This book is divided into two parts that focus loosely on "the system" and "the people," respectively. The first part (through chapter 6) examines what the Soviet defense economy was and how it has become encompassed by the overall reform process since 1985. The discussion in chapter 2 defines what the object of investigation is: what exactly do we mean by the defense-industrial complex? How many people worked there, how many and how large were the enterprises, and where were they located? Chapter 3 summarizes the kind of economic thinking that helped produce, foster, and preserve the defense-industrial sector before 1985. Chapters 4 and 5 examine how the sector was affected by successive policy measures since then, first under Mikhail S. Gorbachev and then under Boris N.

Yeltsin. Chapter 6 looks more broadly at how the behavior of the defense industry was influenced by the general process of market reform.

My objective in the second part of the book (chapters 7 through 10) is to analyze how the behavior of people at the grass roots has helped shape the overall process of demilitarization in Russia. The workers of the Russian defense enterprises are the focus of attention in chapter 7. Chapter 8 describes the peculiar type of organization of industrial relations in the Soviet-style defense enterprise—the notion of a paternalistic enterprise. Beyond the enterprises, there are entire cities and regions that depend on the defense sector. They are the topic of chapter 9. Finally, the future of demilitarization is examined in chapter 10, with attention paid to three levels: the enterprises, the people, and the regions.

Chapter 2

Measuring the
Militarized Economy

How important was Russia's defense-industry sector to the economy and Russian society as a whole? The broader answer to this question is one of the themes of this book. It is developed further in later chapters as I examine the problems of the defense sector's adjustment to market economic reforms and reduced defense budgets. But there is also a narrower answer to the question. It is expressed, for instance, in a measurement such as the percentage of the nation's total economic activity—the amount of physical resources, the number of people—devoted to producing arms. Unfortunately, making such measurements turns out to be extremely complicated. Two features of the Soviet military complex identified in chapter 1 make it so: the extraordinary secrecy that surrounded anything and everything related to the Soviet defense sector, and the absence of market prices. In this chapter I investigate the difficulties of establishing how big the Russian military-industrial complex really was and present some estimates based on the best data available.

Throughout the Soviet period, the nation's leaders consistently denied that the economy was excessively militarized. During the cold war, any argument to the contrary could always be rejected with a simple and convenient response: Anyone who claimed that the Union of Soviet Socialist Republics (USSR) was devoting too many resources to defense—or who, by merely inquiring into facts about defense, could be suspected of making such a claim—was an enemy of the Soviet system and the state. With the new policy of *glasnost'*, or openness, that began in the latter half of the 1980s, Soviet economists and other specialists were permitted for the first time to openly discuss many issues relating to the defense sector that formerly had been strictly taboo. Such discussions were not easy, however. First, even when they had become legal, efforts to call into question the size of the nation's defense sector were still considered downright unpatriotic by many. Second, in contrast with other areas of Soviet society previously declared off-limits to public debate, militarization was not an area in which the facts were generally known but prevented from being made public. Here, the main issue was to obtain those facts. Although the pioneers of reform-era research into the topic showed remarkable boldness and persistence in their inquiries, for the most part the results were meager. In 1989, well into the age of openness, one leading Russian researcher on the defense industry lamented, "Although some progress has been noted in military and space *glasnost'*, the situation has changed very little with respect to facts about the [military-industrial complex]. As before, we know neither the number of employees at military enterprises, . . . nor their geographical distribution, nor the technological potential of individual enterprises, nor their production indices."[1]

In the beginning, not even budgetary data on defense were available. It was not until 1987 that Mikhail Gorbachev broached the idea of having the Soviet government prepare an "open" defense budget—that is, one comparable to those routinely published and debated in the West.[2] And even when Gorbachev's promise was fulfilled a couple of years later, this solved few problems, because with artificial pricing the budget offered little information about cost.[3] Soviet experts made various efforts to interpret and adjust for the scanty budgetary data and compare them to the U.S. defense budget.[4] But the longer they worked, the more apparent it became that the main problem was not that those who knew the correct information continued to conceal it, but rather that no one knew the truth. A Soviet investigator who had tried to tackle the issue concluded in frustration in 1991: "I suspect that the true size of our defense spending is something that not even the generals themselves know."[5]

Meanwhile, in the absence of true measures, representatives of the defense-industry lobby were free to throw around any figure they considered appropriate. The number they chose usually ended up quite close to what the United States said it was spending on its defense. To make things sound especially convincing, Soviet spokesmen even invoked the authority of the U.S. Central Intelligence Agency. The CIA, they claimed, estimated that Soviet defense spending was no more than 6 to 8 percent of the nation's gross national product (GNP)—about the same as for the United States in the mid-1980s.[6] (What was not mentioned was that this CIA estimate referred to Soviet spending in the early 1970s, and that even the estimate for those years had subsequently been revised to 15 to 17 percent of GNP.)[7]

Today there is much greater recognition inside Russia that the defense burden was considerably higher than anyone officially had admitted during the Communist era. In fact, as in many other instances where the taboos of Soviet society have been broken, the media and even some scholars have tried to attract attention to a previously underinvestigated phenomenon by sensationalizing it. In the case of defense spending, the result has been a series of ever-increasing estimates. However, a higher number is not necessarily a more accurate one. Both the methods used in various estimates and the reliability of those estimates vary widely. What is notable is how little substantial new information has been obtained about the defense-industrial complex, even after the collapse of the Soviet government and the accession to power of the democrats in the Yeltsin government.

The lack of information about the Soviet past may or may not change. Meanwhile, a more fundamental problem remains, one that cannot be solved through the passing of time. The USSR was not a market economy, and it therefore lacked the true measure of the cost of any economic activity: market prices. To understand the importance of such prices in the issue of defense cost, let us contrast the problem of ascertaining defense spending in a market economy and in the command economy of the Soviet Union.

The Key Role of Prices

In a market economy, when asking what the cost of defense is, the economist always goes back to the basic definition of opportunity cost: What is it that is not purchased or what are the investments that are not made when society spends on military goods instead? With any given amount now spent on defense—whether $10 million or $10 billion—what could have been bought in the civilian economy if the money had been spent there instead?

For instance, imagine an announcement in the United States that the cost of a new generation of jet fighters would be $50 billion. To the extent that this statement has meaning, it is because we know what that $50 billion could otherwise be used for. It might be used by the government to purchase and deliver other goods and services (education, welfare, roads) to the citizenry. Alternatively, rather than using its tax revenues for such nondefense public goods, the government might choose to lower taxes and leave the money in the taxpayers' pockets to spend as they saw fit. In either case, we assume that the $50 billion spent on the defense project means $50 billion less for other public and private goods and services.

We take it for granted in a market economy such as that of the United States that an additional dollar spent on defense means removing a dollar's worth of resources from the civilian economy. This is not always true. Consider the case of labor power in a nation that has a conscript army. Expanding the armed forces by one soldier will require increasing defense spending by the amount of the cost incurred in keeping him or her in uniform: direct pay, plus the cost of food, housing, medical care, uniforms, training, and so on. But is that soldier's pay a measure of the value of labor power removed from the civilian economy? That is unlikely. Draftees in all countries with universal conscription tend to receive low pay even when in-kind benefits are included. If labor market conditions are relatively normal, the average draftee could expect to earn a considerably higher wage at a job in the civilian economy. In a competitive market, that civilian wage is also a measure of the person's real economic contribution. To the extent that the defense sector gets this individual for less than the market wage, the "defense dollar" is worth more than the "civilian dollar"—that is, defense takes away more from the civilian economy than it pays for. The reason for this, of course, is that draftees have no choice; they are forced to accept the below-market wage paid by the military. (In effect, an in-kind tax is being levied on those young people.)

Normally (that is, not in wartime), labor is the only major resource drafted into the service of national defense in this manner. But we can begin to see some of the difference between the United States and the Soviet Union in this regard by engaging in a thought experiment. Suppose in the previous example about the new U.S. aircraft project that the announcement had then added that the decision to build the planes would be accompanied by a new law mandating that American aluminum producers supply aluminum to the military aerospace industry at one-half the market price. The cost savings would be passed on to the government in the form of a lower purchase price for the aircraft. Calculated on the basis of such prices, the cost of the aircraft project to the government (to the "taxpayer") would clearly be lower than without the new aluminum price regulation. But it is equally clear that the apparent cost would not accurately reflect the cost of the project to the economy as a whole. Part of the cost is merely being hidden. It has been forcibly shifted onto the aluminum industry. As in the case of the draftees, defense prices and civilian prices differ, and the difference is a tax levied on one segment of the economy.[8]

In the Soviet Union, this sort of disparity between civilian and defense-industry prices applied not only to the labor conscripted into the armed forces and to aluminum, but to nearly all the resources supplied to the defense sector of the economy. The inputs purchased by arms manufacturing enterprises were often priced far below those a civilian enterprise would have had to pay. In fact, the inputs were not really "purchased" at all; they were allocated in administrative fashion. Prices were merely a bookkeeping convenience. It is this price problem that helped conceal the true size of Soviet defense spending. Only occasionally was the magnitude of the distortion reflected in official statements. A defense-industry official was once cited in the Soviet press as saying that when the USSR sold aircraft engines abroad, "We receive six or seven dollars for every ruble spent to produce [them]."[9] This was so far more than the ruble was deemed to be worth as to imply profit margins of hundreds or even thousands of percent.

Now, in principle, such unrealistically high profit margins might have been the result of some exorbitant sales prices (perhaps to captive customers in the Soviet empire). But it is more likely that the big differential was due to the artifically low prices of the goods and labor used to produce the planes. That is, prices were not set by supply and demand in a free and competitive market, but by the requirement that the defense establishment be allowed to "buy" equipment more cheaply than anyone else in the Soviet economy. This also meant that prices could be manipulated virtually any way the planners wanted to produce as low a budget as they liked.

Of course, it was not only in the Soviet defense sector that prices were arbitrarily set. The phenomenon of nonmarket, administered prices was a hallmark of the Soviet command economy. Both defense-sector prices and civilian prices were distorted—and, most importantly, distorted to different degrees. This means that any attempt to calculate a ratio of defense output to total output (that is, defense spending as a percentage of GNP) required two adjustments. First, a market price had to be calculated, or estimated, for defense goods. But second, the same had to be done for all the goods and services produced in the civilian sector as well.

Percent of Machine-Building

Although trying to impute market prices to goods not traded under market conditions would seem to be a near-impossible task, a group of Soviet specialists from the prestigious Institute of Economic Forecasting of the Academy of Sciences tried to do just that—at least in a limited part of the economy. They restricted themselves to one branch of industry, the so-called machine-building and metalworking (MBMW) sector.[10] They tried to convert all MBMW output, civilian and military, for one year (they chose 1988) to world prices. This was a monumental task. MBMW was the heart of Soviet heavy manufacturing, a production sector with tens of thousands of major products. Consequently, the calculations made by the Soviet analysts have to be considered a rough approximation at best.[11] But even if they are only approximately accurate, the results are astounding (figure 2-1).

Even the official Soviet statistics admitted that a very large share—30 percent—of MBMW output was in the form of arms. Only 20 percent was said to be consumer goods (cars, television sets, refrigerators, and the like), while the remaining 50 percent was so-called investment goods (*investitsionnaya tekhnika*, or what we would term capital or producers' goods). However, after they calculated what the value of all this would be in world prices, the Soviet specialists concluded that in fact no more than 5 to 6

FIGURE 2-1. *Defense Share of Soviet Machine-Building and Metalworking Output in Domestic and World Prices, 1988*

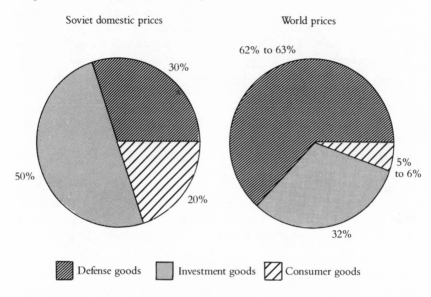

Source: Ozhegov and others, "Konversiya oboronnoy promyshlennosti i preobrazovaniye ekonomiki SSSR," p. 54.

percent of the MBMW sector's output was in the form of consumer goods and that investment goods accounted for only 32 percent. The remaining 62 to 63 percent of MBMW output was arms—direct military orders.[12]

In principle, the method employed by the team of researchers from the Institute of Economic Forecasting could be applied to the entire defense economy. The result would be a calculation of the value of military production as a percentage of all economic activity in the country. But to carry out this exercise, a world market price would have to be calculated for all the goods and services in the Soviet economy—an impossible task. The exercise with the MBMW sector appears to represent the realistic limit of this approach.[13]

How Many People?

If percentage of GNP is not the way to measure Soviet defense industry, what should be used to measure it? One common gauge of the size of economic units is the number of people who work there. Even in market economies, where firms or branches can also be compared by market-based measures such as total assets, sales, or revenue, the statistic that often says more than anything else about who is bigger is the number of employees.

There is no denying that employment, too, is an imperfect measuring tool. In strict economic terms it shares many of the same shortcomings as GNP used as a measurement. Labor is not homogeneous; people work at different types of jobs, and they differ in their levels of skills and productivity. This means that if we only add up numbers of employees, many simplifying assumptions are implicitly being made. Specifically, if we compare the number of defense-industry workers to the total labor force, we are assuming that the quality of labor—that is, the skills and education of the workers—is the same in civilian and military industry. In addition, it is assumed that the number of hours worked and the degree of intensity of the work are the same.

Despite these shortcomings, I believe that measuring Russia's defense industry by the number of people who work there is the most sensible way to proceed. This will be the only way I will try to judge the overall size and regional distribution of Russia's defense industry.

Who Is Considered a Defense-Industry Worker?

There are two basic approaches to defining whom exactly we mean when we speak of a "defense-industry employee." One is to look at what people do; the other is to ask where they work. The first approach might seem more straightforward. In essence, it asks, who makes weapons? But who exactly does? Is it only those people who perform the final assembly of tanks, aircraft, or artillery? Or should those who produce the components and materials used to make those weapons also be included? If so, how far upstream in the production chain does one go—all the way to the mining of ores and extraction of fuels to be used eventually in military plants? What services, especially technical and scientific services, should be included?

The second approach, that of asking where people work, also presents problems. It rests on a reliable definition of "defense plant." In the United States, the definition is a functional one: A defense company is any firm that at a given time is being paid to provide goods or services to the U.S. Department of Defense. In other words, the practice is to examine firms that receive defense contracts. For some companies, this suffices to establish their identity as defense companies: The Pentagon is really their only customer. But for the vast majority of defense contractors, there is more ambiguity. Each year the Pentagon awards prime contracts to more than 35,000 firms.[14] Far from all of them consider defense work to be their main line of business. Where should one draw the line?

The Soviet system provided a much clearer definition of a defense company, one that I use in turn as a basis for defining "defense employees." The Soviet defense-industrial establishment was administered by a ministerial bureaucracy headed by a government agency known as the Military-Industrial Commission (or the VPK, to use the Russian acronym). This administrative structure, which is outlined schematically in figure 2-2, provided for a clear-cut definition: A plant was either under the VPK or not. Can we not then simply count the persons employed in such plants? Assuming that the information is available, yes. But this would also raise new questions. Included among the VPK's "defense enterprises" were some that also produced civilian goods. What, then, to do about the men and women in those enterprises who produced refrigerators, television sets, or other nonmilitary goods? It is evident that any figure for the number of defense employees would need to be carefully qualified as to exactly what definition is being used. Unfortunately, Soviet (or now Russian) sources rarely make such nuances clear. As a result, many seemingly authoritative statements on Russian defense-industry employment are actually quite confusing.

Any number of examples could be cited, but the following situation was typical. In March 1992, the Russian Federation State Counselor for Conversion, Mikhail Malei, stated, "4.4 million people work directly in [the military-industrial complex]. Including subcontractors and suppliers [*smezhniki*], the total comes to 12 million." At virtually the same time, Malei's colleague Aleksei Yablokov, the State Counselor for Ecology and Health Policy, asserted that the number of defense-industry workers in Russia was 7.3 million to 16.4 million.[15] Although Malei and Yablokov may have had a logical explanation for why their figures differed, neither gave enough of an explanation of their figures to know.

In the following sections, I build an independent estimate of employment in Russia's defense-industrial complex and make clear which categories of workers are included.

Direct Data on Employment

I begin my estimation with a set of baseline figures derived from data in an unpublished document of the Soviet State Committee on Statistics (*Goskomstat*).[16] The figures represent a major component of the work force of the enterprises that were subordinate to the Military-Industrial Commission, or VPK. The precise category of employment they represent is something referred to in Soviet economic statistics as industrial production employees. I will explain the definition of this statistical category and discuss how it needs to be qualified to fit alternative notions of defense-

FIGURE 2-2. *Administration of the Soviet Defense Complex, Mid-1980s*

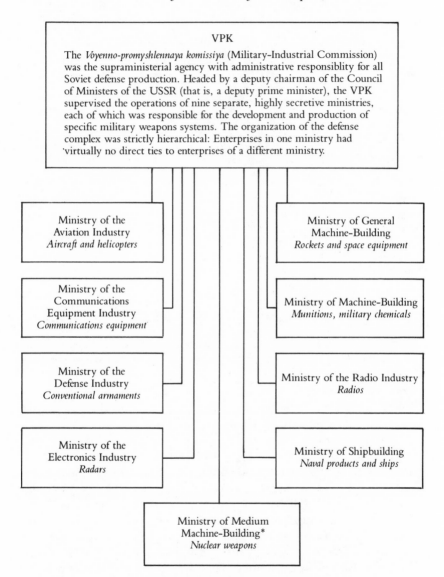

VPK

The *Voyenno-promyshlennaya komissiya* (Military-Industrial Commission) was the supraministerial agency with administrative responsiblity for all Soviet defense production. Headed by a deputy chairman of the Council of Ministers of the USSR (that is, a deputy prime minister), the VPK supervised the operations of nine separate, highly secretive ministries, each of which was responsible for the development and production of specific military weapons systems. The organization of the defense complex was strictly hierarchical: Enterprises in one ministry had virtually no direct ties to enterprises of a different ministry.

Ministry of the
Aviation Industry
Aircraft and helicopters

Ministry of General
Machine-Building
Rockets and space equipment

Ministry of the
Communications
Equipment Industry
Communications equipment

Ministry of Machine-Building
Munitions, military chemicals

Ministry of the
Defense Industry
Conventional armaments

Ministry of the Radio Industry
Radios

Ministry of the
Electronics Industry
Radars

Ministry of Shipbuilding
Naval products and ships

Ministry of Medium
Machine-Building*
Nuclear weapons

*Transferred in 1989 to the newly created Ministry for Atomic Power and Industry, which was given responsibility for both military and civilian applications of nuclear power.

Sources: Harriet Fast Scott and William F. Scott, *The Armed Forces of the USSR* (Boulder, Colo.: Westview Press, 1984), p. 314; Julian Cooper, *The Soviet Defence Industry: Conversion and Economic Reform* (Council on Foreign Relations Press, 1991), pp. 6–11.

TABLE 2-1. *Geographic Distribution of Industrial Employment in Enterprises of the Soviet Defense Complex, 1985*

Republic	Number of industrial employees in defense-complex enterprises	Republic's share of total USSR defense-complex employment (percent)	Republic's share of total USSR population (percent)
Russian	5,416,797	71.2	51.8
Ukrainian	1,327,088	17.4	18.4
Belarussian	245,044	3.2	3.6
Kazakh	128,079	1.7	5.7
Uzbek	109,424	1.4	6.5
Armenian	79,716	1.0	1.2
Lithuanian	60,344	0.8	1.3
Latvian	58,447	0.8	0.9
Kirgiz	46,921	0.6	1.4
Georgian	38,644	0.5	1.9
Azerbaijan	30,824	0.4	2.4
Moldovian	30,152	0.4	1.5
Tadzhik	19,209	0.3	1.6
Estonian	10,992	0.1	0.6
Turkmen	4,370	0.1	1.2
TOTAL USSR	7,606,051	100.0	100.0

Sources: Defense complex employment calculated from unpublished data from the USSR State Committee on Statistics (*Goskomstat*) as explained in note 1 of the appendix. Population data from *Narkhoz SSSR 1985*, p. 8.

industry employment. In the meantime, I will refer to this category of worker as "VPK industrial employees."

Two important points about these data should be noted. First, they are from the mid-1980s, when the Soviet defense industry was at its peak size in recent decades, and certainly before the downsizing that began later. Second, the data are disaggregated to a relatively fine level. They not only refer to the entire USSR but also give totals for each of the fifteen Soviet republics (now independent nations) and the various subunits within the republics. Later discussion in this chapter and elsewhere in the book makes extensive use of the intra-Russian regional data, but for now I will concentrate on the aggregate figures. Table 2-1 shows the USSR totals and the breakdown by Soviet republics. It also shows each republic's share of the total number of VPK industrial employees in the USSR and its share of the total USSR population.

Assuming for the moment that the data accurately reflect defense employment, table 2-1 suggests that the Soviet defense complex was disproportionately concentrated in Russia. Although Russia accounted for only slightly more than half of the total population of the USSR, its share of total Soviet VPK industrial employment was more than 70 percent.[17] The other two Slavic republics of the USSR, present-day Ukraine and Belarus, had VPK industrial employment that was much closer to their shares of the total Soviet population, whereas the rest of the republics had disproportionately small defense-industry shares. Kazakhstan and Uzbekistan stand out as especially "nonmilitarized" by this measure.

Social Sector Employment

It is time to clarify who is and who is not included among "industrial production employees" in table 2-1. For a Western firm, the category of industrial production employees (or PPP, in the Russian acronym) would be fairly comprehensive. It refers not only to production workers but also to white-collar employees, including management at all levels.[18] But in a Soviet-style enterprise, it misses many employees. Many of those employed by manufacturing and mining enterprises of all kinds (not just defense industry) were not classified statistically in the PPP category because they worked in the enterprises' various nonindustrial activities. Such activities could be quite extensive, ranging from farms and construction divisions to hospitals, vacation resorts, day-care centers, and much more.[19]

I estimate that the nonindustrial employees of a typical Soviet defense enterprise made up 25 percent of the total.[20] This means that in addition to the 5.4 million industrial employees in Russia, there would have been about 1.8 million nonindustrial employees of those same enterprises. In other words, total employment in Russia's VPK enterprises would be 5.4 million plus 1.8 million, or 7.2 million.

Scientists

Another type of defense sector employee not included in the PPP numbers in table 2-1 are the employees of the research and development arm of the defense complex. The Soviet VPK administered not only manufacturing enterprises but also two main types of research organizations: scientific research institutes [*nauchno-issledovatel'skiye instituty*, or *NIIs*] and design bureaus [*konstruktorskiye byuro*, or *KBs*]. Around 1.2 million scientists and other research personnel were employed in these institutes in the 1980s.[21]

Like the manufacturing plants, the R&D institutes also had extensive ancillary activities such as day-care centers, housing management, and the like. I estimate that 200,000 more employees of the institutes fell into this social-welfare category.[22]

TABLE 2-2. *Examples of Civilian Goods Produced by the Soviet Defense Complex, 1990*
Percent

Product	Share of USSR total produced by defense-complex enterprises
Sewing machines	100
Television sets	100
Radios	100
Videocassette recorders	100
Cameras	100
Chain saws	100
Tape recorders	98
Freezers	93
Vacuum cleaners	69
Washing machines	66
Motorcycles, mopeds	53
Bicycles	45
Refrigerators	40
Irons	25
Tractors	14
Automobiles	11
All nonfood consumer goods	26

Sources: Cooper, *The Soviet Defence Industry*, pp. 38–39; I. Morzharetto, "Chudo, kotoroye poka ne proizoshlo [The miracle that has yet to happen]," *Argumenty i fakti*, no. 41 (October 1990), p. 6; Kokoshin, "Defense Industry Conversion in the Russian Federation," p. 45.

Civilian Manufacturing in Defense Enterprises

I have now expanded the definition of who is a defense sector employee by estimating the numbers of the enterprises' social sector workers and staff of R&D institutes—two categories of defense complex employees that were *not* included in the PPP figures of table 2-1. But among the PPP of the defense enterprises there were also people who did not produce weapons. Alongside their primary role as arms producers, Soviet defense plants produced substantial amounts of civilian products. As for the shares of products produced, like everything else about defense industry, the data vary here as well. But sources concur that the defense sector produced all the civilian aircraft in the country, virtually all civilian ships and communications equipment, and up to 80 percent of the equipment used in other select sectors of the economy, such as medicine and the food industry. In all, defense plants reportedly produced one-quarter of all the (nonfood) manufactured consumer goods in the USSR in 1990.[23] Table 2-2 lists some major categories of consumer goods for which defense enterprises were responsible. What stands out is the remarkable role of the defense industry in producing nearly every major type of household appliance and consumer electronics.

Clearly, this civilian production activity occupied a large number of persons employed in Russia's defense plants. Russian sources put the figure as high as 50 percent of the manufacturing labor force in the defense enterprises in 1988.[24] This would imply that of the 5.4 million industrial production employees listed in table 2-1, only 2.7 million were engaged in the manufacture of military hardware and the other 2.7 million in the production of civilian goods.

Defense-Related Employment Outside the VPK

Finally, there is the problem alluded to earlier of people who worked for subcontractors and suppliers to defense enterprises whose own enterprises were not formally subordinated to the VPK. This category of indirect defense employment is the most difficult one to define, and only rough estimates can be made. In the U.S. economy, analysts believe that the indirect employment effects of defense spending are quite large. By one estimate, each job directly attributable to defense spending generates an additional 0.66 jobs.[25]

What sort of ratio of direct-to-indirect employment effects could be expected for the Soviet defense economy? On the one hand, we know that a large proportion of some key primary processing sectors of industry—especially nonferrous metallurgy, special steels, and chemicals—served defense industry almost exclusively. Many metallurgical and chemical plants and their workers were therefore producing for defense purposes, even if they were not formally classified as part of the defense complex. But would the number of such employees have been relatively more or less than in the United States?

It could be argued that because U.S. firms are less integrated vertically than Russian enterprises, the indirect effects are necessarily greater in the United States. That is, many more of the goods and services required in the production process must be brought in from outside contractors. Especially in the defense industry, it appears that the degree of integration in the Soviet Union was much higher. The tank industry can serve as an example. In both the United States and the Soviet Union, the industrial base required to produce a major weapons system such as a tank was an extensive network of production and service facilities that produced all kinds of components needed for making a tank. The number of subcontractors to a final tank assembly plant in either country was therefore large. Still, the difference is astounding. The Soviets' main battle tank, the T-80, contained materials, components, and parts supplied by some 700 plants throughout the Soviet Union. This sounds like a huge number until it is compared to the construction of a comparable tank in the United States. In the United States, making every Abrams main battle tank required the participation of no fewer than 18,000 firms![26]

The tank industry example strongly suggests that a coefficient of indirect versus direct effects of defense employment in the Soviet Union would be lower than the figure of 0.66 cited previously for the United States. The U.S. coefficients were rigorously generated by input-output techniques. Without the same sort of full-scale input-output analysis of the Russian economy, including data on defense industry, there would be no way to know what the proper coefficient for indirect employment effects would be for Russia. I am therefore limited to crude, back-of-the-envelope calculations. But to give a rough range, I will take the U.S. ratio as an upper bound, and for the lower bound assume that the indirect effects in Russia may be only half as great as in the United States (that is, a coefficient of 0.33). This would imply that the 5.4 million production workers in the defense-complex enterprises (direct employment) are matched by another 1.8 million to 3.6 million jobs (5.4 million times 0.33 and 0.66, respectively) generated indirectly.[27]

Figure 2-3 summarizes these calculations and estimations. How many defense employees were there? Again, if we are asking how many people worked to make weapons, the answer (allowing for the indirect effect) is roughly 6 million to 7 million. If we want to know how big the "VPK system" was—that is, how many people worked in all capacities in enterprises and research institutions supervised by the secret defense-industry ministries—the answer is 8.6 million. If we want the broadest definition of all—how many people's jobs depended directly or indirectly on the defense-industrial complex and its activity, whether military or civilian—the answer would be about 10 million to 12 million.

A Comparison with the United States

How do these totals compare with those for the United States? Given that the Russian data are such rough approximations, it might appear fruitless to attempt such a comparison. I will do so, but with careful qualifications.

U.S. agencies that publish authoritative estimates of defense employment share a definition of defense industry and the methods they use to estimate employment. Their broad definition of defense industries and workers encompasses prime contractors of the Department of Defense and their major subcontractors, as well as all other private sector suppliers of

FIGURE 2-3. *Estimated Defense Complex–Related Employment in Russia, Mid-1980s*

Millions of employees

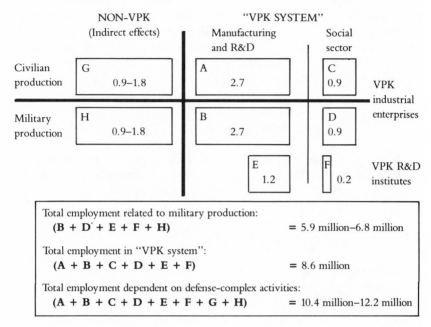

Total employment related to military production:
(B + D + E + F + H) = 5.9 million–6.8 million

Total employment in "VPK system":
(A + B + C + D + E + F) = 8.6 million

Total employment dependent on defense-complex activities:
(A + B + C + D + E + F + G + H) = 10.4 million–12.2 million

Source: Author's calculations; see p. 22.

goods and services to defense firms. Their modeling systems employ input-output techniques to estimate the indirect spending and employment effects of defense contracts.[28]

The Department of Defense's own estimates of what it terms "defense-related industry employment" (a category that does not include active-duty military personnel or civilian employees of the Department of Defense) show that at its peak in the latter half of the 1980s, U.S. defense production accounted for 3.3 million to 3.7 million jobs.[29] This translates into about 4 percent of the U.S. civilian labor force in the same period and can be compared with the various categories of defense complex employment derived for Russia and presented in figure 2-3.[30]

The Russian civilian labor force in the mid-1980s was about 68 million people.[31] The estimated 6 to 7 million Russians who worked in arms production translates into about 10 percent of the labor force—two and a half times the U.S. ratio. A different comparison, though, would be one that viewed the 3.3–3.7 million Americans in defense-related industry

(4 percent of the labor force) as the number of people whose jobs depended on the defense budget. In other words, we would consider defense employment more from the social point of view than the purely economic. In that sense, we would need to take the broadest definition of Russian defense-related employment cited here—all the people whose livelihoods depended on the defense complex and its activities, both military and civilian. In Russia, this meant 10–12 million people, or 15 to 18 percent of the labor force outside the armed forces. In terms of jobs, this implies that the defense complex was four times as important in Russia as in the United States.

Concentration and Distribution

The total number of employees in defense industry fails to reveal a critical dimension: How concentrated was this employment? In other words, how many defense enterprises were there? How big were they? Where were they located?

The Enterprises: How Many and How Big?

The military-industrial complex of the USSR comprised more than 1,100 industrial enterprises and around 920 R&D institutes and design bureaus. About 900 of the manufacturing plants and 800 of the research facilities were in Russia.[32] From the results of the previous section on industrial employment in the sector, this implies that the average size of the Russian defense enterprise was extremely large: 6,000 industrial employees (the PPP) and as many as 8,000 if nonindustrial personnel are included.[33] In contrast, the typical nondefense industrial enterprise in 1985 employed only around 700 to 800 persons.[34]

SIZE DISTRIBUTION.   Another way to think of the huge size of Russian defense enterprises is to focus not on the average-size ones but on the very biggest. In an earlier section I described the phenomenon of the highly integrated manufacture of tanks in the Soviet defense economy. The largest of the Soviet tank plants—not surprisingly, the largest tank plant in the world—was one with the innocent-sounding name of *Uralvagonzavod*, or the Urals Railway Car Factory, located in the city of Nizhny Tagil in the Urals region.[35] This gigantic facility employed more than 40,000 workers, or more than one-third of all the industrial workers in the city.[36]

In terms of sheer size, *Uralvagonzavod* was one of the biggest plants in the Russian defense economy, but it was not unique. A half-dozen enterprises were bigger. My own database lists more than two dozen with at least 25,000 employees.

TABLE 2-3. *Size Distribution of Defense-Complex and Other Industrial Enterprises in Russia, 1991*

		Size class (number of employees)					
	<200	201–500	501–1,000	1,001–5,000	5,001–10,000	10,000+	Total
Percentage of enterprises[a]							
Nondefense	66.2	16.2	8.2	7.7	1.1	0.6	100.0
Defense complex	0.3	1.6	3.9	49.8	29.3	16.1	100.0
Number of enterprises							
Nondefense	18,154	4,443	2,249	2,112	302	165	27,423
Defense complex[b]	2	10	23	299	170	97	600
TOTAL	18,156	4,453	2,272	2,411	472	262	28,023

[a]The percentage size distribution for both civilian and defense enterprises is from Tsentr ekonomicheskoy kon"yunktury i prognozirovaniya, *Rossiya—1992: Ekonomicheskaya kon"-yunktura* [Russia—1992: Economic situation], (Moscow, November 1992), table VI. 5, p. 114. The numbers do not include nonindustrial employees.

[b]The distribution for defense enterprises is said to be for "converting" defense enterprises. According to "Konversiya voyennogo proizvodstva [Conversion of defense production]," *Vestnik statistiki*, no. 12 (1992), p. 46, the number of such enterprises in 1992 was "more than 600." The total number of industrial enterprises in Russia in 1991 was 28,023. Goskomstat Rossii, *Narkhoz Rossiyskoy Federatsii 1992* (Moscow: Republic Information Publishing Center, 1992), p. 347. The number of enterprises in each size class was calculated by applying the percentages to the assumed total number of civilian and defense enterprises in Russia.

The defense enterprises not included in the data reported in the table tend to be in the smaller size classes. Adding them would alter the percentages in each size class but would not substantially change the number of large enterprises.

In 1992 an analytic unit attached to the Russian government released a set of information that complements this picture of large enterprises in the defense sector with data on the size distribution of defense and civilian enterprises (table 2-3).[37] One fact that is immediately apparent from table 2-3 is the large proportion of defense enterprises in the two largest size categories: More than one-third of all industrial enterprises in Russia with at least 5,000 employees were arms manufacturers.

These size distribution data, together with other information, permit further calculations that show the remarkable degree of concentration of employment in a small number of enterprises:[38]

—Virtually all of the people employed in the manufacturing arm of Russia's "VPK system" worked in only about 600 enterprises (out of Russia's mid-1980s total of more than 26,000 industrial entities).

—Some 60 to 70 percent of the defense labor force was concentrated in fewer than 300 enterprises. Ranging in size from 5,000 to more than

TABLE 2-4. *Comparison of Size Distribution of U.S. Mining and Manufacturing Establishments and Russian Industrial Enterprises, 1991*

	Number of establishments/enterprises by employment-size class				*Total number of industrial establishments/enterprises*
	< 250 employees	*250–999 employees*	*1,000–4,999 employees*	*5,000+ employees*	
United States	390,471	12,106	1,739	128	404,444
Russia	22,000[a]	2,500[a]	2,411	734	28,023
Total defense complex			299	267	730–900

Source: For U.S.: Bureau of the Census, *County Business Patterns, 1991* (Government Printing Office, February 1994), tables 1b and 1c. For Russia: Estimations in table 2-3 above.

[a]Approximations based on the estimates in table 2-3 of the "up to 200," "201–500", and "501–1,000" employment-size classes for Russia.

50,000 employees, these 300 enterprises directly employed 3.2 million to 3.6 million people—about one out of every six industrial employees in the country.

—Finally, the real core of the industry consisted of about 100 giant enterprises that averaged 18,000 to 20,000 industrial employees, with several thousand more in supporting functions.

COMPARISON WITH THE UNITED STATES.   Compared with the United States (and all other Western countries), Russia had an extraordinary number of giant production facilities but few small manufacturers (table 2-4).[39] Russia's industrial sector (mining and manufacturing) employs about the same number of people as that of the United States—roughly 20 million. But as table 2-4 shows, in 1991 the United States had roughly thirteen times as many mining and manufacturing firms as Russia, and seventeen times as many small firms (those with fewer than 250 employees).[40] Russia, on the other hand, had more than five times as many very large enterprises (those with more than 5,000 employees) as the United States. In 1991, there were only 128 U.S. mining and manufacturing establishments employing more than 5,000 workers at a single site. Russia's defense industry alone had more than twice that many (267). In matters of enterprise size, the United States simply has nothing to compare with the Russian defense sector. In the entire U.S. economy it is hard these days to find a single manufacturing establishment—civilian or defense—with as many as 10,000 employees.[41] Russia's defense sector had 150 or more.[42]

Finally, we can return to a comparison of average size. The comparison of mean number of employees in U.S. establishments, Russian civilian enterprises, and Russian defense enterprises makes the point. The average U.S. manufacturing establishment in 1991 had 49.2 employees.[43] The mean num-

TABLE 2-5. *Russian Regions with Heaviest Concentrations of Defense-Complex Employment, 1985*

			Indicator			
			Defense-complex employment as a share of			
	Industrial employment in defense-complex enterprises		Total industrial employment		Total population	
Rank	Region	Thousands	Region	%	Region	%
1	Sverdlovsk	350	Udmurtia	57.0	Udmurtia	10.7
2	St. Petersburg (City)	318	Kaluga	46.9	Vladimir	9.3
3	Moscow (City)	300	Mari-El	45.7	Kaluga	7.7
4	Nizhny Novgorod	257	Novosibirsk	45.3	Sverdlovsk	7.5
5	Moscow (Oblast)	225	Omsk	42.5	Tula	7.3
6	Perm	213	Voronezh	40.2	Nizhny Novgorod	7.0
7	Samara	212	Novgorod	39.2	Perm	7.0
8	Novosibirsk	172	Perm	37.8	Novgorod	6.8
9	Tatarstan	172	Vladimir	37.0	Mari-El	6.7
10	Udmurtia	168	Bryansk	36.0	Samara	6.6

Source: See appendix, Note 1.

ber of employees in a Russian civilian industrial enterprise in 1991 was 542 to 602 (depending on whether only industrial employees or total employees were counted).[44] Russian defense enterprises averaged 6,000 to 8,000 employees.

Regional Distribution of Defense Employment

The final exercise in this chapter is to use the data on VPK industrial employment to characterize the regional distribution of defense industry within Russia. Here, I take advantage of the fact that the data set described earlier presents totals of VPK industrial employees for Russia's subnational units, or oblasts.[45] By various measures of concentration, the differences among the oblasts were large. They range from no VPK industrial employees at all to 350,000; in relative terms, this category of defense-industry employment in the region's industrial labor force accounts for a range from zero to a high of 57 percent.

Table 2-5 shows the ten most defense-industry–dependent regions by three alternative measures: absolute number of VPK industrial employees; VPK industrial employment as a percentage of all industrial employment; and VPK industrial employment as a percentage of the population. Figure 2-4 shows how the absolute measure (total VPK industrial employment) and one of the relative measures (percentage of population) correlate. The scatterplot of figure 2-4 also provides a simple way of ranking the regions

FIGURE 2-4. *Russian Regions Ranked by Relative and Absolute Defense-Complex Employment*

Defense employment as percent of population

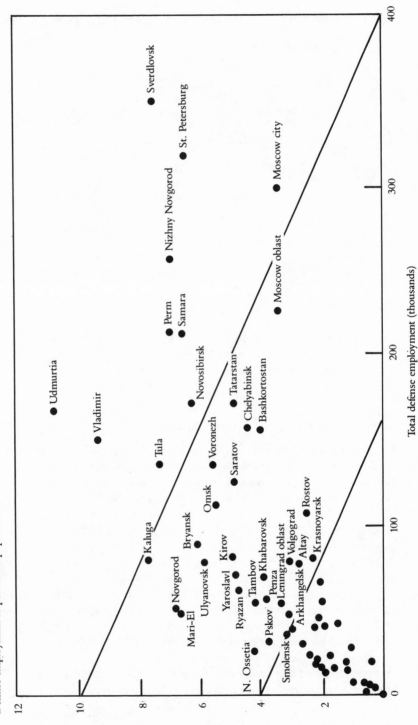

Total defense employment (thousands)

Source: See appendix, Note 1.

FIGURE 2-5A. *Defense-Industrial Regions in Western Russia*

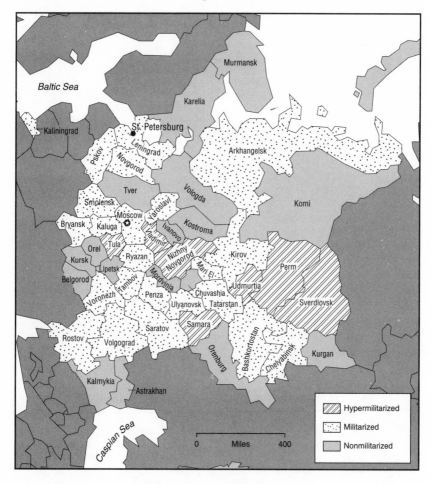

by a combination of the absolute and relative concentration measures. Somewhat arbitrarily, I have grouped the oblasts into three categories, as shown by the dotted lines: ten oblasts into the category of "hypermilitarized," twenty-seven more into "militarized," and the remaining thirty-six into "nonmilitarized."[46]

The maps in figures 2-5A and 2-5B show how this rough classification of the regions appears geographically. As the maps indicate, Russia's defense industry is concentrated in a belt that stretches from the western-most border eastward to western Siberia. Although central European Russia is a mixture of oblasts with and without defense industry, the territories in the Far North, the Caucasus, and the entire eastern half of the country (eastern Siberia and the Far East) are generally less militarized.

FIGURE 2-5B. *Russia's Defense-Industrial Regions**

*Based on the rankings in figure 2-4.

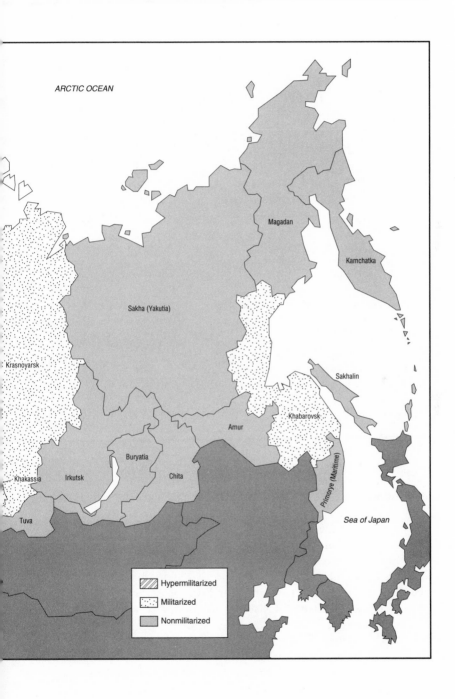

Chapter 3

The Logic of a Hypermilitarized Economy

F ew other nations in the twentieth century have been so dominated by wars—either fighting them or preparing to do so—as has Russia: from the war with Japan in 1905, to World War I, through the civil war following the Bolshevik takeover, to World War II (including its preludes with Japan and Finland in the 1930s) and finally the forty-year-long cold war.

From the time they seized power in 1917, the Bolshevik leaders had an explicit policy of gearing the economy to the needs of national defense. The fate of the new regime rested from the beginning on success in increasing military production. To defeat the anticommunist opposition militarily and consolidate their control over the country, the Bolsheviks had to build up a war industry to replace the large proportion of the military industry that had supplied the Tsarist army in World War I and that was either destroyed or in the hands of the anticommunist forces. Victory in the civil war temporarily relaxed the stress on military production. But within the 1920s, by the time of the launching of the first Five-Year Plan, military industry was again emphasized as an economic priority. This was reflected in the directives for drafting that first plan: "Taking into account the possibility of a military attack by the capitalist states on history's first proletarian state, it is necessary in drafting the Five-Year Plan to devote maximum attention to the most rapid development of those branches of the economy in general and of industry in particular on which falls the main role in the matter of ensuring defense and economic stability of the nation in wartime."[1]

The 1930s saw the forced build-up of a "second military-industrial base" in the regions of the Volga Valley, the Urals, and Siberia. With the German invasion of June 22, 1941, those projects were accelerated and new ones developed. In the post–World War II period, and for the next thirty years of its adversarial relationship with the United States, the Union of Soviet Socialist Republics (USSR) tried to compete militarily with an economy several times its size.

Viewed in a historical light, the militarization of the Soviet economy may appear to have been inevitable. Yet other nations, if perhaps not as frequently involved in conflicts as the Soviet Union, have passed in and out of wars without their economies' becoming so totally and lastingly dominated by the military sector as did the USSR. My purpose in this chapter is not to outline the actual historical process of why or even how the Soviet Union turned so much of its economy into an arsenal. Instead I examine the logic behind the particular way the policy of militarization of the Soviet economy was implemented. The fundamental question this brief excursion seeks to answer is: In the absence of a notion of cost and an open debate on choices based on weighing costs against benefits, what was the nature of the discussion in the Soviet Union about the military economy? That is, what did people say should be done, and how did they justify it?

The approach taken here is to look at this issue from the inside. Each of the historical phases that provided a context for the actual build-up of the Soviet military economy also helped shape a way of thinking about the economy and its relationship to the military. Particularly after World War II, reflections on that traumatic experience led to the evolution of an explicit theory of a war economy, advanced by several important Soviet military economists. Not everything they wrote or proposed was put into practice; they themselves were neither policymakers nor planners. But what is important is that these economists provide insight into the kind of thinking that to one extent or another was reflected in the actions and decisions of many others. The virtue of looking at what military economists wrote is the way in which they have distilled this logic and made it explicit.

The Role of Economics and Economists

In light of some of the observations made in chapter 1, the very idea of a "Soviet military economist" may seem to be an oxymoron. Without a notion of cost, how could there be a role for anyone who might balance costs against benefits (the role that, after all, falls to economists in the West)? Because national defense was a moral absolute, it could hardly be part of anyone's job description to object that there might have been costs or trade-offs involved—that is, that any resources devoted to defense would be unavailable for other uses. But what then was left for the "military economist" to do?

The most succinct answer to that question was offered in a book, *Strategy and Economics* [*Strategiya i ekonomika*], published in 1957.[2] Among other things, it explored the respective roles of the military strategist and the military economist. Strategists, it stated, are to give directions for future development of arms and needs—that is, to define the overall system and mix of weapons and the level of demand for them. The only task left to economists is to organize that arms production. (The Russian word is *nalazhivat'*, a verb that suggests the process of adjusting the settings on a lathe or other machine so that it can turn out the products for which it was designed.)

The author of that 1957 work was Andrei N. Lagovsky, at the time a colonel in the Soviet Army and a professor of military economics at the Soviet General Staff Academy. His was the first major work after World War II that tried to generalize that experience for the future development of the Soviet economy. The main argument in *Strategy and Economics* was that World War II had marked a profound change in the ancient truth that a nation's military potential derives from its economic strength. Whereas in earlier wars, through the nineteenth century, wars could be waged and won on the basis of the munitions and equipment produced and accumulated in peacetime, this was no longer the case. Armies in the midtwentieth century needed huge amounts of military hardware ready to be used from day one of a war *and* they needed ongoing production, at even higher levels than before, to replace losses during the war.

Lagovsky argued that the Soviet Union, though victorious in World War II, had paid a huge price for its failure to recognize these new laws. Completely apart from the fact that the USSR had been caught off guard by the Nazi attack in June 1941, earlier preparations for industrial location and the like had not been ideal. It was not until the middle of 1942—a full year after the invasion—that the Soviets had completed, as Lagovsky put it, "the conversion of the nation's economy to a war footing" [*perestroika ekonomiki strany na voyennyy lad*].[3] His conclusion was that the Soviet Union must never again be caught so economically ill-prepared for war.

Lagovsky made two important recommendations to achieve that goal. The first was to be more realistic in taking stock of the actual requirements of the huge material capabilities needed to fight the next war. Nations had consistently underestimated the sheer scale of those resources. The second urgent task was to structure the Soviet economy itself for mobilization. In effect, just as an army can pre-position certain hardware and equipment ready to use, the nation must also "pre-position" military production and have it ready to operate at full capacity as soon as possible.

Lagovsky believed it was an iron rule that the physical volume of resources needed for war grows exponentially over time. He cited the example of artillery. In the Austro-Prussian War of 1866, the Prussian army expended forty rounds per artillery piece. By the Franco-Prussian War of 1870–71, that figure was already 190 rounds. In the Russo-Japanese War of 1905, the average rate of consumption of ammunition was 720 rounds per piece. Less than ten years later, as World War I began, Russian strategists, at least somewhat aware of this trend, extrapolated from the 1905 experience to project a need for 1,000 rounds per gun. But their estimates fell far short; had their projections held, given the duration of the war, Russian forces would have used a total of 7 million artillery rounds. The actual figure turned out to be 55 million! Finally, in the most dramatic increase of all, by World War II the Soviet Army used an average of 17 million rounds *per month,* with the monthly figure in 1944–45 considerably higher than that average.[4]

To Lagovsky, the implication of trends like this—which he insisted applied to all areas—was that producing and stockpiling large quantities of arms and ammunition *before* the war was not enough (though that is important). Indeed, to build up the necessary stocks of all weapons systems and munitions would be impossible; most production would have to occur during the war itself. Therefore, even more important than stockpiling finished inventory was to have maximum *production capacity*—the ability to produce *during* the war. This is something that could be precisely calculated.

Lagovsky took combat aircraft as an example. If the nation's military strategy dictated an active combat force of 10,000 airplanes, and it was known that, owing to combat losses, the average life of a plane was only six months, industry had to be prepared to deliver 20,000 new aircraft per year simply to replace those destroyed in battle.[5] Add to that the replacement needs stemming from technical losses and obsolescence. Such a calculation could be carried backward to deduce production capacity requirements. For all this and for every other item in the inventory, military planners had to know the precise material and manpower requirements and see to it that they were guaranteed.[6]

Awareness of these requirements implied an approach on the part of "strategy"—the military leadership—to the nation's economy and to the field of economics that went beyond the passive one of simply ordering the requisite numbers of weapons and other military hardware. "The production of an artillery round," Lagovsky noted, "does not begin at the ammunition factory, but rather in the ore field, in the mine, and on the cotton field, and it then proceeds through the metallurgical, gunpowder, chemical, and many other factories."[7] The military therefore had to exert an active influence on these and other branches of the economy. The most direct way it could do that was to ensure that all sectors of industry vital to the conduct of war were not allowed to atrophy in peacetime.

The organs of strategic leadership must . . . know the demands of the country itself, its population, the nonmilitary sectors of industry, transportation, etc., so that, by placing orders for the armed forces, they can prevent a sharp decline in the capacity of, say, machine-building industry, rail mills, or railroad car repair factories. [Such a decline] would have a severe effect on renewal of the stock of machine-tools, on the restoration and repair of railways and rolling stock, and on the provision of the minimum needs of the population in wartime.[8]

For Lagovsky, the key was the timing of these steps. He repeatedly emphasized that they needed to be undertaken "already in peacetime." Lagovsky tried to get military people to understand the difference in timing for decisionmaking and action in the military and economic spheres. The military approach during war was characterized by flexibility and capability of rapid adjustment. *"But this is not how things happen in the economy* [emphasis added]. Production cannot react so rapidly to a change in demands by the armed forces with respect to supplies of materiel and armaments. To steer production onto a new path, to restructure [*perestroit'*] its program, even partially, and to introduce new technology—this is far from a simple matter and one which in any event requires a great deal of time."[9]

The only solution here, Lagovsky believed, was to plan in advance. He identified two important points in particular that related to the organization of the nation's peacetime economy. The first concerned the physical location of military production plants. They needed to be built far from what might become the front lines in the event of war, and deep enough into the country to defend against enemy aviation. Although Lagovsky admitted it would be ideal if economic and military interests could somehow be reconciled, it is "occasionally necessary to sacrifice some economic interests if they should come into conflict with strategic considerations."[10]

In addition to geographic dispersal of military manufacturing, the country also had to have multiple backup facilities producing major weapons systems and their components. "Under contemporary conditions of active impact of aviation on industry, it is impermissible to have one-of-a-kind plants [*zavody-unikumy*]. The same products, the same part or assembly must always be manufactured at several plants located in different economic regions. The duplication of production, even many times over, is absolutely essential."[11]

The second type of advance planning was to influence what was produced in the civilian economy, to ensure that no opportunity for military application was missed. To take one example, Lagovsky noted that modern armed forces make massive use of various types of heavy vehicles in earthmoving, road construction, transportation, and the like. Such equipment should be standardized. That is, one must ensure

> that they can be used both in the [civilian] economy and in the armed forces without significant design modifications. Strategy should always be abreast of the creation of new designs and improvements of existing technologies used in the [civilian] economy in order that each new invention and each new or improved design can be used for the needs of the armed forces. Strategy is also interested in ensuring that special designs of military technology—for instance, automobiles, tractors, light trucks, mobile electric power plants, and so on—can always be used in the [civilian] economy, and that the serial production of such vehicles can be established in the country already in peacetime.[12]

The Real Costs

Lagovsky's casual edict that all heavy vehicles used in the civilian economy should be built to military specifications, without hinting at what the cost of such a measure would be, was typical of his reasoning. But his demand was not new. Already in the 1920s, Soviet military thinkers had advocated the same approach. For instance, in an oft-quoted statement, the early Soviet military leader Mikhail Frunze stated, "In any new undertaking—economic, cultural, and so on—we must always ask ourselves: how do the results of this undertaking correspond to the goal of ensuring the defense of the country? Is it not possible, without detriment to peacetime requirements, to do this in such a way as to also ensure the attainment of specific military tasks?"[13] The idea sounds appealing, and it is economically rational—as long as the qualifying phrase, "without detriment to peacetime requirements," is taken seriously. If not, it becomes that bane of economists, the "free lunch": benefits without costs. Yet in all his writings, Lagovsky ignored the issue of what it would cost to keep a peacetime economy in a constant state of maximum readiness for war as he proposed. Those costs would of course be enormous.

One such immediate cost was the vast quantities of economic resources of all kinds that would need to be stockpiled and kept out of current production in readiness for instant use in wartime-scale production. Less obvious were the cost implications of Lagovsky's various recommendations regarding the structure of the economy. Three examples are worth noting: the duplication and geographical dispersal of production facilities; the near-total subordination of the civilian sectors of the economy to the military sectors; and the phenomenon of what the Soviets called "extensive development" that logically flowed from the Lagovskian concepts.

Mobilization Reserves

Lagovsky's calculation of the scale of Soviet aircraft production in the event of war not only dictated having the plant, equipment, and labor force ready to begin production immediately, but also called for massive stockpiling of materials.

The Soviet mobilization system provided for two types of strategic stockpiles. The first were the national stockpiles called the state strategic reserves (*gosudarstvennyye strategicheskiye rezervy*). In contrast with the national stockpiles in the United States, which contain only a severely limited number of strategic raw materials, the Soviet government also hoarded vast stocks of all sorts of finished goods needed for the survival of millions of people. These included not only minerals and oil products, but also food as well as rails, rolling stock, and the like.[14] The state strategic reserves were under central control and in centralized locations, and statistics were kept on their exact size and value.

But more critical to the implementation of rapid industrial mobilization were so-called mobilization stockpiles [*mobilizatsionnyye zapasy*], which ensured that each enterprise was supplied with the means to produce autonomously as soon as mobilization orders were given. Those stockpiles, which comprised a full complement of material inputs, including machinery and equipment, for each key weapons type, were usually located at the site of the plant that would use them. All the inputs were measured in physical units (such as numbers of products, tons, or meters) rather than rubles, because their sole purpose was to be used in the event of war to produce a specific number of weapons in a fixed period of time. In such a system, cost had absolutely no meaning.[15]

According to Vitaly Shlykov, a former insider in the Soviet defense establishment, the actual value of these mobilization stockpiles was never calculated. (Nor of course could there have been any accurate notion of how great was the cost—in terms of buildings, land, and personnel—of maintaining it all.) Shlykov's own claims regarding the size of the stockpiles are mind-boggling. He states that they were designed to provide enough production inputs to ensure that defense plants could operate at full-scale wartime production levels for four to six months (six months in the Asian part of the Soviet Union, four in the European part) even before the rest of the economy had geared up for a total mobilization effort. The implications can be seen in the example of tank production. The Soviet mobilization plan foresaw production of 30,000 main battle tanks a year. That implies that the stockpiles for the tank factories alone had enough materials for the production of at least 10,000 tanks. Presumably, a similar situation existed for every major weapons system in the Soviet arsenal, and thus at every plant producing those weapons.[16]

Geographical Location of Industry

On the surface, it might seem that one area in which the costs of Lagovsky's ideas would be most evident was the proposal to disperse the nation's defense industries to remote regions of the country, far away from existing population centers and from the front lines of a future war. "Normally," of course, major industries and population centers do not tend to get built in remote regions precisely because the expenses involved in doing so are so great. Transportation—not only for the initial construction of the industry, but also for sustaining it later—is more costly. Labor will not be cheap, either, because people have to be given an economic incentive to move to and remain in a region that remote.

But all of these were precisely the kinds of things that the Soviets believed underscored the advantage of their system over capitalism. They *could* build industries wherever they wanted, regardless of cost. For Lagovsky, it was not current or future costs that were a constraint, but only the problem that the Bolsheviks still had a way to go to overcome the industrial structure they had inherited from Tsarism. "In the process of construction of socialism, the ugly legacy of capitalist location of the productive forces has gradually been liquidated, although even to this day it has not been conclusively eliminated, since that takes a rather long time."[17]

And what, exactly, was this "ugly legacy"? It was that industry, especially heavy industry, was concentrated in old and established regions of the country. At the beginning of World War I, some two-thirds of all heavy industry—whether measured by employment or by output—in the USSR was concentrated in the central, northwestern, and southern parts of European Russia. This was exactly where Soviet defense enterprises should *not* be located, argued Lagovsky.[18] These locations were too close to the front lines of a future war. But the worst thing was why the ugly legacy had been passed down. "Industry developed spontaneously in those regions," he wrote, because it was there that "it was possible to obtain the quickest and biggest profits."[19]

Another desired feature of locations of industrial enterprises was their proximity to raw materials deposits. This was a double advantage in the Soviet Union, noted Lagovsky, because the deposits of raw materials were also in remote regions; he believed that gave them more value![20]

Part of the reason cost could be ignored in the Soviet system was that so much of the burden fell on individuals and households. In some cases, especially during the Stalinist era, outright coercion was used to induce people to move to remote areas. In the first phase, some cities were built with forced labor—an extreme cost borne by only one segment of the population. But later, such coercion was replaced with a complicated system of residence permits and careful rationing of housing, as well as purely economic incentives such as higher wages and better benefits.

Because this system did not allocate industry or labor naturally, some ongoing hidden cost had to be paid every year to maintain this distorted distribution of resources. This was especially needed to resist the powerful natural forces that would otherwise prevail—in short, to keep labor from reallocating itself.

Even as late as the 1980s, however, the Soviet Union continued to pursue and even aggravate this costly policy of dispersal of industry. Writing of the defense build-up of the 1980s, Andrei Kokoshin noted that increasing spending in those years "went not only toward the modernization and expansion of existing enterprises, but also toward the creation of new ones in, amongst other places, Siberia, the Transbaikal region, and the Far East, regions far from the potential zone of large-scale war in Europe." He added: "From the economic point of view, the construction of these enterprises was unjustified."[21] But, exactly as Lagovsky had said twenty-five years earlier, economics took second place to strategy.

Subordination of the Civilian Economy

Perhaps the biggest cost of all imposed by the conception of a war economy was the way in which the entire Soviet civilian economy was negatively affected by the requirement that it actively serve the militarization of the economy. Large sectors of the civilian economy were never allowed to develop (or indeed even exist) on their own terms. They were constantly being subjected to the dictates of the military economy. This happened on three different levels.

Most directly, the military planners demanded that a whole range of what would normally be considered civilian industrial products be designed and manufactured to military specifications. "Civilian production must absolutely be required to meet military standards with respect to strength, dimensions, speed of movement, and so on," emphasized Lagovsky.[22] Means of transportation of all kinds and communications networks come to mind immediately, he noted, but there are many less obvious ones. He encouraged the military to make a thorough inventory of the technologies existing in the civilian economy to see which would be useful to the military and then to insist on the necessary design modifications. The result was that a large number of products manufactured in the Soviet Union nominally for civilian use were in fact only "on loan" by their real owners, the military. These products were often heavily overengineered and far from ideally suitable for the civilian purpose intended. At the same time, they cost more to produce.

The Russian economist Viktor Belkin offered examples. Writing in 1992, he pointed out that even at that relatively late date, most of the trucks, tractors, and airplanes being turned out by Russian factories were still being manufactured according to military specifications. The most common type of truck seen on Soviet roads, for instance, was a four- to six-ton model—the size deemed most useful for the Soviet Army. But such trucks were not suited for most everyday civilian uses. They were too large for transporting small commercial loads inside urban areas and too small to be efficient for long hauls and large loads.

Similarly, the tractors shipped to Soviet farms were huge, heavy, and powerful—not so much because that was what the farm sector wanted, but because that would make the tractors usable for the military in wartime. Meanwhile, in their peacetime applications these behemoths not only wasted fuel but also compacted the soil, rendering it completely infertile. The excessive size and weight of Soviet-made passenger airliners—once again due in part to Soviet military requirements—made them extremely fuel-inefficient. Even the official Soviet airline, Aeroflot, calculated that it would be worth using scarce foreign currency to buy Western-built planes, because the fuel saving alone would be equal to up to twice the cost of the plane over its lifetime.[23]

Another way in which the civilian manufacturing sector served a dual-use capacity was by being structured so as to be capable of immediately switching over to military production in a mobilization. Many civilian manufacturing plants were intentionally not equipped with the specialized tools and machines best suited for the product they manufactured, but rather with so-called universal machines. These were machines that could be easily adapted, if need be, to produce a wide range of products (especially, of course, military goods). The problem was that although such machines could indeed do many different things, they did none of them as well as more specialized machines would have. The effect was to guarantee that the civilian products manufactured with these machines were inefficiently made and of poor quality. As Yevgeny Kuznetsov wrote: "Almost any strictly civilian enterprise (although to a widely varying degree) was affected by the constraints on product design and plant layout imposed by the requirements of the military. Civilian technologies were supposed to be designed in a way guaranteeing easy conversion to military manufacturing. Plants producing agricultural machinery were to be converted to the production of tanks (that is one of the reasons why Soviet tractors were of excessive weight and capacity) and other heavy military equipment."[24]

Civilian production facilities within the defense-industry complex itself were especially susceptible to this dual-use production demand. They
were the ones that would be expected to convert most quickly and easily
to defense production. As a result, their civilian production often suffered
most from the external demands of the plant's "main production."

Finally, a third way in which the concept of dual use negatively affected civilian industry was when military and civilian industry used identical components or materials. Once more, this usually meant that the
designs of the civilian products had to be modified. The operative mechanism here was the way products were separated into those destined for
the military and those for civilian industry. A peculiar and extremely costly
form of quality control was used. Large quantities of a product would be
produced. The military would choose those units that met their rigorous
standards, and the rest would be left over for the civilian sector. In some
cases, the same component might be passed down an entire chain: If the
defense sector rejected it, it was passed on to the "civilian producer goods"
sector. If rejected there, it would be considered for use in the consumer
goods sector. Then, if it was not deemed totally worthless, it might finally
end up as part of a toaster, television set, or the like used in a Soviet
household.

Often only a tiny percentage of the products would pass muster for
the military's quality control staff stationed in the plants. Hedrick Smith
quoted a worker in such a plant: "Military officers sit in each factory—in
the big factories, these are generals—and they operate with strict military
discipline. They are empowered to reject *brak* [junk or substandard items],
and they reject great quantities of *brak,* often at great expense. . . . I have
seen how they made transistors. They would make 100 and the military
representative would select only one or two. Some would be thrown out
as defective and the rest would go to the [civilian] market."[25]

An analogous process was going on in every plant that had to supply
products to the military directly or as a subcontractor. The system was
extremely costly to the economy as a whole, but nearly all the costs were
being absorbed everywhere in the economy *except* the military sector.
Although everyone tried to pass the cost on down the chain, no one could
do so fully. The manufacturers of consumer goods had to work with
substandard inputs, and the defective products that were shipped on to
the household sector represent a cost borne by individual Soviet citizens.
Even the original supplier of components incurred costs, especially if it
did not have some obvious channel to dispose of the output rejected by the
military.

Special hardened aluminum sheet designed for the "skins" of Soviet
military aircraft, for instance, was typically rejected if there was the slight-
est scratch on the metal. The air force officer in charge of quality control

could take delivery of the high-quality sheet, but what of the rejected aluminum? "That was another headache for me," the director of one such aluminum mill later told an American businessman. "Where was I to find someone who wanted defective military-grade aluminum sheet?"[26] And so, a substantial amount of his time was spent trying to unload the *brak*.

Ironically, in light of future discussions about conversion of military industry in the Soviet Union, the greatest extent of conversion of military products into civilian uses occurred during the heyday of the military-industrial complex in the decades before reform. It was just that this conversion was in the form of countless daily small instances in the system—and at huge expense in terms of efficiency.[27]

Civil Industry Manpower: Yet Another Residual

Because the civilian economy was forced to claim whatever components and raw materials were left over, it was said that it operated "on the residual principle" [*po ostatochnom printsipe*]. That principle applied to the use of Soviet labor power as well. In much the same way that the defense sector had first pick of the economy's physical resources, it also was allowed the best of the labor force. The central planners recognized that even minimal competition for labor from the civilian sector could not be tolerated. Their solution was a simple ban on hiring by civilian industries until the defense sector had its pick of the labor crop.

The director of a pharmaceuticals factory in Chelyabinsk described how for years his plans to expand employment had regularly been vetoed by the labor planning office in the city. Every time he submitted a list of the kinds of workers he needed, he was told that it would not be possible, since "Defense Plant X" or "Defense Plant Y" had also submitted a declaration that it needed personnel with those very qualifications. "They got the workers, and I didn't. The health industry ranked low in priority in those days," he remarked. "Our leaders obviously felt that what I like to call the 'antihealth industry' [military industry] was more important."[28]

This tracking of workers into a dual labor market began even before people left their schools and institutes. The higher education systems of many large Soviet cities dominated by defense industry were highly regulated. Not only was the choice of curricula heavily skewed toward defense-industry–oriented specializations to begin with, but the number of university graduates in any year who were permitted civilian careers was also limited. A faculty member of one such defense engineering school, the Izhevsk Mechanical Institute, described how the staff was forced to hold what was in effect a two-tier job fair for the graduating class each year. In the first round, only recruiters from the area's defense plants were allowed to attend. Only later could representatives of civilian industry come in to talk with those students who were left over.[29] The young person who "chose" a defense industry career in Izhevsk (or Sverdlovsk or Perm or Chelyabinsk) therefore did so only in a highly constrained and limited environment.

Finally, there was another way the military-industrial complex reached into the civilian sector to pick its labor, or at least the fruits of it. Whenever anything that might remotely be considered of military value was invented, developed, or discovered by civilian scientists, it was simply appropriated by the defense sector, often disappearing as if into a black hole. This phenomenon has been described as "a scientific-technological *barshchina*."[30] In old Russia, the *barshchina* was the labor service Russian peasants had to perform for their lords. In the same fashion, military industry was exacting its own special tax or a "labor-service duty" on the individual scientists.

Extensive Development

A final way in which the military economists' logic adversely affected the Soviet civilian economy was how it reinforced one of the worst systemic flaws of the Soviet economy: so-called extensive development. This was the practice of continuously expanding the scale of production by enlisting additional resources as opposed to using existing ones more efficiently. Even when new technologies were to be applied in the Soviet economy, it would not mean reallocating resources to them, but finding new ones to be brought into the production process. The real root of that problem was not the military economy but the lack of market prices. Without market prices to signal the changing relative values of all inputs, there was no incentive for healthy "recycling" of existing resources in other more efficient ways.

But the views of people like Lagovsky encouraged putting even more pressure on promoting extensive development. The goal of maximizing military production capacity in quantitative terms dictated a policy not of replacement of capacity through modernization, but of linear addition. The ultimate aim, after all, was to maximize the ability to produce more physical units, regardless of costs. This kind of thinking was partly responsible for the notion that old weapons systems should be kept; new ones would be produced, but the old ones would not be scrapped. In fact, not only were old weapons kept, but the plants and equipment that produced them were as well, and they continued to produce more. So, rather than retool existing plants to manufacture a new generation of jet fighters, an entire new factory might be built—and the old plants kept as well. The real victim here was the civilian economy. For even if the old defense plants were not as high a priority for labor and other inputs as the new one, they still ranked higher than most civilian industry in the demand for workers, materials, and capital equipment. In effect, then, the addition of every new generation of weapons to the Soviet arsenal meant that the search would be on for new resources to be brought in. And those resources would come mainly from the nonpriority sectors of the economy: civilian manufacturing, agriculture, and the household sector.[31]

A New Conception of Economic Flexibility

The discussion on military economics continued long after Lagovsky. His 1957 book even helped institutionalize the importance of the discipline. One of the specific recommendations he had made was for the establishment of a separate department [fakul'tet] of military economics at the General Staff Academy, where he taught. Such a department was in fact set up shortly after his book was written, with Lagovsky as its first chairman. His first academy classes included the generation of Soviet military leaders that would head the country's defense establishment in the late 1970s and early 1980s.

At the same time, new ideas were introduced. Lagovsky's own book was revised in a second edition (published in 1961) to reflect changes in military economic thinking dictated by the new era of nuclear missile warfare. A particularly important new idea was introduced in the late 1970s. A 1981 publication for the Soviet General Staff, *The Economic Foundations of the Military Power of the Socialist State [Ekonomicheskiye osnovy oboronnogo mogushchestva sotsialisticheskogo gosudarstva]*, written by Aleksandr I. Pozharov, summed it up.[32]

The basic notion that had governed Soviet military economic thinking until the 1980s was that mobilization capacity of the economy implied the ability to rapidly move from the peacetime state of the economy to a *known* end state—a war economy. That idea had straightforward implications: Because you know what you will need in war and what the economy will look like, go ahead and do as much as possible in advance. This could be accomplished in two ways: by producing in advance, and by creating the production potential that would allow for such production during wartime.

The latter point, ensuring the proper structure of the economy so as to make it easily mobilizable for war, meant finding the ideal structure for the economy—ideal in the sense of what would be most readily "restructured" to a war footing—and then putting that in place in peacetime. This made sense in a world of static or slowly developing technologies. But in an era of rapid technological shifts, it would be impossible to forecast one particular structure of the economy, and dangerous even to try. If there were a radical technological shift, having committed too many resources to the outmoded structure could then be a drawback rather than an advantage.

This was Pozharov's insight. He concurred with Lagovsky on the idea of preparing for rapid conversion to a war economy but challenged the idea that anyone can know what the *end state* would be: that is, "it should not be assumed that there exists some ideal structure of the economy" from the military point of view.[33] There are simply too many military products (several million, noted Pozharov), and their life cycle was too short (a mere five to seven years) to think about a fixed structure. The problem of the structure of the economy is therefore intimately connected to the problem of its *mobility*, or its ability to adapt to changing circumstances. "Thus, raising the mobility of the economy is also one of the ways of increasing the military economic potential."[34]

Read with historical hindsight, Pozharov's summation of this point is particularly ironic: "The greater the mobility of the economy, the more rapidly it can undergo restructuring"—or *perestroika*, to use the phrase traditionally employed by military economists in describing the conversion of a peacetime economy to one of a nation at war.[35]

Chapter 4

Perestroika *and* Defense Industry

B efore Mikhail Gorbachev came to power in the spring of
1985, there was little reason to think he would devote as
much attention to the defense-industrial sector of the Soviet economy as
he eventually did. Gorbachev had no background in industry, and certainly
none in the defense complex. But his concern for the general problems of
the Soviet economy inevitably drove him to examine defense industry more
closely.

Perhaps because of his previous unfamiliarity with it, over time Gorbachev seemed to become more fascinated with defense industry. He was
perplexed that one economic sector could accomplish so much that the rest
of the economy seemed incapable of replicating. In one sense, much of his
groping toward reform of the Soviet economy was based on an effort to
resolve that paradox—to discover the "secret" of defense industry and
apply it to the rest. But all that was to come; his immediate concern was
defense spending.

Gorbachev's position was straightforward: The defense budget was
too big. He was hardly the only person in the Union of Soviet Socialist
Republics (USSR) who knew the country was spending more on its military than it could afford. But most others justified such spending as a
necessary burden. Gorbachev challenged that conventional wisdom by saying that world leadership, and implicitly national security, did not come
entirely (or perhaps even primarily) from military power but from the
strength and dynamism of the national economy. What the Soviet Union
therefore needed was modernization of its economy, not more arms.

Of course, there were problems with cutting back on defense spending. One was the obvious political obstacle. There was no doubt that the
uniformed military and the military industry, and the political allies of
both, would vigorously oppose a simple reduction of defense spending.

But the other reason why Gorbachev was reluctant to just pare down
the military sector was somewhat more subtle. Simply reducing it might
mean losing the "secret" he searched for in the economic sphere. Much

47

better than to eliminate large chunks of defense industry would be to somehow use it: to learn from the defense sector, or harness it directly for civilian ends—he was not yet sure which. So while Gorbachev was reining in the military on the political side, his economic policy incorporated various schemes for co-opting defense industry into his program of economic renewal of the Soviet Union.

Initially, none of these proposals threatened the status of defense industry. In fact, most of them called for giving the defense sector *more* power and responsibility. This changed over time as a critically deteriorating economic situation forced the Soviet leadership to consider a more drastic approach. With military opposition to serious demilitarization removed, Gorbachev finally talked about redefining the mission of defense industry—plants would be retooled to produce civilian goods. Thus began a series of "conversion" programs that seemed endless in number, variety, and scope and that have continued to define the discussion on the future of defense enterprises to this day.

The Rest of the Reforms

Changes in the size and structure of the armed forces and in military-industrial policy were only one aspect of Gorbachev's policy changes that would profoundly affect defense industry. Other reforms initiated by him had a less direct but equally serious impact on the defense complex. Politically, the new policy of *glasnost'* permitted dissemination of information about and criticism of defense policy, including defense industry, which was unprecedented in the Soviet Union. In foreign policy and foreign economic policy, the breakup of the Soviet bloc's military alliance, the Warsaw Pact, and its trade organization, COMECON (Council for Mutual Economic Assistance), and a shift away from subsidization of former socialist trading partners and client states in the third world decimated the huge captive foreign market once enjoyed by Soviet arms manufacturers.

But the most significant change was the general trend toward removal of constraints on economic activity. By opening up vast new opportunities for both individuals and firms who had been vassals of defense industry, it fundamentally altered the industry itself. Few realized how important these constraints had been.

Meanwhile, defense industry saw many of its hidden advantages being eroded. Although it was not clear at first, what was actually happening was that the industry was on its way to becoming a "normal" sector of the Soviet economy. The problem was that no one in or out of defense industry knew what "normal" meant in the USSR after about 1988. At the same time, and in equally dramatic fashion, the rest of the economy was undergoing unprecedented changes. The trend toward decentralization and depoliticization that had begun with a package of reform measures in 1988 put the Soviet economy on a path toward change that was unalterable.

In this chapter and the next two, I examine these policy changes to create a background against which we can examine how people and institutions behaved in the reform period. It was the changes described here that they were reacting to. I begin by assessing how Gorbachev viewed the military economy and how he dealt with the Soviet military itself.

Gorbachev on the Military Economy

Gorbachev entered office with a focus on the economy, not military might. The calculation was simple. Whatever the Soviet Union gained by spending so much on its military was being threatened by its inability to make the rest of its economy work, especially in attempting to raise the living standards of its people. The failure to raise standards was not merely a domestic policy concern but also an issue fraught with foreign policy and even national security implications. World leadership no longer simply devolved from raw and static military power; it was economic strength that counted most. This was one of the lessons Gorbachev had learned from his patron, Yury Andropov. Both Andropov and Gorbachev were fond of quoting V. I. Lenin's aphorism: "Socialism will exert its main influence on the surrounding world through its economic policy."[1]

Gorbachev was even more explicit about the supremacy of economics over military power than Andropov had been. In a Communist Party Central Committee conference in May 1986, he said: "We are encircled not by invincible armies but by superior economies."[2] And yet he did not want to suggest the dilemma was one of mutually exclusive alternatives: Choose the defense economy *or* the civilian economy. Circumstances were more complicated than that. There was something good about the way the defense industry functioned; could it be applied to the rest of the economy?

Gorbachev asked this question many times and in various ways. A typical case was in public remarks he made in September 1985, when he spoke of the paradox that one sector of the Soviet economy could do so well while others could not: "I can understand the consumer who simply cannot grasp why we are able to produce spaceships and nuclear-powered vessels at the same time that we turn out defective household appliances, shoes, and clothing. This is hurting us not only materially, but morally and politically as well."[3]

The Military Reaction

The natural tendency of most people in the military-industrial complex was to be wary of this kind of talk. Military strategists, as we have seen, were happy to discuss the economy—provided they set the discussion agenda. But experience had taught them that too much talking about the economy by political leaders—especially if the gist was that the economy was not in good shape—could be dangerous. Sooner or later, it always seemed to degenerate to the level of choosing between guns or butter.

Most recently, Leonid Brezhnev had provoked such a debate in the mid-1970s when he announced that the prospect of new arms control agreements with the United States meant it would be possible to reduce defense expenditures.[4] Although that statement triggered unprecedentedly open opposition from the military, the conflict never became as serious as it might have, thanks in part to fortuitous external circumstances. The increase in world oil prices in 1973 gave the Soviet military (as well as the economy as a whole) extra breathing room. It was a boon to the military-industrial complex in two ways. First and most obviously, the USSR was itself an oil exporter, so the price increase meant more direct revenues for the country. This took the pressure off the defense sector from those who would have called for diversion of resources from military to civilian ends. A second benefit of the oil price increases to the defense-industrial complex was that the biggest paying customers for Soviet weapons abroad were also oil producers. In these years, Soviet arms exports soared. (In contrast with both earlier and later periods, many of these purchases were actually paid for in hard cash.)

As the 1970s drew to a close, however, the postponed debate about the affordability of defense resumed. Already by mid-decade, the growth rate of the Soviet economy was in a steady downward slide. Gorbachev himself dated the onset of the decline in Soviet economic performance to the early 1970s.[5] Although there is some disagreement among Western specialists on the extent and timing of the downturn, depending on the indicator used, the overall trend is clear. Figure 4-1, which is based directly on official Soviet statistics, shows that from 1974 to 1980 the rate of growth of industrial output dropped continuously, except in 1977.

The deterioration in national economic performance in the second half of the 1970s affected the daily lives of Russians profoundly, especially in the ever-worsening chronic shortages of consumer goods. Although citizens knew from their daily experience that all was not well, official statistics largely ignored or concealed the true extent of the crisis. Information published after the Soviet era, however, is more revealing. To take one example, data from 1993 show that in 1980 Russian industrial employees and their families were eating less meat per capita than they had in 1975

FIGURE 4-1. *Declining Rates of Growth of Soviet Industrial Output,
1970–80*

Percent increase from previous year

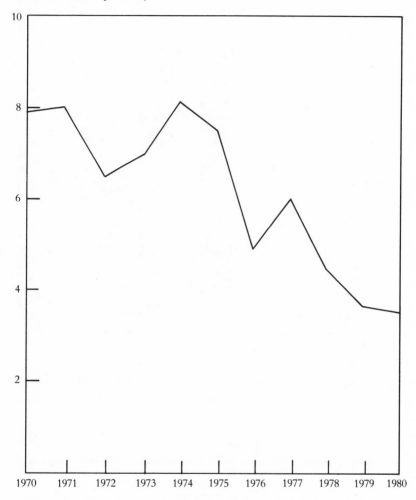

Sources: Calculated from data in Goskomstat SSSR, *Narodnoye khozyaystvo SSSR v 1970 g.
Statisticheskiy yezhegodnik* [The national economy of the USSR in 1970: Statistical yearbook]
(Moscow: Statistics, 1971), pp. 130–33 (hereafter *Narkhoz*); *Narkhoz SSSR* 1975, pp. 190–
91; *Narkhoz SSSR* 1980, pp. 122–23; *Narkhoz SSSR* 1985, pp. 92–93.

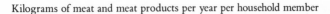

FIGURE 4-2. *Meat Consumption in Households of Industrial Employees in Russia, 1965–90*

Kilograms of meat and meat products per year per household member

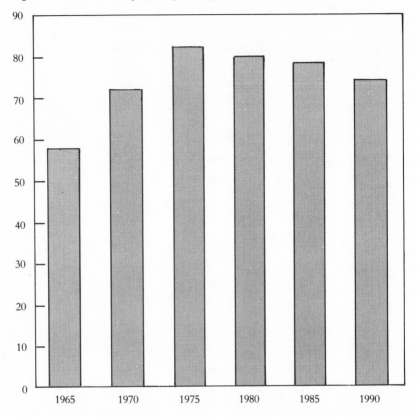

Sources: See table 5, "Potrebleniye osnovnykh produktov pitaniya naseleniyem Rossii [Consumption of basic food products by the Russian population], in "Sotsial'no-ekonomicheskoye polozheniye respubliki (yanvar'–avgust) [Socioeconomic situation of the republic (January–August)], *Vestnik statistiki*, no. 8 (1993), p. 15.

(figure 4-2). The early 1980s was not a good time to talk of devoting even more resources to the military. And yet, at that very point, the world was changing in ways that put new demands on Soviet defense needs. The USSR had gotten itself involved in a hot war in Afghanistan; meanwhile, there were potentially costly military challenges from a new U.S. administration. In principle, then, there was the potential for a broad coalition of forces to welcome a leader like Gorbachev who offered an approach to economic management that promised the Soviet Union both more guns and more butter.

Possible Allies in the Military?

From the discussion in chapter 2, it is clear that to at least some military thinkers, abandoning the approach of simply spending more on arms would not necessarily be a bad thing. Gorbachev was not saying that military power was unimportant, only that it had to be approached differently. It had to be built on a modern and flexible economic base. The term Gorbachev used was *uskoreniye*—accelerated economic development. That was consistent with the military economists' concern: to "raise the mobility of the economy."

In fact, this was the way the concept of *uskoreniye* was initially marketed across the country. In one early presentation of the new idea, Gorbachev stressed that the most urgent problem *uskoreniye* was designed to solve was to provide Soviet citizens with more food, consumer goods, and housing. But he quickly added that the need for a new, more dynamic economic policy was also dictated by the necessity of maintaining strategic military parity with the United States.[6]

Apart from the economists, was there anyone in the military hierarchy with real power who might understand and support Gorbachev's commitment to economic modernization? The military figure most closely associated with an emphasis on technological development, especially nonnuclear high technology, as a key factor of modern war was Marshal Nikolai Ogarkov, chief of staff of the Soviet armed forces from 1977 to 1984. In a series of articles toward the end of the Brezhnev era and during the Andropov and Chernenko interregna, Ogarkov had repeatedly written about the urgent need to reorganize both the structure of the Soviet economy and its management. Such a reorganization would ensure the most rapid transition possible to wartime production levels. In a 1981 article in *Kommunist*, the Communist party theoretical journal, that gained much notoriety at the time for its highly alarmist tone about alleged U.S. plans, Ogarkov urged greater emphasis on technological development in the armed forces. In the modern era, scientific and technological progress was proceeding so fast that "the basic systems of armaments are changing practically every 10 to 12 years."[7]

Because of his emphasis on modernizing the economy, some observers have speculated that Ogarkov may have been an early supporter of Gorbachev for the post of party leader.[8] But there was much that divided Gorbachev and Ogarkov. They disagreed on whether a durable peace between the USSR and the United States was at all possible. Ogarkov's alarmist articles ran counter to Gorbachev's effort to back off from the arms race. But in economic thinking, too, Ogarkov would have made a difficult ally. For even as he emphasized technological development, he put even more import on some ideas that, if implemented, would have altogether ruined Gorbachev's campaign for technical modernization. An examination of a couple of these ideas serves as a reminder of how detached from economic reality were even those in the Soviet military most in favor of modernization in the early 1980s.

During World War II, Ogarkov pointed out, political, economic, and military leadership in the Soviet Union had been tightly coordinated on the local level in a way that deserved to be emulated today. There had been special organizations known as defense committees in the cities of those regions of the USSR closest to the front lines of battle. They were composed of the top leadership from the Communist party, the state administrative apparatus, and the military. Ogarkov proposed that such committees be set up in peacetime throughout the country, not only in frontline regions, for the purpose of coordinating economic and military policy.

One of the important tasks of these new regional management bodies would be to ensure that regions could function more autonomously during wartime. Perhaps the single most radical and concrete measure Ogarkov proposed in this regard was also one of the most costly (although he himself, of course, never hinted at the cost). The plants producing the main types of weapons system, he wrote, should be able to operate independently if the nation were at war. Specifically, this meant not only that the final assembly plants—most of which were already huge—should be further integrated with their suppliers. But it also meant that they should have independent power plants and water supplies and that the existing, immensely costly program of stockpiling raw materials and reserves of equipment should be greatly expanded.[9]

In short, in whatever respect Ogarkov may have been in opposition to a faction of so-called metal-eaters within the military who openly called for continuing traditional military spending, many of his own proposals were hardly less wrongheaded in economic terms. His calls for enlarged mobilization reserves and autonomous production complexes would have been especially (and prohibitively) expensive. For that reason, it was perhaps fortunate for the prospects of demilitarization of the Soviet economy that Ogarkov was removed as chief of general staff in September 1984, several months before Gorbachev came into office. Whether or not his ouster was (as has been suggested) engineered by traditionalists in the military, it was the metal-eaters who remained. Dealing with them was probably simpler for Gorbachev than dealing with Ogarkov, and not only politically. Those who simply called for more weapons were easier to handle than someone who proposed handing over the authority on important economic decisionmaking to the military.

Gorbachev's March to Take Over the Military

The attitude of the Soviet military toward Gorbachev's accession to power is unclear and was probably fragmented. In any event, Gorbachev perceived many of the leading military personalities as being opposed to his programs for both political and economic reform. With remarkable haste he proceeded to remove them as real or potential obstacles to his plans to demilitarize the Soviet Union and streamline its economy.

When Gorbachev was named general secretary of the Soviet Communist party on March 11, 1985, the military leadership he inherited from his predecessor, Konstantin Chernenko, was already in disarray. The chief of staff, Sergei Akhromeyev, had been in his position for only half a year, having replaced Marshal Nikolai Ogarkov the previous fall. The minister of defense, Sergei Sokolov, had even less tenure. Although Sokolov and other military figures put up some resistance to Gorbachev and his calls for tightened military spending, their positions grew weaker as Gorbachev dismissed top generals and systematically replaced their political supporters over the next two years. The dramatic highlight came when Sokolov himself was forced to resign after an embarrassing episode in May 1987, when a West German teenager made an uncontested solo flight across Soviet territory and landed in Red Square.[10]

By that time it was clearly not the military that entertained any hopes of acquiring a voice in Soviet economic policy. Rather, it was the civilians—first the foreign policy specialists, but later on the economists as well—who were muscling in on military policy.[11] No longer were military officials talking about ways of imposing their authority on the civilian economy. Instead, they were fighting rear guard battles to keep civilian experts—not just leaders of the Communist party—from encroaching on *their* territory. Concepts of *glasnost'* that would once have been totally alien were being applied to the military economy.

Meanwhile, Gorbachev had not waited to remove his military opponents before tackling the problems of the Soviet economy. From 1985 to 1988, a succession of approaches was considered, tested, and (usually) rejected. There were many reasons for Gorbachev's reluctance to commit to a genuinely radical economic reform plan. But one was his stubborn belief that a key to reform was to take what he perceived to be the defense-industrial complex's secret of success and apply it to the rest of the economy. He did not know that in trying to extend the methods of the military economy to the civilian sector, he was doing exactly what would not work. The "secret" was that the military cannibalized the rest of the Soviet economy—to what extent no one knew, as costs had never been measured. The old system had harnessed the civilian economy to serve defense production as much as the Russian serf of old had been harnessed to serve his master. To ask the military industry to apply its methods to serve civilian industry was not simply politically impossible but also illogical.

Dealing with the Military-Industrial Complex

From 1985 to 1988, Gorbachev's approach to military industry had two parts. The first was to enlist key personnel from the defense complex and have them apply their administrative methods to the rest of the Soviet economy; the second was to call on defense industry directly to produce goods for his modernization programs. During these years Gorbachev did not touch defense spending. It actually rose to its highest levels ever and did not stop increasing until 1989.

Personnel

Gorbachev's most senior economic policymaker, Nikolai Ryzhkov, was a logical choice to lead the campaign to draw both the personnel and the methods of the defense complex into the economic reform campaign. Ryzhkov had long-standing links to defense industry. He graduated from engineering school in Sverdlovsk (now Yekaterinburg) in 1950 and lived in that city for the next twenty-five years, working his way up in the legendary Urals Heavy Machine-Building Plant, or *Uralmash*. In his last five years in Sverdlovsk (1970–75), Ryzhkov served as *Uralmash*'s general director. With its work force of roughly 50,000, *Uralmash* was one of the real giants of Soviet heavy industry.[12] Although it was not administratively part of the core Soviet defense-industrial complex, *Uralmash* did produce some military products and was subject to many of the mobilization requirements imposed on such industries. So, although Ryzhkov would have been well positioned to understand the status and operations of defense industry, he was enough of an outsider to be able to gauge what was lacking in the nondefense sectors of industry.

Ryzhkov had served as Central Committee secretary for economic affairs under Andropov. Gorbachev brought Ryzhkov on as a full member of the Communist party's leading body, the Politburo, in April 1985. Then, in the fall of that year, he made Ryzhkov prime minister.[13] This in effect meant that Gorbachev's economic policy was placed in the hands of a former director of one of the biggest military-related plants in one of the most heavily militarized regions in the USSR.

A second key recruit was Lev Zaikov. Zaikov had worked in defense industries in Leningrad from 1940 to 1976. He was appointed as the key Communist party official in charge of defense industry in July 1985 (replacing Grigory Romanov, Gorbachev's rival and ally of the "metal-eaters" in the military).[14]

Both Ryzhkov and Zaikov enthusiastically embraced Gorbachev's *uskoreniye*. Zaikov in particular stressed the importance of the machine-building sector (read: defense industry) and of scientific and technological progress. But the Ryzhkov and Zaikov appointments were only the tip of the iceberg. Throughout the Moscow bureaucracy, defense-industry executives were appointed to positions in which their expertise in making one part of the economy work could perhaps rub off on the rest. By the summer of 1989, eighteen of fifty-eight newly appointed government ministers had defense-industry backgrounds. This number included six of thirteen first deputy and deputy chairmen of the Council of Ministers.[15]

Methods

Two important early reform initiatives were based on emulating the defense industry: the creation of a number of so-called superministries, and a program to upgrade quality control in civilian industry.

Gorbachev and Ryzhkov attempted to restructure the administrative apparatus of key sectors of the civilian industry on the defense-industry model. They created a group of superministries, bodies that would coordinate entire sectors of the economy the way the Military-Industrial Commission had coordinated the defense sector. The Machine-Building Bureau, perhaps the most important of these, was headed by another defense industry insider, Ivan Silayev. For more than twenty years, Silayev had worked in a major defense plant in a leading defense-industry city (an aviation plant in Gorky, now Nizhny Novgorod). He, too, rose to general director before joining the Moscow ministerial apparatus.

The next step was to apply the methods that made defense industry work. The first choice was quality control. Nothing so clearly illustrates Gorbachev's apparent lack of understanding of what made the defense sector work than his failure to understand the true nature of its quality control methods.

Quality Control

Of all the problems of the consumer sector in the USSR, perhaps the most painful for ordinary citizens was the abysmal quality of the goods they could purchase. There were certainly not enough of these goods; shortages abounded, and the choices available to Soviet citizens were abominable. But variety is something that is hard to miss if you have never experienced it. What was really humiliating for ordinary Soviets was the experience of waiting for a deficit good—whether "only" for a few hours in a queue outside a store, or for years on a waiting list for big-ticket items such as automobiles—only to discover that the product they had earned the right to purchase was junk and to know that they had no recourse. This was the kind of resentment that Gorbachev had noted.

Gorbachev was convinced that the defense sector had solved the quality problem. The defense sector produced high-quality goods that worked, so quality in civilian goods could be had, the reasoning went, by using the defense industry's method: powerful quality control inspectors known simply as military representatives (in Russian, *voyennyy predstavitel'*, or *voyenpredy* for short). The *voyenpredy* were not employees of the producer plant. Rather, they answered to the plant's client: the Ministry of Defense. Most were uniformed officers whose rank depended on the importance of the product they were inspecting, and they had the power to reject anything that did not meet the rigid military standards.[16] This was quite literally their method: take what they wanted, leave the rest, and let the plant worry about what to do with it. As we saw in chapter 3, that meant that the rejected items would be cycled down the priority list until they ended up in household appliances and so on as precisely the *brak* Soviet consumers complained about.

So now, the new tactic was to set up something like the *voyenpredy* in the civilian plants. In the civilian sphere, the name would be *gospriyemka*, or "state acceptance." Quality control became Lev Zaikov's issue. Beginning in the summer of 1986, Zaikov pursued a "virtual crusade" for *gospriyemka*.[17] Soon others in leadership, including a highly enthusiastic Gorbachev, took up the drumbeat.

The problem is obvious: if the civilian products are built of the *brak*— junk—rejected by the *real voyenpredy*, what good will it do to have an imitation *voyenpred* standing along the assembly line in a civilian plant and rejecting the *brak* one more time? If the new inspectors do their jobs conscientiously, the result will simply be huge quantities of civilian goods that fail the quality control test, but with no one having the possibility to correct the situation. (That would require stepping back one more stage, to the military plants—but they were off-limits.) In short, the draconian quality control method did work fine for the military; the whole system was geared to producing that small percentage of quality goods that would be acceptable to the defense sector. But it simply could not work in the civilian sector. In fact, if the only civilian goods to be sold had to pass a rigorous quality standard, then there would be even greater shortages than before. And it would mean havoc inside the producer plants.

That is exactly what happened. After a special kickoff rally in November 1986, quality control became the major economic theme in Soviet media for several months. Then, just as suddenly, the campaign fizzled out. The reason was not that it did not work, but that it worked too well. Throughout the economy, a substantial proportion of products was rejected. Output in the key civilian machine-building sector dropped drastically as quality inspectors shut down production lines for days. Worse still, workers and managers lost bonuses for quota fulfillment. Under overt and latent pressure, the leadership backed off from the experiment.

Anders Åslund observes: "It is difficult to establish the precise reason for the quick reversal, but the overall social strains appear to have become intolerable. One possible explanation is strikes that erupted in the wake of eliminated bonuses. Did the advocates of *gospriyemka* not understand what the effects would be, or were they prompted to moderate the campaign by skeptical colleagues? *Gospriyemka* was advocated almost entirely by Zaikov and Gorbachev, and the other leaders were not overtly committed to it."[18]

It was typical of Gorbachev that even after the campaign was perceived as a failure and essentially abandoned, he continued to mull over why a system that worked so well in defense could not work equally well elsewhere. Speaking in Murmansk in October 1987, Gorbachev expressed his regret that so many people had given up on *gospriyemka*. The quality problem was still the number one issue in the economy. He cited cases of brand-new harvesters in such sorry shape that they had to be subjected to a complete overhaul before they could be put to work in the fields, or television sets that broke down "after a few days or hours."

> So, comrades, how then can we back down from quality, from *gospriyemka*? If we do, then what's the point in spending our working hours, effort, raw materials, and energy, when the only result is that it's all transformed into a useless final product? I don't want to blacken everything. *We do produce a lot of good things in our country. Take defense. There we are second to none.* That means that we can work. But there, I have to say, the quality inspectors work in a way that puts the heat on everyone: both the workers, the designers, the engineers, and the managers. That's how the [civilian] state quality inspectors should work. Then we'd get both the machines and the consumer goods that we want. [Emphasis added.][19]

Thus, months after the campaign for civilian quality control had been generally recognized as a fiasco, Gorbachev still had not understood why the military industry's quality control really worked. He defended the defense-sector approach as a way to stop the waste of "working hours, effort, raw materials, and energy." But what, then, of the waste involved when a *voyenpred* rejected and junked 99 of every 100 units produced? The *voyenpredy* never eliminated *brak*. They only pushed it out of their sight and dumped it back on the "residual" sector: the civilian economy.

Direct Production

But Gorbachev, with his blind faith in the efficacy of the defense sector, pushed on. If defense sector methods could not be transplanted into the civilian sector, the obvious solution was to let the defense sector itself produce the high-quality consumer goods he wanted. Of all the ways he sought to use the defense sector, this seemed to be most clearly destined to fail. One obvious point was that defense *already* was producing civilian goods, and ones that did not work that well, either. (In fact, one of the examples of a shoddy product that Gorbachev had cited in Murmansk— television sets that break down in a few hours—was produced *exclusively* in Soviet defense plants!)

A second reason why the leadership should have moderated their expectations was that the idea had been tried before. Throughout the 1970s, for instance, there had been efforts off and on to encourage defense industry to produce more civilian goods. The idea then was the same: because those in the defense industry knew how to meet quality standards for military goods, they could take over more civilian production and do just as well there. But the trials were just lip service or wishful thinking, with predictably fruitless results.[20] Despite all the rhetoric, civilian production could never be allowed to take priority over military goals. When conflicts arose—whether over allocation of resources and labor or simply for management's time and attention—the civilian side always lost out. The plant managers may have had a civilian production quota in addition to their military one. But, in terms of both material benefits and prestige, the rewards for fulfilling the military quota were greater and the penalties for failure more severe. In short, just as a defense procurement ruble was worth more than a civilian ruble, the military quota was worth more than the civilian quota.

Nevertheless, Gorbachev persisted. His idea was to use high tech in the defense sector. Thus, in addition to the consumer durables the military plants were already producing, he proposed that they produce more of the *machinery and equipment* used in the lower end of consumer goods manu-facturing, including those for food processing, in restaurants and cafeterias, and in retail distribution. This idea was first mentioned publicly in June 1986. At a plenum of the Communist Party Central Committee, Prime Minister Ryzhkov broached the idea cautiously, as if the role of defense industry were not the central theme. He simply stated that all machine-building enterprises, "including the defense sectors of industry," were to produce more equipment for light industry.[21]

It was the other top defense-industry representative on the Politburo, Zaikov, who seemed to assign the issue higher priority. In a speech in Irkutsk a couple of weeks later, he stated there was definitely a plan to involve defense plants in the "technical re-equipping of light and food industry, public dining, and wholesale and retail trade."[22] This plan led to a formal decision in late 1987. In spring 1988, 230 enterprises previously under the disbanded Ministry of Machine-Building for Light and Food Industries, along with their 300,000 workers, were reassigned to the Ministry of Defense Industry. A further major reassignment followed in the summer of 1989, when several other defense-industry ministries were given entire blocs of civilian enterprises.[23]

1989: Demilitarization and Decentralization

Despite all the changes that had taken place in the Soviet Union, the conversion of Russian defense industry did not truly come into its own until 1989. The first dramatic step occurred in December 1988. Speaking before the United Nations General Assembly, Gorbachev announced a unilateral Soviet decision to reduce the nation's armed forces by 500,000 (out of 5 million). In addition, the USSR would withdraw 50,000 troops from Eastern Europe, reduce troop strength in the Asian part of the country, and withdraw troops from Mongolia. Gorbachev also mentioned conversion of defense industries to civilian production. Indeed, the way he formulated it made it sound as if the purpose of announcing the reduction in forces was only a prelude to the real mission—conversion: "By this action of ours, as by all our activity on behalf of the demilitarization of international relations, we would also like to draw the attention of the world community to another urgent problem: the problem of a transition from an armaments economy to a disarmament economy."[24]

Gorbachev proclaimed a giant international campaign. The Soviet Union would take the lead by developing its own domestic conversion plan; other countries should then follow suit. An international group of experts would make an in-depth analysis of the problem of conversion and make recommendations for various countries and regions. A special United Nations session would then be held on this issue.

In contrast with the rhetoric, though, the actual plan for conversion in the USSR announced by Gorbachev was remarkably modest. During 1989 the USSR would be prepared to draft experimental plans for conversion of "two or three" defense enterprises and to "publish its experience in retraining and job placement of specialists from defense industry, and in using [defense industry] plant and equipment in civilian production."[25] As it turned out, it was not long before the program was greatly expanded. But the fact that Gorbachev made such anticlimactic promises may indicate how politically explosive the issue of actually *converting* defense capacity was. It was one thing to have the defense plants do extra civilian work on the side, or even adopt a relatively small number of poor civil cousins, although this provoked enough opposition. It was quite another matter to suggest that the plants stop producing some weapons systems and use those facilities to produce nonmilitary goods.

Now things were getting serious. On this count alone, 1989 promised to bring significant changes for defense industry. Few realized how quickly those changes would come and how profound they would be. Demilitarization was part, but only part, of the problem; 1989 was also the year when serious economic reforms came to the Soviet defense industry.

End of Spending Growth

From 1985 to 1988, whatever else Gorbachev had said or done, defense industry had not been hit in the pocketbook. Each year in that period the Soviet state continued to spend more on the research, design, and production of arms. But with Gorbachev's 1988 United Nations speech, the rise in defense spending came to a halt.[26] At the same time, both the talk and the demands for conversion increased. But worst of all was the shift in opinion. In the eyes of defense industrialists, Gorbachev's speech at the UN legitimized criticism of the Soviet defense industry.

Drop in Foreign Military Sales

At the same time that domestic procurement stopped rising, there were signs that things might change for export orders as well. World oil prices had dropped dramatically during the early Gorbachev years—a 40 percent decline between 1985 and 1989, nearly all of it in 1986.[27] As a result, the Soviet Union had already suffered substantial losses on actual revenues from arms sales. Oil-producing countries that had been able to pay in dollars for arms could not any longer. In most cases, however, this did not lead to suddenly decreased orders or deliveries; the arms kept flowing. It took some time before payment was due. But that was not a concern for the producer plants—just the government's worry. As far as the enterprises were concerned, it was business as usual. What did affect even them was the collapse of the USSR's Eastern European empire in 1989–90. At that point, actual orders dropped as well. In 1990 there was also a shift in the Soviet policy of foreign aid. This made it more difficult to justify subsidizing arms sales even to Soviet non–oil client states.[28]

Loosening Controls

More important than any of the policies directly aimed at defense industry, though, were the general changes in the Soviet economy. In 1988 Gorbachev adopted the critical components of an economic reform policy. Two of the most important elements of the overall policy were also the ones that most affected defense industry: the Law on the State Enterprise and the Law on Cooperatives. The first gave greatly expanded autonomy to enterprises, and the second to individuals. Both affected defense enterprises because they allowed enterprises and workers previously constrained to serve defense industry to make choices—including the choice *not* to supply their products to or to work for defense industry.

The Law on the State Enterprise, which went into effect on January 1, 1988, did not on the surface appear to affect defense enterprises. They were among the category of enterprises exempted from its provisions—at least directly. But as it turned out, they were substantially affected indirectly. Every defense enterprise was dependent in some way on enterprises outside the military–industrial complex.

The May 1988 Law on Cooperatives spurred development of legal small businesses. Their numbers skyrocketed, as individuals leaving the state sector of the economy, including defense industries, went into business for themselves. The pent-up demand for meaningful and well-remunerated job opportunities outside the defense sector led some defense workers to leave their old firms almost immediately. Stories circulated of workers who walked home from work the day the law went into effect who never came back.

Though the absolute number of such cases was probably small, the effect was shocking; never before had defense plant executives had to deal with such a thing. In the past, most defense plants in the larger cities had at worst faced competition for labor from other defense plants. Over the years they had been protected from real competition by the lack of any alternative outside opportunities.

But this was different. For a significant number of individuals, nothing could entice them to turn down the chance to be free. Defense plants were under pressure to find new ways to compete for labor; much more emphasis was placed on both material and nonmaterial incentives. The more savvy managers tried to join the process, creating cooperatives within their companies. Yet the overwhelming majority were either unwilling or unable to join in the new process in any way at all.

Conversion

Although the conversion program Gorbachev announced at the United Nations in December 1988 seemed modest, it was expanded considerably in 1989—no longer for international acclaim but for purely domestic reasons. Apparently this was partly because of the further deterioration of the economy. In a Communist party plenum in April 1989, it was already obvious that a more aggressive conversion program had been adopted.[29]

As the new official "campaign," conversion received the customary constant coverage by the official Soviet media. By the fall of 1989, there was at least one story a week on conversion, either in the Communist party–controlled national press or on television.[30]

In the beginning, the articles and stories were upbeat. But it was difficult to describe conversion without examining the negative aspects of defense industry. In this respect the conversion campaign differed from previous efforts propagandizing defense-industry efforts to produce more civilian goods. Those were actually based on the assumption that defense industry was good and praiseworthy. Recall Gorbachev's comment in Murmansk: "I don't want to blacken everything [in our economy]. We do produce a lot of good things in our country. Take defense."[31] In fact, defense had been so good that it was being given extra responsibilities. This time it was different: the media found it hard to talk about the plans to convert military capacity without leaving the impression that the military had taken too much from the Soviet economy.

The second aspect of the conversion campaign that irritated defense-industry executives and others was that defense industry was no longer being given prestigious high-tech projects. It would not be producing machinery or even electronics, but ordinary household items. This was far beneath the dignity of the captains of defense industry. They complained about being told what to produce. But it was clear that the compulsory nature of the programs was only part of the reason they were considered so distasteful. Had not defense plants always been "told" to produce every major product they had ever made? What was galling was that the products were now so mundane. Never had the prestige of defense industry been so low. The comments of Deputy Minister of Defense Yury Yashin in an interview in early 1990 were typical:

> It seems to me totally impermissible that certain enterprises in the military sectors of industry are not being charged with the production of the sort of consumer goods which those enterprises ought to be producing. For example, is it sensible when aviation [plants] . . . manufacture saucepans? . . . Is it sensible when rocket works, that is,

space rocket works, manufacture some kind of bedsteads or something else? Do we need these household items? Of course we do. But, surely, the military sectors ought primarily to address and tackle tasks at the level of technology which these defense enterprises have achieved, and where this technology has been developed.[32]

This criticism was implicitly directed at Gorbachev. Yet he himself was saying the same thing. The references to "saucepans" and to the need to use defense plants for higher technology were repeated endlessly, not only by the industry's own representatives but even by Gorbachev. In the spring of 1990, in a speech before defense plant workers in the Urals, Gorbachev accepted the criticism. "You can't just try to casually solve the problem by irrationally assigning the manufacture of saucepans to specialists who are experts at building complex machines and equipment. If we do that, we'll destroy much of what has been accumulated in the sector."[33] Only "advanced products" would suffice.

The lowly saucepan became the symbol of resistance to conversion by the defense-industrial complex. In effect, the message they sent was: "If we are going to convert, it has to be on our terms, in a way commensurate with our status. Otherwise, we won't convert at all!" Gorbachev admitted that the Soviet leadership had made numerous errors in the "first stage" of conversion. But things would get better, he promised.[34]

Protests

In the rest of 1990, if defense industry did perceive any change, it was for the worse. The tolerance level of the industry leaders fell to a new low in the fall of 1990. In an open letter that September to Soviet parliamentarians, published in the Communist party newspaper *Pravda,* several dozen directors of defense enterprises raised a great hue and cry about their current situation. Theirs, they wrote, was a "crisis situation moving out of control." Interestingly, conversion policy in itself was not a target of their criticism. The signatories to the letter even proudly cited the success of the defense complex in producing consumer goods in 1990.

But even though a complaint about lack of funding was implicit in some of their demands, this was not their principal grievance. Two other issues were more disturbing. The first was what they perceived to be a conscious policy by the government to destroy the tightly managed system of privileged supplies and the command economy that formerly had prevailed in their sector of the Soviet economy. Recent laws and decrees, they claimed, were "directly aimed at shattering our [defense] complex." Worst of all was the new freedom of choice of subcontracting enterprises that no longer had to obey the dictates of a strong central government. Supplier enterprises now had the freedom to choose their partners and charge prices they themselves set ("a significant number of suppliers are arbitrarily raising prices on their products"). Sounding almost shocked, the defense-complex executives complained that if they wanted a product, they might be asked now to pay bribes, pay in hard currency, or make other forms of extra, quasi-legal payments. These were, of course, common practices in the "normal" Soviet economy, so it is hard to take their indignation too seriously. But this was precisely what was most disturbing to these executives: they were becoming part of the "normal" economy—that is, if they continued to exist at all.

The second major complaint that the letter writers expressed was that they were being subjected to "crushing criticism and attacks" by outsiders. Authorities at all levels were attempting to interfere in the management of defense enterprises, they wrote. "In individual cases, the very necessity of having a national defense complex under contemporary conditions is being called into question. A situation has been created in which our enterprises are compelled to prove the necessity of their existence."[35]

As it turned out, what the defense-industry representatives were feeling in 1990 was mild compared with what was to come. Spending on hardware procurement and on research and development (R&D) in 1990 declined by about 8 percent from 1989—even before adjusting for inflation. The hardware procurement budget for 1991, though, was an estimated 25 to 27 percent lower in real terms than in 1990. Spending on R&D dropped even more.[36] The defense-industrial complex stepped up its own political activity in response. The culmination of that overt and desperate activity was the active participation of defense-industry representatives in the attempted coup against Gorbachev in August 1991. Of the small circle of conspirators in the self-appointed State Committee for the State of Emergency, two were directly associated with the military-industrial complex: Oleg Baklanov, the Communist party's top official in charge of defense industry; and Aleksandr Tizyakov, general director of a major manufacturer of sea-launched cruise missiles and antiaircraft missiles.[37]

Even though the coup attempt failed, it was the beginning of the end for Gorbachev and for the Soviet Union. He did not complete the task he had set for himself, but the process of demilitarization was now in full swing and had taken on a life of its own. Formal policy on defense industry, as in all other sectors of the economy and society, was now in the hands of Russian President Boris Yeltsin.

Chapter 5

Defense Industry in the New Russia

Having compromised themselves so greatly during the August 1991 coup, those in the defense-industrial complex had no reason to expect that their lot would improve under the new Russian leadership that effectively took control in the fall of 1991. Russian President Boris Yeltsin clearly intended to take on economic reform in a new way.

Yeltsin's attitude toward defense industry and its role in reform was also distinct from Mikhail Gorbachev's, as could be seen in his major reform speech of October 28, 1991. Outlining his plans for the Russian economy, Yeltsin devoted little attention to defense industry. His message was simple and direct: The problem was that defense industry needed to be drastically reduced. There was no talk here about how well defense industry worked and how it needed to serve the Russian economy. Although he used the word conversion, Yeltsin's term was "deep conversion" (to distinguish his policy from one of mere diversification): "We propose to shut down a certain proportion of the enterprises, and to totally reorient a number of military plants to the production of [civilian] output and consumer goods."[1]

The initiative in the government in this case, as in other key policy areas, was in the hands of the economics minister, Yegor Gaidar. Gaidar and his team of young reformers showed early on that they were more than ready to pursue the direct assault on defense industry Yeltsin had hinted at. They did so almost immediately, by slashing the 1992 defense procurement budget by more than two-thirds! Many defense enterprises received no new orders at all.

Not only the enterprises but also the central defense-industry bureaucracy was caught off guard. For their part, the bureaucrats tried to carry on as before, and on the surface, it may have appeared that little had changed. The old central planning establishment continued to draft plans, elaborating more programs for conversion, industrial policy, and arms export promotion. But the big difference now was that there was not just less money, but virtually none at all for any of this. The plans and programs suddenly counted for almost nothing substantively. Even their purported beneficiaries—the defense enterprise managers—disparaged them as nothing but mere pieces of paper.

But if the conversion programs and other plans did not do much to change anyone's behavior, there were other policies that did. Again, as in Gorbachev's last years, it was the overall environment of economic reform that mattered above all. The trends the defense enterprise managers had complained about so much in the final year of Gorbachev's regime—decentralization and deregulation of economic behavior—had dramatically intensified.

In this chapter I begin the examination of changes in the environment under Yeltsin: those caused by the dissolution of the Soviet Union, and the policies that were debated and elaborated on during 1992 and 1993. Finally, there are the unquestionably more important changes brought about by Russia's move to a market economy. That is the subject of the next chapter.

Dissolution of Economic Ties

Like all the other assets (and liabilities) left over when the USSR ceased to exist in December 1991, the Soviet defense industry was simply divided among the successor states according to geographic location. Russia inherited a disproportionately large share. Although Russia accounted for about half the population of the USSR, as much as 70 to 80 percent of the Soviet defense complex—both the number of industrial enterprises and the volume of output or employment—was in Russia. Its share of military research and development capacity was even higher.

As extensive as it was, Russian defense industry could not stand alone. Each plant had had vital links with the rest of the economy; now some of those suppliers of materials and components to Russia's arms manufacturers were no longer even in the same country. The defense plants in the other post-Soviet states were in even worse shape, but that was little consolation to the affected enterprises in Russia.[2] The economic consequences of the collapse of the Soviet Union were enormous for both the military and the civilian product lines of the Russian defense-industrial complex.

It was not as if the shock caused by the dissolution of the USSR was completely unanticipated. Russian defense industry had noticed disruptions as independence movements had sprung up in the republics of the USSR. For instance, the separatist-minded Baltic republics, though small in size, had had some key defense components manufacturers, which they talked of removing from Moscow's jurisdiction. This was a threat fraught with potentially serious consequences. With the tightly integrated Soviet economic system, and without a competitive market to provide alternative suppliers, all it took was one missing link to upset the entire system. The Soviet defense managers had made this important point in their open letter of September 1990 (discussed in chapter 4). One of the concrete steps they called for was clarification of the links among defense enterprises in the new Union Treaty then being discussed.[3]

Dismantling the Central Bureaucracy

The second major consequence of the USSR's demise was the dismantling of nearly all central institutions that had governed the Soviet defense-industrial complex (see figure 2-2). Under the Soviet system, the nine defense-industrial ministries had been organized and had operated exclusively at the national level (that is, across the USSR). There had been no provision for regional delegation of responsibility to republican branches.

As it reorganized the central bureaucracy, the new Russian leadership had a critical choice to make. They could either take over the old defense-industrial ministries of the former Soviet Union, effectively doing nothing but giving them new names (which happened with many other parts of the Moscow bureaucracy), or they could seize the opportunity to radically reorganize the entire defense sector. At first, it appeared that they chose the latter course. The old defense-industrial ministries were formally abolished, with no Russian counterparts set up in their stead. Rather, their functions (and personnel) were subsumed under a newly established Ministry of Industry. What had been nine separate ministries, headed by the powerful superministry known as the Military-Industrial Commission (VPK), were now departments within a single Ministry of Industry, which had departments for many other civilian branches of industry as well. This was clearly an attempt to eliminate the defense industry's special status.

But like the phoenix, the central defense industry bureaucracy emerged once more as a distinct body out of the ashes of the Soviet defense complex, and almost from the moment it disappeared. The Ministry of Industry was an unwieldy giant and was disbanded in early 1992. In its place sprang up one main State Committee for Industrial Policy and four committees of lesser status for various sectors of the nation's industry. One of these four committees was specifically for defense industry: the Russian Committee for the Defense Sectors of Industry, or *Roskomoboronprom* by its Russian acronym. The committee was subdivided into eight departments that replicated the old secretive ministries exactly.[4]

Keeping a single government body responsible for all defense enterprises and their activities, both military and civilian, later proved to be important. Although it was much weaker than the old ministries and the Military-Industrial Commission, *Roskomoboronprom* did provide a place for the old bureaucracy to retreat and regroup. From the time this committee was created, the military-industrial bureaucracy consistently waged a campaign to upgrade the status of *Roskomoboronprom*.[5]

Retaining the structure of the old defense-industrial complex had another consequence as well, because it helped preserve the special status of defense enterprises. In his October 1991 reform speech, Yeltsin had promised to keep the civilian and military activities of the defense complex separate. From the picture of the Soviet defense-industrial complex presented so far, this clearly would have been a huge and perhaps impossible goal to realize quickly. But any significant steps taken in that direction would have been important.

As it turned out, nothing happened at all, and *Roskomoboronprom* remained in charge of both military and civilian activity in the defense sector. In effect, that meant that many components of the new government's economic reform program could not be applied to defense enterprises, at least not in the same way as to other sectors of the Russian economy. Given the enormous size of defense enterprises, this exempted a substantial portion of the *civilian* economy from the reforms as well. Land reform, bankruptcy, and other reforms would be fundamentally different if defense enterprises were not included. As will soon be seen, this is precisely what happened in the case of industrial privatization.[6]

Policy toward the Industry

One of the main complaints of defense industry during the "conversion" period of the Gorbachev era—that is, after 1988—had been that the country's leadership was not giving defense enterprises any definite guidelines about the future. (This was another theme of the September 1990 open letter from Soviet defense-enterprise directors.) The enterprise managers argued, quite logically, that as the people responsible for equipping the nation's armed forces, they could not decide on their own policies and strategies until the nation had a clear, coherent set of military-industrial policies.

The highest priority on the list of those policies, according to the defense-enterprise managers, must be to establish a military doctrine, a statement of the purpose and mission of national defense. Such a doctrine would provide a basis for knowing which weapons the country needed, now and in the future. How can we be expected to convert arms production capacity to other uses, the managers argued, if we do not know how much of that capacity needs to be *kept*? The doctrine would then be followed by a program for how those weapons were to be obtained—how they were to be developed, from whom they would be bought, and how. This in turn would mean delineating active military production and resolving related issues (for example, mobilization capacity). This would also provide a basis for making decisions about public versus private ownership. Finally, and not until this point, could the country's leadership talk meaningfully about "conversion" of those defense plants deemed eligible for it.

And so the desired sequence of policymaking emerged:

—Military doctrine, including principles of force structure and weapons requirements, and general directions of weapons development.

—Weapons development and procurement programs.

—Related issues such as the definition of mobilization capacity, conversion policy, and ownership issues (state versus private).

—Budgetary funding of annual procurement, decisions on procurement, and issuance of the state defense order.

The problem, of course, was that none of the preconditions was in place for defense policymaking to proceed in this way. Various bureaucratic interest groups controlled policy relating to the different components of the program. Some of the groups had achieved relative consensus and could act promptly, but for others there was no prospect of quick action. As a result, changes in policy moved forward all at once, but at varying speeds and with no coordination between groups.

Final policy pieces were completed all out of sequence. For instance, the scheme called for the budgetary decision to be the final one made, because it was supposed to be based on more general principles and frameworks. But in 1992, the budgetary decision was the very first one made. A military doctrine was also developed quickly, with the General Staff presenting a first draft in May 1992. The reason the military was able to work so fast was that they changed very little of the old doctrine. Consequently, the framers of the doctrine were told to come up with a new version, which was not presented for another year and a half. Meanwhile, a third policy track occupied those working on a conversion law. In short, during the first months in post-Soviet Russia, there were three separate and highly contradictory tracks of policy on military industry, each controlled by a different group: the radical reformers, who controlled the procurement budget; the military, which tried to develop a military doctrine; and the defense-industrial establishment, which worked on legislation and programs for conversion.

The Procurement Budget

The fact that a defense procurement budget was presented early in the process, even prematurely, was not surprising. The budget had its own deadline. What was unexpected was the nature of the budget. Instead of keeping defense spending to a noncommittal, business-as-usual level until more fundamental decisions had been made, the procurement budget presented by Yeltsin's government in January 1992 was a dramatic shock. Funding for purchases of military hardware would be cut by two-thirds. This was so low that it might have had possibly irreversible consequences.

In fact, this was the conscious intent. Even if the team headed by Yegor Gaidar had believed in the efficacy of grand policy pronouncements—and they did not—they knew they were not in control of policy-making regarding military doctrine and national security goals. Yet they knew that if there was no funding, there would be no meaningful policy made by anyone. The situation clearly resembled their position with respect to the broader reform process. Cutting funding, like "liberalization"—that is, removing controls and regulations—is a way to break down the old system, but it does not in itself build new institutions. For the defense-industrial establishment, this offered some hope that the process of demilitarization might eventually be reversed. Meanwhile, the defense complex was under powerful pressure to cope with what they hoped would be a temporary situation.

Military Doctrine

No one really expected economic policy to appear in the draft military doctrine that was presented in the spring of 1992. This had not been the case in the past. But though a new doctrine was not expected to answer all (or even many) questions of relevance for defense industry, some clarity was needed on basic issues. After all, Russia was not just a country with a new name. This was a new country, one with a fundamentally different place in the world than the former Soviet Union and with new relationships with other nations. The most recent Soviet military doctrine had been prepared in 1990, and it did not reflect the new political and economic realities of the country.

THE MAY 1992 DRAFT. The new Russian draft in 1992 came swiftly, some would say suspiciously so. The packaging certainly looked new. The military had paid strict attention to public relations. A special issue of the journal *Voyennaya mysl'* [*Military Thought*] contained not only the text of the doctrine, but also unprecedented user-friendly features such as a three-page glossary of terms, an explanatory appendix, and a set of flowcharts showing how the doctrine would work.[7] But as far as the relationship between defense and the economy was concerned, the substance of the doctrine was old-fashioned. No explicit attention was given to defense industry at all. The new doctrine did conclude that because budgets were being reduced year by year, priorities would change. There would be no more mass spending on huge quantities of serially manufactured arms; rather, there would be more R&D projects and the creation or maintenance of production capacity capable of producing top-level weaponry. Existing full-scale mobilization capacity also would need to be maintained. However, the doctrine did not suggest what this implied for defense industry. No mention was made of important related issues such as procurement or conversion.

The May 1992 draft was debated within the military hierarchy for nearly a year and finally passed on to the Russian parliament for debate and approval in March 1993.[8] The parliament never approved it and apparently demanded a new version. This probably had little to do with the draft's failure to address economic issues. But it is worth noting that the next time around, the major changes included a more explicit—and much more realistic—treatment of economic issues.

THE NOVEMBER 1993 DOCTRINE.   When Russia's new military doctrine was officially adopted on November 2, 1993,[9] some of its political and military provisions were viewed with concern in the West. Some observers concluded that the new doctrine heralded "the resurgence of the armed forces" in doctrinal issues.[10] Whether or not that conclusion was warranted, there was at least one important way in which the new doctrine reflected not the military's omnipotence but their awareness that there was now one force in Russia much stronger than they: the economy. In contrast with the spring 1992 draft, which had contained almost nothing on the economy, the 1993 version added an entire section on "the economic foundations of the military doctrine." It mentioned conversion, procurement, arms sales, foreign cooperation, and industrial policy.

Most important, for the first time, military goals were put in the context of other societal goals and of economic reality. As was discussed in chapter 2, Soviet thinking had nearly always regarded national security considerations as absolutes. The idea of a trade-off between military considerations and other possibilities was unthinkable. But this doctrine acknowledged a truly revolutionary concept: It asserted that the state's first task in guaranteeing military security was to "maintain the defense potential of the country on a level appropriate to existing and potential military threats while taking into account the country's economic possibilities and the availability of human resources."

In a press conference presenting the doctrine on November 3, Yeltsin's defense minister, Pavel Grachev, reinforced this emphasis on the economy when he stated what was unique about the new doctrine. Two of his four points related directly to the economy. He stressed that the new doctrine was based on the real political, economic, and military possibilities of the

Russian state. He then said that force development was taking place "under conditions of a transition to a market economy, when the role of the Ministry of Defense in shaping and implementing military-technological policy is being radically altered."[11]

Conversion

While the Gaidar government was taking action, the old and new defense-industry establishment was acting as well. Through the autumn of 1991 and into 1992, successive drafts of a law on conversion were debated and rewritten. Finally, on March 20, 1992, President Yeltsin signed the new law. (It was not made public until April 27.[12]) This was a conversion law in name only. It was actually the first chance the central military-industrial bureaucracy had had to make certain statements about the future of defense industry, and so they took it. They turned it into a law providing the framework for and the first steps toward the comprehensive defense-economic policy they sought.

The March 1992 Law

Despite its title, the March 1992 Law on Conversion had less to do with conversion than with protecting the rights of all defense enterprises in the prevailing climate of downsizing and market transition. The law was a wish list from the defense-industrial establishment. It made no attempt to divide the old defense-industrial complex into segments, with "converting" enterprises somehow classified as more progressive or worthy of support. The definition of a "converting" enterprise was literally any defense enterprise that had had a reduction of military orders and had taken measures to produce civil output—a definition that included every defense enterprise in the country. It would be up to each enterprise to define itself.

What was key in the law was that there was essentially nothing but promised benefits for a converting enterprise, with no obligations. As if winning revenge for everything they resented about Gorbachev's conversion effort, the drafters of the law filled it with rhetoric about the "main principle" governing conversion being "the use of high-technology capacities of the defense complex to produce output capable of competing on the foreign market" (Art. 2:2). There would be "priority targeted state programs for socioeconomic development" that, the law stipulated, were to be appropriate to the scientific and technical level of the enterprises and to the professional skills of the work force (Art. 2:3).

A list of the other provisions seems downright silly when one considers that the law appeared just as the government had cut defense procurement spending to less than one-third of the previous year's appropriation. Enterprises were to be protected against circumstances that reduced their profits (Art. 8:3). In some cases, they would be subsidized so that prices on their conversion products would remain below world market prices (Art. 8:5). Plants would be given at least two years' notice before receiving any cutbacks in orders (Art. 3:3). They would be compensated for keeping their mobilization capacities (even for creating new ones; Art. 2:4).

Although the law recognized that enterprises would be responsible for developing their own conversion programs, it made no provision for any real assistance in this regard. The law quite literally defined conversion as the antithesis of the market. In the introduction, with the sole use of the term "market" in the entire text, the law stated that its purpose was to "guarantee protection of all participants [in conversion] under conditions of market relations."[13] Logically, there was not a word in the law about programs or measures to facilitate or assist enterprises in adapting to the market—for instance, by finding new civilian products or customers. The purpose instead was protection from the market. Nor would the market, according to this law, play any role at all in an enterprise's conversion programs. Those programs were to be developed solely on the basis of information about the national arms production program, the necessity to preserve mobilization capacity, and government procurement orders for both civilian and defense goods (Art. 4:1).

Programs

Whether any conversion legislation could have been meaningful in the economic environment prevailing in Russia in 1992 is open to doubt. But by being so totally divorced from reality, the March 1992 law merely heightened the enterprises' cynicism toward and distrust of the leaders of the central government, whether radical reformers or old-line defense-complex bureaucrats. If the management and workers in the plants had not already stopped believing that their old patrons in the Center could bring them relief, the law should have convinced them.

And yet, the charade continued. This is somewhat understandable; the problems of the defense enterprises and the regions they formerly supported were real and acute. Clearly, advice and strategies were needed—but not the ones these enterprises received. Unfortunately, after the formal demise of the old Soviet planned economy, "conversion" seemed to become a magnet for every planning expert at every level who was looking for a new task. Ministries, research institutes, universities—all were full of underemployed economists who could hardly wait to present a "conversion program" for the country, for a region, for a city, or for an enterprise. During 1992 and 1993, *one thousand* conversion programs were developed, reviewed, and approved for implementation in Russia.[14] A large number were presumably for individual enterprises, but many were grand, highly comprehensive programs, including fourteen so-called federal programs.

Although there have been scattered reports of success stories at the enterprise level, none of the larger conversion programs is generally believed to have produced results. One of the biggest problems with these programs was the expectations they raised and the incongruity between their goals and the financing available. Most of the blame for unfulfilled expectations and broken promises fell on the federal government. The government, including Yeltsin himself, continued to approve programs with one hand (presumably encouraging enterprises to take them seriously) and then refuse financing for them with the other.[15] The enterprises understandably resented this. And yet as long as there was hope of some funding, they had to continue to play the game. It seemed that no matter how many times conversion had been pronounced dead, it was the issue that would never die.

Privatization

Among the many realities facing defense enterprises that the conversion law almost completely ignored was privatization. Yet privatization, as opposed to the grand plans for industrial policy and the like, was actually happening. Military doctrine, conversion policy, and budgetary policy were areas where each of the three main Moscow groups—the military, the reform politicians, and defense-industrial bureaucrats—could stake a claim and pursue policy in relative isolation from the others, but privatization was a potential battleground. All had some immediate interest in it, and all had some leverage. Moreover, this was an area further complicated by the fact that the enterprises (that is, both the managers and the workers) were in the middle. They did not agree among themselves on privatization policy, and in some cases the same people did not agree with either the reformers or the bureaucracy and wanted both off their backs. To the extent that formal decisions had to be made, the arbiter, as usual, was the Russian president. In most cases, however, practice rather than law or decrees decided the issue.

What Was at Stake

Privatization was an issue that would affect each of the central players in the game for the future of Russian defense industry differently. Each player—the uniformed military, the reformers in the Yeltsin government, the central defense-industry bureaucracy, and the enterprise managers— saw something different in privatization. Each had a general idea of what the others wanted, and therefore a sense of who could possibly ally with whom. A game of alliances and de facto coalitions emerged.

THE MILITARY.   The military wanted guarantees that Russia would continue to have a defense-industrial base in the normal sense of the term. It was not essential that the enterprises that produced and developed arms be state-owned, but there had to be some way to ensure they would not just abandon arms manufacture altogether. Yet it was hard to see how to do that without substantial direct state ownership. Given all the other uncertainty, it seemed risky to trust that market mechanisms and incentives could guarantee the defense-industrial base. The military understood that if, in principle, defense contracts could be made financially attractive enough, the market would work. But the reality of Gaidar's 68 percent cut in procurement for 1992 did not make this appear realistic.

The only real leverage left with which to influence enterprise policy was continued state ownership rights. The military tended to support highly restrictive policies to privatize the defense sector. They spoke of keeping a nucleus or core of defense enterprises that would be responsible for Russia's future defense production. This was roughly estimated as one-third to two-fifths of the total defense industry. The rest of the defense enterprises (or the residual assets, as some called them) could be allowed to privatize.[16]

The choice of which enterprises would be kept in the core (and not allowed to privatize) was a source of potential conflict with the enterprises themselves, or at least with their directors. Although the military did not care to see large but otherwise unviable enterprises remaining as part of the core, many weak enterprises wanted to be on the core list for lack of any other alternative, especially in the market. In contrast, many of the best enterprises did not want to be on the core list, given all that implied about lack of autonomy and interference from Moscow.

THE DEFENSE-INDUSTRY BUREAUCRACY.   The position of the central bureaucracy was simple: It wanted power. This meant two things. First, and obviously, *Roskomoboronprom* should have some de facto ownership rights over enterprises. Not exclusive rights, of course; it was too late for that. Enterprise managers had already acquired much greater independence than they had had under the old system, and they were not going to give that up. But *Roskomoboronprom* needed to make sure that it had a decisive say in managing the defense sector.

Second, the sector itself had to remain influential. It was obviously not appealing to be in control of a sector of the economy that had no real status and weight. This latter goal meant that *Roskomoboronprom* consistently fought for two things: to uphold the special status of the defense industries, especially that they be given special treatment in key reform legislation; and to keep the defense sector as large as possible—that is, with the maximum number of enterprises defined as defense enterprises and with individual enterprises themselves as large as possible.

THE REFORMERS.   The radical reformers naturally realized that the defense industry was a large and important part of the Russian economy. But they did not see it as the salvation of the economy and tended to view it as a burden—an economic sector that was draining the country's budget without any direct benefit to living standards. These defense enterprises definitely needed to be weaned from the budget and exposed to market discipline. The reformers' basic approach was to use budgetary power to cut them off and reduce them to the status of "normal" enterprises. In the long run, this could only happen, the reformers believed, if the Russian state had as little ownership interest in these enterprises as possible.

In the meantime, the reformers took a pragmatic approach. They could live with the status quo. If a hard push toward privatization of defense industries was destined to provoke heavy opposition by a still-powerful political force, they would ignore it for the time being while going about other urgent tasks.

In principle, the reformers agreed with the military that the right way to proceed was to separate the old defense industry into core assets and residual assets. But they wanted a much smaller core. Most defense industries should be privatized and subunits should be encouraged to separate. To the reformers, the talk in some circles in defense industry and the defense ministry about consolidating several enterprises into "financial-industrial groups" sounded dangerous.

ENTERPRISE DIRECTORS.   Finally, there were the enterprise directors. They tended to want two things: survival of their enterprises and control over them. Their motives therefore resembled those of the bureaucracy. The two groups differed only on the issue of *who* would control the enterprises. The managers would get into disputes with *Roskomoboronprom* over outside interference from Moscow, but *Roskomoboronprom* was in general a good ally, as long as the reformers were the main enemy.

The directors remained ambivalent about privatization. Few of them argued strongly in favor of rapid privatization; for most, the prevailing situation was just fine. They already had de facto property rights—that is, though they may not have had legal property rights, they had economic property rights.[17] In fact, that was the preferred situation. It ensured them the most benefits and the fewest obligations of all alternatives. Privatization was bad for them not only because it might lead to loss of control, but also because it might mean a loss of their monopoly on information about what was going on. Much of the managers' behavior was based on maneuvering regarding privatization, but not to either block it or make it happen. Lack of clarity was preferable to either sure alternative.

If they absolutely had to privatize, the managers wanted to privatize their own way. As early as 1991, defense enterprises were planning for privatization. But most of that planning consisted of organizing worker support for what has been called *nomenklatura* privatization. This was privatization done internally, with an absolute minimum of oversight from the public or any federal or local authorities.

Reformers Take the Initiative

The first move in the struggle over defense industry privatization was made by the reformers. When Yeltsin formed his new government in November 1991, he put the government agency in charge of privatization of industry in the hands of a determined radical reformer, Anatoly Chubais. Chubais's agency—the State Committee for Management of State Property, or GKI—had the status of a state committee, which meant he was a cabinet member.[18]

As a matter of principle, Chubais would probably have preferred to see all defense industry privatized. However, defense industry was not his main concern. He wanted fast privatization of the bulk of Russian industry. It was apparent that this task was going to be big enough without bringing in the defense industries and their still significant political influence. As the events of the next year would show, Chubais was a consummate tactician. He began by avoiding any head-on clash on the issue of defense industries and then proceeded with the rest of Russian industry.[19]

From the beginning little was said about defense industry in the official privatization legislation. The main thing was that defense enterprises were given special status. In Russia's privatization legislation, the general principle was that all industrial enterprises were to be in private hands. To that end, most enterprises were subject to mandatory privatization by a certain deadline. But there were some exceptions.

First, there was a class of enterprises that would not be privatized under any circumstances. These included the nuclear industry and space sectors, both civil and military. Other nonnuclear and nonaerospace enterprises that were defense related fell into yet another category. They would be permitted (but not compelled) to privatize, but only if they requested and obtained special permission from the Russian government.[20] In practice, this meant they were in limbo while the power struggle played out between the reformers (in the form of the GKI) and the defense-industrial bureaucracy (through *Roskomoboronprom*). It certainly put little pressure on them to privatize.

Compromises

The sharp public debate on privatization during the first half of 1992 therefore had little to do with the defense enterprises. However, during this period, as Chubais maneuvered for support for the general privatization program and made efforts to ensure its speedy implementation, he made a couple of compromises. These would prove indirectly to be of great consequence to defense enterprises, when and if they were allowed to privatize. The first compromise was to give the "insiders"—the workers and management of these enterprises—a large stake in ownership. The second compromise was to ease the pressure to disaggregate large enterprises into separate units.

POWER TO THE INSIDERS.   In his original privatization program of December 1991, Chubais had already made what he considered to be a major concession to enterprise workers and management. Workers were to be given 25 percent of their enterprise's shares in nonvoting stock absolutely free. In addition, they would be entitled to purchase an additional 10 percent of the shares at a discounted price. Managers could purchase 5 percent of the shares at a favorable price as well.[21] But by the time a revised privatization program was approved by the parliament in June 1992, even this mode of privatization had changed. Under strong pressure, Chubais accepted the so-called Option 2, under which workers and management could purchase 51 percent of shares from the outset.

In all privatized enterprises, especially those choosing Option 2 (as some three-quarters of enterprises did), insiders were therefore given a great deal of power. In the case of defense enterprises, this was even more true. Much of the remaining 49 percent of shares not directly held by insiders would, as it turned out, be kept off the open market and unavailable to outsiders.

KEEPING THE GIANTS.   The second significant compromise Chubais made was to leave the large enterprises alone. Again, the privatizers would have preferred to break up some of the industrial giants into their constituent units and be liberal about allowing sections to break away on their own. But the enterprise managers did not want that, and they were prepared to fight. Rather than risk delaying the entire process, Chubais once again opted to let the enterprises privatize any way their directors wanted. They were not broken up.[22]

Here, too, there were important implications for defense enterprises. In effect this meant that the largest defense enterprises would remain tightly under the control of their old directors, with less chance of splitting off smaller units as viable new firms. The effect of this was to close (or at least substantially constrict) one of the most promising avenues for restructuring of defense companies. It blocked the best and most ambitious workers from being given the opportunity to identify the parts of their defense enterprises they thought viable and to run them as separate, autonomous units. As a result, many of those workers who had hoped to change the direction of at least part of their enterprise were again faced with the choice between two less than satisfying alternatives: either to stick around with the hopeless old dinosaur of an enterprise or to leave altogether.

The GKI Strengthens Its Hand

Chubais succeeded in getting the privatization program passed by the Russian parliament in June 1992. It looked as though his GKI was obtaining more formal power in relation to defense industries. A presidential edict on industrial policy issued in November 1992 allowed the state to keep control of blocks of shares in certain state enterprises (including defense enterprises) for as long as three years, during which the GKI would play a significant role in their governance. The GKI would, for instance, have the right to appoint executive officers of the enterprises to represent the state's interests on each board of directors.[23]

There was also a significant provision concerning arbitration in disputes between defense enterprises and subunits that sought to transform themselves into separate entities through privatization. The edict stipulated that the GKI would be on the arbitration boards but not the branch agencies (that is, in the case of defense enterprises, not *Roskomoboronprom*).[24] This meant that in disputes over the breakup of large defense enterprises, enterprise management would have to face the pro-fragmentation GKI with no protection from the defense-industrial committee.

The favorable results in the April 1993 referendum on Yeltsin's government and economic program strengthened privatization efforts generally and Chubais personally. (Just before the referendum he had come close to losing his job.[25]) A Yeltsin edict in May 1993 even seemed to suggest that mandatory privatization might loom for many defense enterprises. The edict ordered the GKI to review various categories of enterprises whose privatization had been restricted in the original privatization program. Defense enterprises fell into those categories. The GKI, decreed Yeltsin, should aim at achieving "the overall reduction of the number of such enterprises." Regarding defense enterprises, the edict also stated that any defense plant for which defense orders constituted less than 30 percent of total sales could be fully privatized; that is, there would be no state ownership of that plant at all. Similarly, a plant's obligations with respect to mobilization programs, state secrets, or security were not to be obstacles to complete privatization.[26]

In sum, by the spring of 1993 the GKI's position of advocating rapid and full privatization of as much of defense industry as possible was strengthened considerably. All of these measures weakened the hold not only of *Roskomoboronprom*, but also of the enterprise managers. But their counterassault was already under way. At a conference of the main lobbying group of the defense enterprises—the League of Assistance to Defense Enterprises—in the spring of 1993, the participants focused on the issue of privatization. They sharply criticized the entire program, accusing the GKI of applying "command-administrative" methods. In a resolution, they condemned the speed, scope, and overall "destructive effect" of privatization of Russian industry. They were especially upset by cases of privatization in which large amalgamated enterprise complexes were fragmented. "Things had even reached the point where an enterprise would be artificially broken up into parts that then would be included in a list of enterprises subject to privatization, each individually. The consequences are obvious: the enterprise as an integral unit ceases to exist, while one more link is removed from the system of division of labor."[27]

The executives of defense plants also deplored their own dependence on the GKI. Then-current legislation had made the GKI the entity that concluded employment contracts with managers. The GKI was therefore the directors' "employer"—an intolerable situation. The GKI could, and did, use its position to pressure directors to privatize, they claimed. As a result, the united front had been broken: Many directors were giving in and submitting applications for privatization.

The conference of defense managers adopted a resolution with four demands. Their first and primary demand was that all issues relating to privatization of defense enterprises should be taken out of the hands of the GKI and given to *Roskomoboronprom*. Second, the contracting party for employment of managers should be *Roskomoboronprom*, not the GKI. Third, in the event of privatization, the state's controlling package of shares should be handed over under a trust agreement to the "operative management of the workers' collective in the person of the directors." Fourth, the list of enterprises prohibited from privatizing should be expanded to ensure that not only the main enterprise but all the enterprises "technologically linked to them" in the production of military output were prohibited from going private.[28]

The Decree of August 19

Given the climate that prevailed after the April referendum, when privatization seemed to have gained renewed force, the demands raised at the conference of the League of Assistance to Defense Enterprises would seem to be utopian. Even the participants themselves did not have much faith that anyone would listen to them.[29] Yet within only a few months, their dreams were realized. On August 19, 1993, Yeltsin issued an edict specifically devoted to defense industry privatization.[30]

This document was remarkable for several reasons. It was the first time a legal act had dealt directly with the issue of defense industry privatization in Russia. Previous provisions applying to defense industry had been parts of other laws. Having a separate law meant that the defense complex had achieved its standing goal of gaining special status for defense industry. The edict was also secret. The reason given for this was that there was a list attached to it giving the name, location, and type of weaponry produced by 482 Russian enterprises and design bureaus where privatization would (pending further review) not be allowed.

But the substance of the edict was even more significant, because its other provisions were a fulfillment of everything the League had demanded and more. The edict was a major victory for both the directors of the defense enterprises and for *Roskomoboronprom,* both of which received important new powers allowing them to control and manage the assets of the defense complex. There was even a concession to the Ministry of Defense, which would be allowed once again to place its quality control inspectors in defense enterprises. The loser in all this was clearly the GKI.

The edict put both money and power in the hands of the managers. Any profits that accrued to the state from its shares in the defense enterprises would henceforth be plowed back into the companies.[31] The state also relinquished its own voting rights for those shares (for up to 20 percent of total shares of each enterprise) to the enterprise director and other members of the board of directors.

But though the edict did grant defense enterprise managers these direct concessions, there was a catch. Other apparent gains for the managers were conditional on the support of *Roskomoboronprom. Roskomoboronprom* was designated as the protector of management from both the GKI and outside financial interests. Whenever any defense enterprise was privatized (that is, transformed into a joint-stock company), it would now be up to *Roskomoboronprom* to decide who could be that enterprise's director. Only those individuals who held a special "qualifying certificate" issued by the government would be eligible to be general directors of joint-stock companies producing arms.[32]

Roskomoboronprom would also recommend appointments as the state's representatives on the boards of these companies. In response to the defense managers' complaint that their employment contracts were with the GKI, the new edict stipulated, "All contracts with managers of state-owned defense enterprises shall be concluded and terminated by the chairman of *Roskomoboronprom* as authorized by GKI."

Roskomoboronprom would play a much more prominent role in all future decisions regarding defense-industry privatization as well. A representative of *Roskomoboronprom* would be included in the standing arbitration commissions for resolving disputes in privatization of defense enterprises. (Normally, it was only the GKI and the Antimonopoly Commission that had seats on these boards.) *Roskomoboronprom* would set conditions for privatization regarding maintenance of mobilization capacity, defense orders, and the like. Permission to privatize any defense enterprise that was fulfilling its state defense order could not be granted by territorial agencies of GKI.[33]

The greater influence of *Roskomoboronprom* over the enterprises was a mixed blessing. Although nearly all managers welcomed any attempt to keep the hated GKI from meddling in their affairs, most were not enthusiastic about *Roskomoboronprom*. They simply did not want *anyone* from Moscow telling them what to do. Moreover, the attitudes of the various enterprises differed from one another in many respects. Some enterprise managers wanted to be protected from privatization; others were annoyed to find that they had been included on the list of enterprises prohibited from privatizing. Some had assumed they could privatize if they wanted to and had made far-reaching plans to attract outside capital. They found they now had to devote more time and effort to lobbying efforts to be removed from the list.

The August decree on privatization of defense industry obviously did not resolve all privatization issues. For the time being, most enterprises may have had a somewhat better idea about where they stood on the issue of privatization. But in the context of the overall economic environment in Russia, that was slight progress indeed. In the two years since the coup attempt of August 1991, the really big changes that had occurred were not in specific policies directed toward defense industry but in the overall economic environment. In chapter 6, I retrace the history of some of those changes and the reactions of defense enterprises to them.

Chapter 6

Responding to Market Rules

The series of radical reform measures introduced by the Russian government in January 1992 brought changes to all sectors of the economy. The most immediate change to which Russian defense industry (both the central military-industrial bureaucracy and the enterprise directors) had to adapt was the decision to cut funding for defense procurement by two-thirds. No other major sector of the economy was affected so suddenly and directly by a policy decision from the new government. At the same time, the defense enterprises had to adjust to a very different economic environment overall. Although it could not yet be described as a "market" economy, it was characterized by vastly less regulation and centralization than even in the previous year. Traditional suppliers of goods and materials to defense plants were freer than ever to choose their customers and set their own prices. The liberalization trends that defense industrialists had decried back in 1990 and 1991 under Mikhail Gorbachev gained new force.

Defense-industry managers continued to protest the changes, but as much as they disliked them, the reforms could not be wished out of existence. The enterprises had to adjust simply to survive. Did they succeed? It depends on the definition of success. But if mere survival was the goal, they did remarkably well.

Figure 6-1 shows that despite the decision to cut military procurement funds by 68 percent in 1992—a measure that would appear sufficient to break the back of Russia's defense-industrial complex—by the end of the year, the defense sector still retained a remarkable share of its assets. It lost only 9 percent of its total work force while continuing to expand its physical plant and equipment. And it had accomplished this with no increase in civilian production—indeed, output of civilian products by the defense-industrial complex dropped by 7 percent. In the aggregate, "conversion" had not taken place at all. How was this possible? The many adjustment mechanisms that allowed the sector to survive, and survive in this particular way, are the subject of this chapter.

FIGURE 6-1. *Shock and Response: Russian Defense Industry, 1992*

1992 levels as a percent of 1991

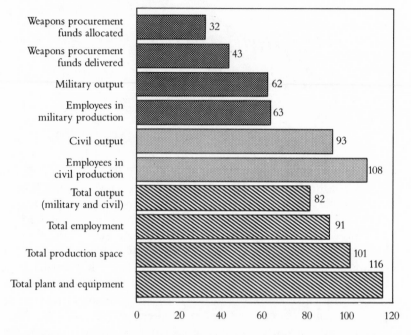

Source: Materials provided to author by Russian government sources, April 1993.

Formation of New Structures:
Big Business in the Center

In the summer of 1991, certain segments of defense industry seemed to have accepted that change was imminent. But they assumed it would be carried out in the grand style to which the defense-industrial establishment had been accustomed. If the new game was the "market economy," they could learn to play that game quickly. Indeed, it was as if they had been waiting for the opportunity. Already in 1991, individuals from the defense-industrial ministries, the VPK (the Military-Industrial Commission), the defense ministry, and various enterprises had begun creating new entities—sometimes explicitly on the basis of their official government bodies, sometimes formally detached from them. In each of the former defense-industrial ministries, personnel who had been the bulwark of what previously was undeniably an antimarket military complex began setting up what they called "commercial structures." Variously described as "holding companies," associations, or industrial groups, they were an effort to retain control over the assets of the military-industrial complex, not least of all the network of personal contacts and proprietary information.

One of the earliest and most spectacular examples of the new structures was the Military-Industrial Investment Company (or VPIK, according to its Russian acronym). The VPIK was set up in the fall of 1991 by individuals connected mainly with the aerospace and missile industry. This particular part of the defense-industrial establishment was well suited to lead the way. Its political influence—and hence its access to people and information—was enormous because of its size and weight in the defense program. It was centered in the Moscow suburb of Kaliningrad, one of about nine "science cities" surrounding the capital. The location was ideal for contacts both with government policymakers and with Westerners. And the aerospace and missile sector did have impressive assets. With its far-flung computer and communications networks, it was the embodiment of Russian high tech, and its personnel were used to thinking in terms of grand plans.

The VPIK was the result of ongoing cooperation between the space-missile group and Russia's leading new capitalist, Konstantin Borovoi. Their partnership had begun in the summer of 1991, when one of the space sector's research institutes had helped computerize operations at Borovoi's new Russian Raw Materials and Commodities Exchange, one of the early symbols of the new Russian market economy. Part of the idea of the VPIK was to expand on this concept and use the computer resources of the military-industrial complex to mediate financial and other business transactions throughout the country. The former mission control center for the Soviet space shuttle was even set up as the "Big Board" of a stock and commodities market and was proudly displayed to foreign visitors.

When the VPIK was founded, its management was shared between individuals associated with Borovoi and top representatives of the military-industrial complex. The general director was a former minister in the Soviet aerospace and missile sector, and the chairman of the board was a Borovoi lieutenant.[1] The other positions on the board of directors were apportioned similarly. The juridical entities that founded the VPIK ranged from some of the leading space and missile producers and design bureaus to military entities (including the highly secretive Dzerzhinsky [Rocket] Academy, which trained officers in the strategic missile forces).

The rapidly shifting tactical approaches of enterprises in the defense sector in these months of change are illustrated by the case of three of the VPIK's founders. In September 1990, during the Gorbachev era, three of the enterprises founding the VPIK—the Khrunichev Works, and the Energiya and the Pleshakova Scientific and Production Groups—had signed the letter protesting the damage the military-industrial complex was enduring as a result of market economic reform.[2] Then, less than a year later, they founded the VPIK. Their investment prospectus described the new company as "a practical vehicle for implementation of conversion of enterprises of the military-industrial complex of the country in accordance with market laws of development of the economy."[3]

The subsequent histories of the three enterprises are equally interesting. Khrunichev and Energiya joined with the American aerospace firm Lockheed to form Lockheed-Khrunichev-Energiya International (LKEI), a marketing consortium for the Proton booster, which Khrunichev and Energiya make. Meanwhile, Pleshakova's general director, Aleksei Shulunov, became the president of the League of Assistance to Defense Enterprises, a main conservative lobby of the industry.

Western Investment

The grandness of the VPIK was admittedly an extreme case for Russian military industry in late 1991 and early 1992. This was a special sector of defense industry, with special contacts, and it was located in Moscow. The overwhelming majority of the defense-industrial establishment was more concerned about survival. The enterprises were nervous about the implications of radical economic reform and Boris Yeltsin's "deep conversion." Still, even among certain enterprise directors at lower levels, there was a noticeable change in attitude following the coup. Some directors turned their attention to the West. Now that Russia was a democracy and open to the world for business, they thought Western businessmen would be ready to come in and invest.

This attitude began to firmly take root after the restrictions that had limited foreigners' travel to defense cities were lifted in the autumn of 1991. During the later Gorbachev years, some defense directors had already hosted delegations of Westerners in the Soviet Union (and had traveled to the West themselves). But this effort was limited almost exclusively to Moscow and Leningrad. In 1991, however, it had spread to the provinces, as one big defense city after another officially opened to foreign visitors. Western business executives began to come in, and although their actual number was not great, the delegations represented a flood in comparison with the past. By the end of 1991, the last of the regions were opened.[4] According to one estimate, managers from some 300 defense enterprises had had foreign contacts to one degree or another by the spring of 1992.[5] Much of the foreign contact was through a small number of Western firms that systematically searched for potential partners for Western investors and corporations for joint ventures.

The results of this unprecedented mutual searching by Western businesses and Russian defense manufacturers are interesting. Russian enterprise directors were under the impression that they had opened themselves and their enterprises up in unprecedented fashion. But the Western perception was quite different. Western executives were not sure they were being shown very much at all. Ostensibly, the discussions on cooperation were about converting military to civilian production; yet most military production lines remained closed to outsiders. The civilian production facilities that were displayed were often shockingly outmoded. More fundamental was the lack of agreement on what was really important about each Russian enterprise. The Western business executives were interested in products and markets, the Russians in engineering and production. American visitors would often be subjected to interminable displays of technological achievements without learning what the Russians wanted to do with them. An innocent question such as "Tell me about your company" would generate hours-long parades of venerable scientific prize winners and citations of their successes. Most of the Americans, with their attitude that time is money, did not have the patience for this.

What probably irritated Americans the most, however, was what they perceived as the Russian inability to think in realistic terms about the scope of cooperation. The Americans were entering totally uncharted territory. Although they were intrigued by Russia and wanted to learn more, almost no one was willing to risk huge amounts of money. The ideal, from the Western point of view, would have been to start with some small-scale ventures. The partners would get to know and trust each other; it would be a learning experience.

Few Russians were prepared to think this way. They wanted big deals and had no lack of big plans: after all, almost every enterprise had several major investment projects on the drawing board left over from the Soviet period, ready to go or even standing half-completed. It did not matter that they were entirely unjustified in a market-driven economy. Largely cut off from the flows of investment credits from Moscow that had sustained them for decades, the directors urgently looked for replacements. Western executives were reluctant to play that role. If they discussed cooperative ventures at all, they were much more modest ones.

The Russians, convinced of the great value of their technology and work force, could not understand why these Americans, who were supposed to be so powerful, could think so small. More than one American had the experience of offering a proposal to a Russian counterpart, only to have it pushed back across the table with the admonition, "Add on three zeros to all your figures and maybe we can talk." Those Americans often hustled themselves nervously out the door, never to be heard from again.

Especially frustrating was the lack of feedback and the misunderstandings—even bitterness—such encounters engendered. The Russians described the situation as a flood of visitors and nothing but a trickle of responses. Americans (and other Westerners) would arrive, "kick the tires" of the Russian enterprise, and walk away without comment. In some cases, the Russians made proposals but never got a response. Not knowing that this is the style of American business and nothing reflecting on them, Russians concluded this indicated something strange, or perhaps dishonest, about the whole effort of opening up to the West. Why are all the Westerners interested in us, they asked, if clearly not for the purpose of doing business? Many Russians concluded that the entire campaign of interest in their defense industry was a Western intelligence operation.

In retrospect it is easy to say that these attempts at business cooperation were destined to be considered failures simply because expectations had been much too high.[6] One of the big problems was that the negative effects were asymmetrical. American company executives may have been disappointed when deals did not materialize, but the fate of their Russian experiment was hardly seen as a life-or-death matter for their businesses. The Russians tended to view things more seriously. Many of the Russian defense-industrial managers had actually placed high hopes on cooperation with Western firms. In frustration, they looked elsewhere for a way out of their predicament.

Foreign Arms Sales

One alternative being offered was arms exports. Leading defense-industry representatives and others whom defense-complex managers presumably trusted to tell them the truth were raising enormous (and unrealistic) expectations that the real future of Russian defense industry was in arms exports. Both those from defense industry's own lobbying group and from the government itself (even including Yeltsin) were proclaiming that there was a huge potential international market for Russian arms.[7]

There seemed no limit to the dreams. In June 1992, a vice president of the League of Assistance to Defense Enterprises, the defense-industry lobby, claimed that Russia could earn up to $30 billion a year from sales and service of arms.[8] The discrepancy between the illusion and the harsh reality was huge. By the end of the year, Russia had exported less than $2 billion worth of weapons.[9] Undaunted, advocates of foreign arms sales continued to project a huge market. In September 1993 an economist from the Ministry of Economics cited projections of $20 billion to $30 billion in annual sales.[10] But the 1993 totals were once again under $2 billion.

The reasons for this phenomenal misjudgment of prospects for export success are complex. Part of the story is that the former Soviet (now Russian) arms manufacturers were entering a world market vastly different from that of even a few years earlier. Shrinking defense budgets worldwide—largely the result of the collapse of the Soviet Union and the end of the cold war—had left excess capacity in all the main arms-producing nations. Albeit to a lesser degree than those in Russia, defense firms in the West were also hungry for export markets, and competition became keener than ever. The Russians simply could not compete in the defense market for new systems with the most advanced technical products of Western manufacturers. Moreover, the end of the cold war had also brought a flood of used but still serviceable equipment from downsizing Western forces.

In addition to a misperception of the harsh realities of the current world market, the Russians also had illusions about the arms market of years past and their role in it. The Russian arms manufacturers were persuaded that they were losing a great market when in fact they never had much of one to lose. It is true that during the Soviet era, huge amounts of arms were shipped abroad, with substantial growth from the mid-1970s to the mid-1980s. Figures from U.S. government sources suggest the importance of Soviet exports relative to domestic procurement. For every 100 tanks delivered to the Soviet armed forces in 1974–85, another 55 were exported to other countries. The corresponding figures were 72 for fighter aircraft, 77 for artillery (including multiple rocket launchers and antiaircraft artillery), and 28 for helicopters.[11]

For all of these arms deliveries, a nominal price was attached, and so revenues appeared enormous on paper. However, in reality many of the weapons exported in the Soviet era had been given away to (or even forced on) client states. Substantially less income was taken in than was officially recorded. In table 6-1 this can be seen in the balance of revenues from Soviet arms sales to countries outside the socialist world from 1975 to 1990. The table shows the proportion of nominal Soviet arms exports that actually sold for hard currency, the proportion that was exchanged for barter goods, and—by implication—the proportion that was simply given away free.

The bottom line is that a substantial proportion—about 44 percent—of the reported sales revenue of the Soviet arms was fictitious. This portion was accounted for either by arms delivered free or by inflated prices. The "real" receipts included hard currency actually received (even if late) plus the imputed market value of barter goods such as oil, natural gas, cotton, foodstuffs, clothing, and other consumer goods.

But the full picture in table 6-1 is something few if any Soviets knew. At the level of the manufacturing enterprises in particular, no one either knew nor cared to know the price for which the weapons sold, the terms of payment, and to what degree those terms were fulfilled. All anyone knew was that foreign countries were ordering huge amounts of Soviet weapons. The arms may have been shipped to Angola or Iran, but payment came from Moscow.

TABLE 6-1. *Soviet Arms Exports to Nonsocialist Countries, 1975–90*
Millions of current US$

Year	(1) Total nominal sales	(2) Cash actually received	(3) Value of barter goods	(4) Total value actually received
1975	2,720	800	836	1,636
1976	3,250	956	999	1,955
1977	5,285	1,554	1,625	3,178
1978	6,319	1,858	1,942	3,800
1979	6,725	1,977	2,067	4,044
1980	6,979	2,052	2,145	4,197
1981	7,984	2,347	2,454	4,802
1982	10,007	2,942	3,076	6,018
1983	9,957	2,927	3,061	5,988
1984	9,183	2,708	2,817	5,525
1985	7,497	2,056	2,417	4,473
1986	10,401	2,740	3,189	5,929
1987	11,225	2,891	3,497	6,389
1988	11,745	2,999	3,682	6,681
1989	11,889	2,942	3,806	6,748
1990	9,410	2,374	2,974	5,348

Source: Derived from Alan Smith, *Russia and the World Economy: Problems of Integration* (Routledge, 1993), tables 5.5 and 8.5, with adjustments as explained below.

Column 1 above is taken directly from table 5.5. The years 1984–90 in column 2 above are computed from table 8.5, and the years 1980–83 by applying a 42 percent rate to column 1 above for hard currency–designated sales as a proportion of total sales to nonsocialist countries.

Then, various assumptions are made about the actual mode of payment of these dollar-designated sales:

1980–85 assumes 25 percent cash, 75 percent credit (with 60 percent of credit repaid).

1986–90 assumes 25 percent cash, 75 percent credit (with 50 percent of credit repaid, because of fall in Mideast oil incomes from 1986).

The 25 percent cash assumption may be too high in some years. Assuming a rate of only, say, 20 percent cash sales would lower total revenues slightly (by a maximum of $120 million in 1988).

Because enterprises had no idea of the real cost of producing the weapons, it was impossible for them to calculate whether any profit had been made on arms sales abroad. Of course, in the Soviet-era system, knowing whether or not arms exports were profitable was irrelevant to the enterprise producing the arms. But in the new economic system that prevailed in 1992 defense enterprises were paying for their previous lack of participation in and knowledge of the foreign trading process. Many enterprises demanded that they be allowed to sell directly instead of channeling exports through a central agency. But then, when the enterprises were finally on their own, they did not know where to start. In at least some cases, they did not even know what prices had been charged for their products. A brisk market in information sprang up. Shadowy figures were seen wandering the halls of various government office buildings in Moscow, seeking out information from this or that mid-level official—information that could be sold in turn to an arms-producing enterprise.[12]

When the hoped-for substantial foreign sales failed to materialize, enterprises rarely blamed themselves. Instead they often tended to believe they were being victimized. The industry's disastrous export record was due, they thought, either to the political ill-will of the Yeltsin government (which they were sure was only too happy to see post-Soviet defense industry fail), the incompetence of the foreign trading authorities (who were not taking advantage of obvious opportunities), or corruption in Moscow (by bureaucrats who skimmed profits or undercharged customers in return for kickbacks).

It took time for the economic reality to sink in. In the meantime, there were mutual recriminations between the enterprises and the trading authorities. Yet all the while the dreams of success on the world arms market had real consequences in the arms enterprises' behavior. Like the illusion of Western investment, succeeding on the export market became an excuse for these enterprises to avoid embarking on the inevitably painful process of internal restructuring: finding new products to market and sell and new ways to produce existing civilian products better and more cheaply. In response to any inquiry about progress in that direction, it was not unusual to hear a plant director ask defensively: "How many pots and pans would we have to make and sell abroad to earn as many dollars as we could get from a single tank or airplane?" The irony was that this was often being said by directors of plants that made neither tanks nor airplanes. But somehow, in their eyes this argument justified that *they* should not have to stoop to produce pots or pans—for export or otherwise.

Surviving without Cash

Neither Western investment nor success in the export market could replace the lost domestic funding of the Soviet defense-industrial complex. Survival depended on other mechanisms. In one case, Moscow-based bureaucratic allies of the defense-industrial complex took the initiative by simply continuing to order weapons, despite the declaration that procurement would be cut. Elsewhere, the enterprises themselves devised the strategy. Joining together with their subcontractors, they continued to produce and even deliver weapons, without any orders at all. In both cases, the expectation was that the government would lose its resolve before the defense enterprises did, and funds would flow once more.

DOMESTIC WEAPONS ORDERS WITHOUT BACKING.   Technically, the agency that ordered weapons was the Ministry of Defense; the agency that paid for them was the Ministry of Finance. In a government under firm control and with a unified direction, this would not have been a problem. Such was not the case in Russia. As a result, it was possible for the Ministry of Defense to keep ordering weapons in excess of what the payer, the Ministry of Finance, had been authorized to pay for.

The tactic seemed to be a conscious one on the part of the Ministry of Defense: It had nothing to lose. The defense enterprises would be demanding payment elsewhere—from the Ministry of Finance. If payment was not made, the Ministry of Finance would be the villain. The Ministry of Defense could even pose as the great ally of the military-industrial complex. In any event, the Ministry of Finance did not have the funds to pay for all the weapons produced in 1992. Payments presumably were made to the enterprises only as long as the money lasted. By the end of 1992, military output was 37 percent below that for 1991 (see figure 6-1). This was a significant drop, yet it was far less than the procurement funding cut of 68 percent. And even though the flow of procurement funds to the enterprises exceeded the amount actually decided on by the Russian government at the beginning of the year (see figure 6-1), a large volume of weapons had been ordered and produced but not paid for. This practice continued in 1993. By the end of that year, the Ministry of Defense reportedly owed the defense enterprises 870 billion rubles for arms.[13]

EXPORT ORDERS WITHOUT BACKING.   The Ministry of Defense was not the only agency seeking to undermine the decision to cut funds for the defense-industrial complex. The ministry had allies in the Ministry of Foreign Economic Relations (MFER). The agency within the MFER responsible for arms exports—the Main Technical Administration, or GTU—continued to order arms for export, even though it should have been clear that there was no paying market.[14] The head of the GTU, Admiral Sergei Krasnov, had been among those claiming that Russia could export huge amounts of arms in 1992.[15] According to one report, 32 percent of the total state procurement order to Russian defense industry in 1992 came from the MFER for exports. Allegedly, weapons worth 37.1 billion rubles (in 1991 prices) were ordered and produced for foreign customers—but never paid for.[16]

The practice of placing what essentially were phony domestic and export orders was clearly a way of providing subsidies to the Russian defense-industrial sector. What was particularly insidious about this was how well it evaded public monitoring. If the government had tried to fund the defense plants by means of ordinary defense orders, it would have been obliged to show where the financing came from, as part of the budget. But in the case of export orders, the central arms exporting authority could sign agreements with a foreign country (or claim that it was going to) and then issue orders to Russian arms producers. The plants, of course, believed what they wanted to hear: that there were real customers out there. In fact, few of the arms they produced were shipped anywhere.

Interenterprise Debt

While claims and counterclaims for payment on both foreign and domestic defense orders were being hurled back and forth between government ministries and defense enterprises, the enterprises themselves still had to find a way to continue producing arms without money. The method they used was known as building up "mutual arrears." On the surface, this appeared to be a spontaneous development. For example, an assembly plant that did not receive payment from the Russian government for weapons delivered was unable to pay its own suppliers; those suppliers in turn could not pay theirs, and so on. But what happened was often not a natural development at all. Rather than trying to avoid becoming entangled in this web of mutual indebtedness, many defense enterprises actively sought it. The more enterprises that depended on payment from the Russian state, they reasoned, the more likely it was that the government would eventually buckle under and pay. Eventually this degenerated to the point where goods were being produced and delivered and the "customer" charged, even without orders.

This mechanism was not confined to defense enterprises. It went on throughout the Russian economy, and—thanks to a major loophole in the law—it was legal. The old Soviet law was based on a system where in most cases enterprises never "bought" goods from one another—the goods were administratively allocated. It was assumed no enterprise would order anything without being told by central planners to do so, so no provision had been made in the law for refusing to accept a product on the grounds that it had not been explicitly ordered by anyone. All the Soviet law had required was that the seller notify the "buyer's" bank that shipment had been made and then collect payment from that bank (if funds were available). This was not changed until July 1, 1992, when the so-called interenterprise arrears crisis forced a change in the system.[17]

At the peak of the arrears crisis in mid-1992, enterprises of all types in Russia were estimated to be behind in their payments to one another in an amount equal to 78 percent of the nation's total gross domestic product (GDP). Four-fifths of Russia's industrial enterprises had either overdue accounts receivable or accounts payable, or both.[18] The debt of defense enterprises to their suppliers and subcontractors definitely accounted for much of this—although exactly how much is not known.

A study of the practice of mutual arrears in civilian industry concluded that most enterprises had not merely been drawn into the scheme unwittingly; it was an active and conscious strategy for survival on their part.[19] Statements by one important defense-industry insider support that conclusion in the case of defense enterprises as well. In December 1993 Mikhail Malei, Yeltsin's adviser on defense-industry matters, stated in an interview:

> Back then, in 1992, [Yegor Gaidar's] "zero" option didn't work. He thought that by leaving defense industry without orders and without any means to survive, that he would bring about its natural collapse. He would divide it up into its constituent parts, and from the remains he could fashion a truncated defense complex, converting all the rest simply and cheaply. That didn't happen. Unexpectedly for Yegor Timurovich [Gaidar], the defense complex applied the rule of mutual indebtedness and survived by using its material resources.[20]

Lobbying for Subsidies

When pursued to its logical extreme, the mutual indebtedness routine was like a pyramid scheme: A did not pay B; therefore, B did not pay C, C did not pay D, and so on down the line. As long as everyone kept playing the game—that is, shipping the goods down the production chain—there would be no problem. But this meant that ultimately all the pressure of the scheme was directed downward. At the very bottom of the chain were the workers in defense enterprises and other production facilities all along the way.

Supplies and components might arrive, unpaid for, at a factory, be fabricated into final products and then shipped on, again unpaid for, without consequence. But fabrication required labor. Workers could not remain unpaid indefinitely; they were bound to protest. To some extent, that was the idea: the plight of millions upon millions of unpaid Russian workers was used as an argument by defense-industry leaders to demand a bailout. Defense enterprises declared that they needed "working capital"—mainly funds to pay wages.

By mid-1992, the process had escalated to where every second enterprise in Russia was behind on payments of wages to its workers.[21] At that point, political will to continue the tight budgetary and monetary policy of the first half of the year weakened dramatically. Carrying out decisions made by both the government and the Russian parliament, the central bank sharply increased the flow of credits to all sectors of the economy. The rate of growth of credit issued in June and July 1992 was six times what it had been in the previous two months.[22] The overall amount of subsidies was huge. Official statistics claim that the volume of subsidized credits (credits either interest-free or at extremely low interest rates and probably assumed not to be repaid) in July to September 1992 alone was roughly one-quarter of Russian GDP.[23] Nearly all of this extra credit was covered by monetary emission. The result was a sharp increase in inflation beginning in October. For the next thirteen months, prices rose at a monthly rate of 20 percent.

The conventional wisdom finds that there were three main rivals for funds from the Russian budget: the agricultural lobby, the fuel and energy lobby, and the defense-industrial lobby. Each voiced its particular threat if it did not receive additional funding. The agricultural lobby threatened a food shortage if farms did not get the money needed to prepare for sowing crops in the spring and bringing in the harvest in the fall. The energy lobby threatened power cutoffs as cold weather approached the northern regions in late August. (These two threats were most effective in July and August, so combining them tended to bring a certain seasonality to credit emission in Russia.) The defense lobby's main threat was that without extra money, there would be a social explosion as millions of Russian defense workers, concentrated in a limited number of cities, would take to the streets. In arguing for new infusions of money to the defense sector, defense-industry advocates would consistently downplay the amount of budgeted money used to produce weapons. They argued that the funds were being used to save jobs.[24]

The defense-industrial lobby was blamed for playing a pivotal role in getting the Russian government to abandon its tight budgetary policy in 1992.[25] But the biggest beneficiary of the opening of the credit spigot was the agricultural lobby. Of the 1.5 trillion rubles issued in credits to all branches of the Russian economy in the late summer and early autumn of 1992, 50 percent went to the agroindustrial complex and another 15 percent to the Far North, mainly in subsidies for energy. All other branches of the economy, including defense industry, accounted for the remaining 35 percent.[26]

The relationship among the three lobbies was often ambiguous. On the one hand, they shared a common grudge against a government that was radically reducing subsidies across the board. On the other hand, all realized that they were competing with each other for pieces of that shrinking pie. The gains for one would come at the expense of the others. To the extent that the lobbies recognized Gaidar as a permanent fixture on the scene, even he would have to be a target of their lobbying. At the end of 1992, the defense-industry lobby apparently believed that it had accomplished something in that regard. When Gaidar was replaced as prime minister by Viktor Chernomyrdin, some in the defense-industrial complex feared that the new prime minister might become a bigger threat to them than Gaidar. Chernomyrdin, after all, was a former minister of the gas industry. Because of those previous ties, there was concern that he would support the rival energy lobby. As one longtime defense-industry bureaucrat commented in 1993, "The leadership of the fuel and energy complex [had been] making considerable efforts to prevent any outflow of funds to the military-industrial complex and to win subsidies for itself." Reflecting on the efforts of the defense-industrial complex in 1992, he stated, "After doing a titanic amount of work, we even reached mutual understanding with such a market man as Yegor Gaidar. I fear that everything may now have to be started over, but I can see no other solution."[27]

Market Relations and Freedom of Choice

The idea of continuing to produce arms without orders and without money by using mutual arrears worked as long as everyone kept playing the game. Many enterprises formerly associated with the defense complex did so because they had no choice—they had no alternative customers. But the pyramid scheme broke down when it reached someone who did not want or need to supply insolvent customers, no matter how politically powerful they once had been. This breakdown is exactly what happened in the new environment of economic liberalization.

The Soviet military-industrial complex had been an artificial network of production relations. Its command over resources did not arise from allocation by market prices, but by administratively imposed constraints on suppliers of inputs. Money never mattered in this system, except as an accounting unit. When Russia abolished the tight control over the whole military-production network, enterprises previously constrained to supply their products to military plants were, in principle, free to look for alternatives. If the defense plants still wanted their products, they would have to bid for them along with everyone else. This was one of the issues that had so outraged the defense-industry representatives who signed the open letter of protest back in 1990 (see chapter 4). Prices were being taken seriously for the first time, and those in the defense complex found that difficult to accept.

But the emergence of an economy in which money mattered put the defense industry at a disadvantage. First of all, as the payments crisis showed, its enterprises did not have much money. Moreover, the whole concept of using money implies true market behavior: searching for partners for voluntary exchange, bargaining over prices and other terms, establishing mechanisms of contract enforcement, and the like. Many managers of defense enterprises were unaccustomed to this way of acting. Their civilian counterparts had developed considerable skills over the years in beating the system and finding scarce supplies by their own means (which usually involved market behavior). The natural tendency of powerful defense-industry executives, however, had been to appeal to the political authorities to "make the system work"—that is, to use command methods to ensure that resources were allocated to them. No one had followed all the rules in the Soviet system, but as beneficiaries of the system the way it was *supposed* to work, the defense managers in the old system wanted to enforce the rules, not bend them. But now, with the ultimate enforcer of those old rules, the Communist party, gone, money became even more important in determining how resources would be allocated.

This is what made the pyramid scheme fall apart. The weapons assembly plants were definitely in favor of a "we're-all-in-this-together" approach. The same was true of some of the supplier plants whose manufactured products had little or no value outside the defense production network. It was not worth it for them to defect; if there was no demand for MiG fighter planes, for example, there was even less for the components designed exclusively for those MiGs. But the situation was different for some levels in the pyramid. Certain raw materials and metals, in particular, had high value outside the defense production network. Indeed, the further "upstream" one went, the more valuable the products became. One of the best examples of how the emergence of market economic relations inside the defense-industrial complex affected an important sector of the Russian economy is the aluminum industry. The fate of that industry in 1992 and 1993 is worthy of closer examination.

The Case of Aluminum

Aluminum is an especially appropriate example of how dependent the Soviet economy was on defense industry—and how distorted it was as a result. In the Western world, few commodities better illustrate the consumer economy of the past twenty to thirty years than aluminum. Its principal uses in modern market economies (about 75 percent of all aluminum is used for construction, packaging, and transportation) are at the heart of the consumer society. From aluminum siding on houses to beverage cans and cars, Western societies have found one new use after another for the metal, with demand pushing the industry to expand capacity. For the past twenty years, consumption of aluminum in the Western world has grown at a annual rate of about 2 percent.[28] In Japan, aluminum consumption shot up 49 percent between 1986 and 1990.[29]

What of aluminum production in the Soviet Union? Because all statistics on production capacity and actual output had remained secret since the Soviet aluminum industry began in 1932, there are no exact figures available.[30] Aluminum output appears to have increased sharply in the mid-1980s, rising from slightly more than 2 million tons in 1982 to 3 million tons in 1987.[31] Less information is available about the specific uses of aluminum. It is clear that it was used extensively in military industry. But no aluminum was used in Soviet-made passenger cars, nor were any Soviet beverages sold in cans of any kind—much less any made of aluminum. Cigarette packs with aluminum foil liners, foil-wrapped candy bars or chewing gum—none had been produced in the USSR. Consequently, when aluminum producers were no longer tied to a rigid system requiring them to supply the defense industry and they could choose to whom they sold their product, they found practically no existing civilian market for aluminum inside Russia. But they did find a market in the West. Beginning in 1991, exports from the former Soviet Union (mainly Russia) climbed sharply. Exports rose from around 250,000 metric tons a year before 1991 to more than 1 million tons in 1992 and 1.8 million tons in 1993 (see figure 6-2).

The West was unprepared for the flood of aluminum from the former Soviet Union. In the first place, because of the veil of secrecy, no one had known how much aluminum production capacity the USSR had. But even after *glasnost'*, Western experts seriously underestimated the resilience of this industry.[32] They thought it odd that the "inefficient and largely obsolete" Soviet aluminum industry could swamp Western markets. They did not know why this happened and what was sustaining it. Although it was sometimes acknowledged that the aluminum industry had been built up to satisfy defense needs in the former Soviet Union, little attention was paid to the importance of suppliers now being free to sell to whom they chose. Prediction after prediction was made by Western experts on the aluminum industry who declared that this flooding of the market could not last.[33] Their forecasts were repeatedly proven false.

EFFECTS ON THE WORLD MARKET.   Russian aluminum flooded the world market at a point when the Western aluminum industry was in the throes of a recession. Prices had dropped from $1.60 a pound in mid-1988 to $0.60 a pound in 1991. Russian exports kept that price low. Some alleged that the Russians were dumping aluminum—selling the metal abroad at prices below that on the domestic market. Technically, it was not dumping; aluminum prices were set strictly on the basis of world supply and demand by the London Metals Exchange. But the willingness of the Russian smelters to continue to produce and sell in a glutted market, and to do so when other producers could not, underscored that the entire Soviet industry had not been built up along market principles.

FIGURE 6-2. *Production, Domestic Consumption, and Exports of Aluminum in the Former Soviet Union, 1987–93*

Millions of metric tons

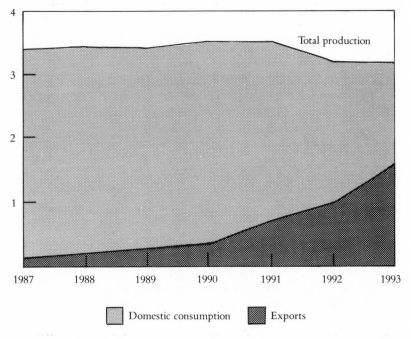

Domestic consumption   Exports

Source: David Humphreys, "Mining and Metals in the CIS: Between Autarky and Integration," paper prepared for the Post-Soviet Business Forum, Royal Institute of International Affairs, November 23, 1993, draft version; Alison Leigh Cowan, "A Squeeze Play by Big Aluminum," *New York Times*, November 24, 1993, p. D1; and "Aluminum Talks Falter," *New York Times*, January 24, 1994, p. D9.

The ongoing cost squeeze on the world aluminum industry led to the closure in 1992 of nearly 1 million tons of production capacity in the West.[34] There were other external effects as well. All of the Western production capacity being shut down was considerably cleaner than that of the Russian smelters. At some smelters in Russia, environmental conditions were so poor that the life expectancy of the workers was only 47 years. "If Russia's own antipollution regulations were enforced, every one of its aluminum smelters would either have to close or curtail output substantially," wrote one commentator.[35]

EFFECTS IN RUSSIA.   In theory, Russian aluminum production should have been a perfect illustration of the gain to the Russian economy that demilitarization was to bring. Aluminum was one of the valuable resources that had previously been poured into the military. Demilitarization meant that aluminum would be used to produce useful consumer goods, not weapons, according to the definition of the so-called peace dividend. In fact, Russian aluminum *was* successfully converted from military to civilian uses, as were copper, zinc, lead, and other metals whose exports had also soared. However, few inside or outside Russia perceived this as true conversion. The failure to do so once again illustrates the fallacy of the conventional notion of conversion.

The assumption had been that Russian aluminum would be used by the same plants that had used it in the past, only now aluminum would somehow be used to produce useful consumer goods instead of weapons. Jobs would therefore be kept in the defense plants. What the conversion advocates failed to understand was that no resource formerly employed by defense industry (including aluminum) had any value independent of the market infrastructure into which it could be integrated. Conversion devotees were unwilling to accept the logical consequence of market reform: The market will allocate the resource to those who are willing to pay more for it than others, precisely because they have a way to use it that will yield a higher value. As it turned out, the highest bidders were outside Russia. Consequently, that was where the "conversion" of Russian aluminum from military to civilian purposes mainly occurred.

A large share of Russia's peace dividend accrued to foreign consumers of canned soft drinks, cars, and other products, which were less expensive because of the added supply of Russian aluminum on the world market. Russians—that is, aluminum smelters and their workers and communities—benefited, too. But what was missing in the eyes of the conversion advocates was value-added activity that used the aluminum inside the Russian plants that had once used it for arms production. However, this could not happen unless those plants could come up with ideas for products that could compete with alternative uses of the aluminum in the rest of the world. The plants simply did not.

The attempts by defense industry to use aluminum and other metals in conversion products failed almost entirely. Titanium, which has broad applications in the aerospace industry, had been used in massive quantities in plants in the Urals. The conversion plans of many defense enterprises in that region featured titanium. One of the legendary examples is the manufacture of garden spades and shovels of titanium by several different defense plants in the Urals in 1991 and 1992. This apparently began as a serious effort to find a practical use for what then seemed to be "excess" metal. But it was based on a complete lack of awareness of how prices would change and how difficult it might become to have continued access to such a valuable metal. Although the initial result was a lot of wonderfully light and strong spades being used to dig potatoes on garden plots in the Urals, more entrepreneurial souls quickly realized that the value of the spades lay in the metal. Thousands of shovels were exported for the value of the titanium alone.[36]

Finally, even some defense plants concluded that the best use of their stockpiled titanium was to sell it directly, rather than waste time (and value) trying to transform it into some manufactured product. In fact, for a period the defense enterprises could themselves benefit from the liberalization of foreign trade. They could draw from their mobilization stockpiles and also benefit from the inertia in the system that allowed them to continue to have privileged access to metals for a while longer.

Not only did Russian defense industry fail to come up with new uses of aluminum and other metals, but they also found that the new prices rendered even existing civilian uses for these metals unprofitable. As Russian aluminum came to the world market, the world market came to Russia in the form of prices. The domestic Russian price of aluminum soared (figure 6-3). It was far beyond the reach of the same defense industries that had once had unlimited supplies. Figure 6-3 indicates that the domestic price of aluminum remained substantially below the world market price through 1993, suggesting that Russian enterprises still would have had a cost advantage. This is, however, misleading. It was extremely difficult for a Russian enterprise to procure aluminum domestically at any price in 1992 and 1993. The manager of the refrigerator-manufacturing division of a Russian defense plant reported in the spring of 1993 that he had faced such pressing problems in acquiring aluminum inside Russia that he was considering turning to the world market to get what his plant needed (each refrigerator used about 1.5 kilograms of aluminum). Nominally, this method of acquiring metals was more expensive, but the more reliable supply was worth it.[37]

One of the reasons for the difficulty in actually obtaining aluminum inside Russia was that much had been contracted for by Western trading organizations already at the smelters. A significant part of the Russian aluminum industry depended on supplies of alumina and other raw materials from abroad. With the breakdown in centralized foreign trade, the smelters were often incapable of managing the financial risk of obtaining those materials. Western metals traders bartered raw materials for aluminum ingot, which they could market internationally. It was the ability of Western organizations to assume the financial risk in obtaining those materials and to deliver the aluminum to market that made it possible for the Russians to become such big players on the world market.[38] As much as some Russians (particularly in defense industry) resented seeing "their" raw materials exported to the West, Russia could have been even worse off. If not for the market-driven intervention of Western trading organizations, even the smelters might have been idle, and Russia would have

FIGURE 6-3. *Domestic and World Market Prices of Russian Aluminum, December 1991–October 1993*

U.S. dollars per metric ton

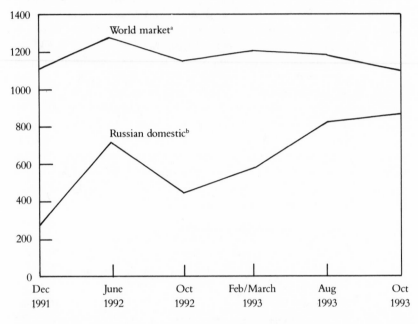

Source: Based on data from selected issues of *Kommersant* and the *Financial Times*, December 1991–October 1993.

a. London Metals Exchange.

b. Moscow Raw Materials and Commodities Exchange.

gained much less than it did from the demilitarization of the aluminum industry.

Consumer Freedom and Defense Industries

What can ultimately be said about those enterprises in the Russian defense-industrial complex that already had civilian production? Were they able to survive? Some have, but there are so few of them that surveys of the defense sector name them individually.[39] The general picture is much gloomier. Figure 6-1 showed that in the aggregate, civilian production by Russian defense industries in 1992 did not compensate for the decline in military output, because civilian production also declined in that year. However, this proved to be only the beginning of a much worse trend.

Defense industry had two broad types of civilian production. It manufactured consumer goods destined directly for households—television sets, refrigerators, vacuum cleaners, and the like—and it produced goods for government and industrial consumers, ranging from bulldozers and airliners to machinery used in plants manufacturing consumer goods. The record in both categories is poor. The collapse of the Russian consumer goods manufacturing industry has been one of the most dramatic developments of the post-Soviet transition. Defense enterprises have been affected directly and indirectly. These plants had been monopoly or near-monopoly producers of a whole range of goods and had had years, even decades, of experience in manufacturing them. Figure 6-4 illustrates how drastic this collapse has been.

Many reasons have been given for this calamitous decline in consumer goods output. For instance, some have attributed it to a breakdown in supply relationships among producing enterprises. But this is the same as with aluminum: Suppliers previously constrained in a command economy were now permitted to choose their customers and set market prices. Another explanation is lack of consumer demand. Yet Russian consumers are purchasing imported goods in great quantities at prices much higher than the competing domestic products.[40] According to government estimates, by 1994 Russian manufacturers of consumer goods had lost 40 percent of their domestic market to imports.[41] (Nongovernment estimates cite an even higher share lost.) The ultimate cause of the collapse of the Russian consumer goods industry mirrors the case of aluminum: freedom for both consumers and producers to make their own choices. The effect on defense industry can be illustrated by the seemingly mundane example of the Russian market for clothing and textiles.

In August 1993, the Ministry of Economics published figures showing that of all categories of civilian goods manufactured by the Russian defense complex, the one that had suffered the greatest collapse during the first half of 1993 was production of the machinery used in the nation's textile industry. The government report attributed this collapse to the "lack of funds for purchase of equipment by purchasing branches on account of their own drop in output."[42] Why? The answer requires tracing networks of production and consumption, supply and demand.

In the Soviet era, the demand for textile machinery was dictated by the decisions of an army of functionaries in Moscow, working in the offices of the state planning commission, *Gosplan*. Using calculations of "scientific consumption norms," they determined how much clothing and cloth the Soviet people needed and then computed everything necessary to produce them, including machinery. Output quotas were issued for the apparel manufacturers, the textile mills, and so on, back to the cotton producers and the manufacturers of spinning machines and looms.

By early 1992, this procedure had changed radically. The decision about how much clothing and what kind was "needed" by Russian citizens

FIGURE 6-4. *Output of Major Household Appliances and Other Consumer Electronics by Russian Defense Enterprises, 1985–94*

1990 = 1

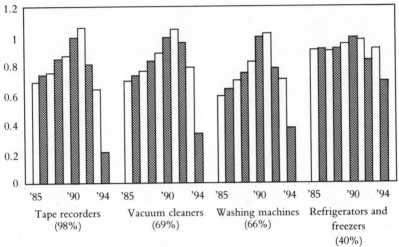

'85 '90 '94	'85 '90 '94	'85 '90 '94	'85 '90 '94
Tape recorders (98%)	Vacuum cleaners (69%)	Washing machines (66%)	Refrigerators and freezers (40%)

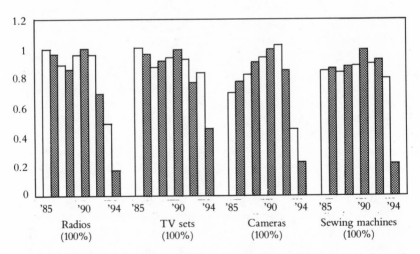

'85 '90 '94	'85 '90 '94	'85 '90 '94	'85 '90 '94
Radios (100%)	TV sets (100%)	Cameras (100%)	Sewing machines (100%)

Sources: Goskomstat Rossii, *Narodnoye khozyaystvo RSFSR v 1988 g. Statisticheskiy yezhegodnik* [The national economy of the RSFSR in 1988: Statistical yearbook] (Moscow: Finances and Statistics, 1989), pp. 417–18 (hereafter *Narkhoz*); Goskomstat Rossii, *Rossiskaya Federatsiya v 1992 godu. Statisticheskiy yezhegodnik* [The Russian Federation in 1992: Statistical yearbook] (Moscow: Republic Information Publishing Center, 1993); *Sotsial'no-ekonomicheskoye polozheniye Rossii, 1993* [Russia's socioeconomic situation, 1993] (Moscow: Goskomstat Rossii, 1994), p. 224; and "Sotsial'no-ekonomicheskoye polozheniye Rossii v 1994 g [Russia's socioeconomic situation in 1994]," *Voprosy statistiki*, no. 3 (1995), p. 66.

was no longer being made by *Gosplan* but by the Russians themselves. They were doing it by buying a shirt or a pair of jeans on the street corner, haggling with the street vendors or kiosk operators rather than shopping in the big government department store. But the street vendor was not selling clothing made from the cotton fabric produced in the Russian textile mills; and the textile mills, not the centralized planning and supply agencies in Moscow, were the clients of the factory that produced their spinning machines and looms. If Russians were not buying Russian shirts and jackets, the clothing producers were not ordering fabric from the mills. The mills did not, in turn, have the funds to buy machinery from the defense enterprise producing the looms.

There was another important part of the story also relating to processes beyond the control of the ministries in Moscow. Under the old Soviet system, 70 percent of the cotton used by the Russian textile mills was grown in the Soviet republic of Uzbekistan. With the fall of the USSR, Uzbekistan became not only an independent country but an independent economic actor. Suddenly it had a real choice in what to do with its cotton. On the world market, cotton could be sold for many times the price the Russians had paid. The mills could not afford those prices—their sales were already suffering. Without funds to purchase the key raw material, production fell even more. By the end of 1992, output of cotton fabric in Russia was already down 38 percent over 1991.[43]

This created a vicious cycle. With acute shortages of fabric and apparel from the domestic mills, the retail sector had an even greater incentive to find imported goods to sell. Private traders streamed across Russia's borders, west to Warsaw and east to Beijing, each taking Russian manufactures such as chain saws or rototillers (ironically, many from defense plants) and bringing back, legally, up to $10,000 worth of Chinese- or Vietnamese-made shirts, dresses, jackets, and athletic wear.

Eventually, this had to affect the next upstream stage, the defense enterprises that produced the machinery used by the textile mills. At first, the drop in textile machinery production lagged slightly behind the decline in cloth output. But by the end of 1993, the drop in machinery production was worse than even that of fabric. The picture was equally grim in many other branches of consumer goods manufacturing linked in this way to defense industry. Figure 6-5 illustrates how output changed for textiles, footwear, and the machinery that produced them.

Conclusion

We have examined several cases of how the removal of constraints on agents in the economy during the reform period altered the economic

FIGURE 6-5. *Output of Cotton Fabric and Shoes, and Machinery for the Textile and Footwear Industries, 1991–94*

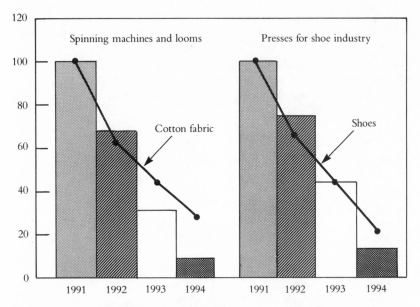

Source: *O razvitii ekonomicheskikh reform v Rossiyskoy Federatsii v 1992 (dopinitel'nyye dannyye)* [On the development of economic reform in Russia in 1992 (supplementary data)] (Moscow: Goskomstat Rossii, 1993), pp. 59, 77; *Sotsial'no-ekonomicheskoye polozheniye Rossii 1993 g.*, pp. 219, 225; "Sotsial'no-ekonomicheskoye polozheniye Rossii v 1994 g. (po materialiam Goskomstat Rossii) [Russia's socioeconomic situation, 1994 (according to material from Goskomstat of Russia)]," *Voprosy statistiki*, no. 3 (1995), pp. 64, 66.

environment for Russian defense enterprises. These examples of freedom of choice for consumers and suppliers also raise a fundamental question about conversion. What exactly is the Russian defense enterprise, the entity that is to be converted? It is, of course, everything that is legally the property of the enterprise, its plant and equipment. But what about all the other components of the production process that had been brought in from the outside?

As we have seen, the idea governing conversion generally was that the same inputs would be used by the same manufacturers to produce different products. But in reality these inputs were *not* part of the defense enterprise. Under the old system, they had been in effect owned by it, but that was no longer the case. The "converting" defense industry no longer enjoyed the privileged access to inputs it once had. One main factor of production the defense complex no longer controlled in the same way was labor.

Chapter 7

New Choices for Workers

O f all the freedoms Russians gained during the reform period, perhaps none has had a greater impact on the nation's economy than the expanded right to choose where they would work and at what. Not only did reform ease regulations and restrictions throughout the labor market, but by introducing the many new occupations associated with a market economy, it also created a whole range of employment opportunities that simply had not existed under the old Soviet system.

The large number of people who took advantage of these opportunities and left their old jobs upset the existing balance of the labor market. This had an especially strong impact on defense enterprises. While the lure of work outside the defense enterprises grew, much of the special attraction of working in the defense sector diminished. Not only the material rewards but also the less tangible benefits—the special social prestige and sense of mission that had once been a part of defense-industry work, or the ability (rare in the Soviet system) simply to have the tools and equipment that allowed an honest worker to do the job—decreased drastically. All these factors contributed to greater mobility in the defense labor force.

Although there is little doubt that the net result has been a substantial reduction in the number of workers in the defense sector, it is difficult to analyze this decline in detail. Determining even the aggregate flows of labor out of the defense complex—much less answering the questions of why workers left, who they were, and where they went—is a challenge.

Mobility of the Defense-Industrial Labor Force

Any analysis of the mobility of the defense labor force during the reform period is plagued by the same problems regarding data as was evident in the discussion in chapter 2 concerning the number of defense workers. The main problem with the data is still a notable lack of clarity, if not outright secrecy.[1] Moreover, those who do have access to data often have political motives for distorting the picture. On the one hand, some claim an alarming rate of loss of skilled labor from defense plants, under-estimating the actual number of highly trained employees still working in them; on the other hand, some exaggerate the size of the labor force in defense industry to underscore its political weight and the threat of dire consequences if these enterprises are allowed to fail.

The result has been a lack of authoritative data, as well as many data that are contradictory and highly inconsistent. To circumvent the problem of the dearth of directly acquired data on the defense-industrial labor market, some of the discussion in this chapter is based on two types of indirect statistical evidence: regional averages of labor market variables (comparing oblasts with high and low concentrations of defense-industrial enterprises), and data on the sector of manufacturing industry most heavily dominated by defense enterprises, machine-building and metalworking (MBMW).

In principle, a standard Soviet statistic would be a good starting point for studying the issue of mobility: the so-called labor turnover rate, or the percentage of workers who each year either quit their jobs of their own volition or are fired by management for disciplinary reasons.[2] Soviet doctrine considered this sort of labor mobility "unplanned" and accounted for it statistically apart from all other movement of labor within the economy. When workers left their jobs for "objective" reasons (military leave, educational leave, maternity leave, or retirement), this was considered "planned" mobility, because it reflected—or at least did not contradict—the social goals of Soviet planners. Another category of planned mobility was layoffs, as enterprises could not collectively dismiss personnel without permission from central planners.

Unplanned mobility or turnover reflected purely individual goals, making it negative on ideological grounds alone. But there was a practical concern as well. The Soviet system of economic management had produced a chronic shortage of labor throughout the economy. At the heart of the problem was the so-called priority approach to economic development described in chapter 3. Certain high-priority economic activities (arms production chief among them) were deemed so important that they were guaranteed no matter what. This dictated keeping both extra physical production capacity and labor reserves on hand, especially in these economic sectors.

But labor differed fundamentally from other inputs. Whereas planners and central bureaucrats had relative control over the allocation of physical resources (plant and equipment, components, raw materials), labor meant real human beings who, even in the Soviet system, had enough freedom of choice to upset planning goals. The planners could issue quotas for output and centrally allocate the material inputs needed to meet them. But generally they could not allocate labor that way. In the end, it was left up to the plant director to obtain the amount and kind of labor required to make the plant run. The result was that for managers in all sectors of the economy, finding enough labor became the biggest headache of all. One thorough study of Soviet management, which surveyed more than 2,000 managerial personnel in 226 industrial enterprises in the 1980s, found that managers ranked "shortage of labor" as the single most critical factor hindering the normal productive work of their plants—even more important than lack of materials or difficulties in dealing with planning directives.[3]

When Soviet managers talked about their chronic demand for more workers, they actually were referring to the demand for different categories of labor. Each enterprise had a productive function to perform; for that, it needed skilled and educated workers. This was especially relevant for defense plants. As the priority sector of the economy, in which failure was not allowed and to which the best material inputs (machines, components, and raw materials) had been provided, successful operation of defense enterprises required an adequate supply of reliable and competent workers. On the other hand, nearly every large enterprise (including high-tech defense plants) needed an additional pool of unskilled laborers. These workers would not only perform the numerous manual chores required at any Soviet industrial enterprise but could also be sent out by the plants to perform civic tasks such as harvest work or fire duty.

The result of this demand for labor of different levels of quality was that to some extent most enterprises ended up with a two-tier system of personnel recruitment and allocation. They used their most productive workers for the plant's highest priority work. But to be able to meet all the other demands on them without interfering with priority work, plant managers also maintained a corps of second-rank workers to do extra, unexpected tasks and to serve as a general reserve (for instance, for the unique Soviet phenomenon of "storming," or exerting frantic effort to meet a quota at the last minute). Special circumstances and tasks might create a demand for even more types of labor. Many defense plants had fairly extensive civilian production, usually in the same facilities. Those plants needed a third category of labor, between their high-priority military work and the lowest priority "civic duties" (harvest work, for example). Even though the concept of productivity in a market sense was absent, enterprise managers did implicitly measure the value of the marginal additional worker by estimating the net contribution he or she would make to the overall welfare of the plant and its management. That calculation tended to show that almost any worker was better than none. Unless the worker was directly disruptive (owing to violent behavior or alcoholism), it was generally considered better to have an additional worker on the payroll than not. Even if these individuals were not needed all the time or at the moment, they were worth having around to meet a quota for farm labor or for some other emergency. In the end, the rule tended to be: "When in doubt, hire!"

Workers were of course aware of this situation, and they took advantage of it. With no fear of unemployment, even a poor worker could walk off one job and right onto the next. In fact, for most of the 1960s and 1970s, as many as one out of every five workers in Soviet industry did just that every year.[4] This sort of "job shopping" was dirt cheap for the worker but costly to employers. If all the workers had been menial laborers, the fact that they frequently left their jobs would not have been so serious a problem. But the more skills and specialized knowledge needed in a job, the more costly it was to hire new people. Workers would have to pass through the often lengthy learning period during which they acquired the particular knowledge and techniques needed in a plant—what in a market economy is known as firm-specific human capital. In short, excessive mobility among skilled workers made it difficult to plan and organize production.

To the extent that they needed more skilled workers, defense plants were more vulnerable to the consequences of excessive turnover. At the same time, they were also in a better situation to solve the problem. As discussed in chapter 3, defense enterprises enjoyed preferential rights in hiring specialists in local labor markets. Another big advantage was their superior ability to offer their employees social benefits such as housing, day care, vacation facilities, and the like. Not only were such benefits often more attractive to workers than monetary wages, but they also served the purpose of increasing the workers' dependence on the enterprise.[5]

The large size of many defense enterprises also helped mitigate the turnover problem. Larger enterprises could offer more opportunity for internal horizontal moves, continuing education under the auspices of the enterprise, and career advancement—all of which might have particular appeal to the younger workers who accounted for most of the labor mobility in the Soviet economy.[6]

Although there was undoubtedly heterogeneity within the defense complex, on balance a lower rate of turnover would be expected in defense enterprises than in the rest of the economy. Indirect evidence from regional labor markets supports this. Figure 7-1 compares average annual turnover rates from 1965 to 1989 in oblasts where defense industry accounted for a large proportion of all manufacturing employment and oblasts with low concentrations of defense-industrial employment. The figure shows that though turnover rates in defense regions fell and rose as in the Soviet Union

FIGURE 7-1. *Employee Turnover in Industry in Defense and Nondefense Oblasts, 1965–89*

Percent of workers changing enterprises each year

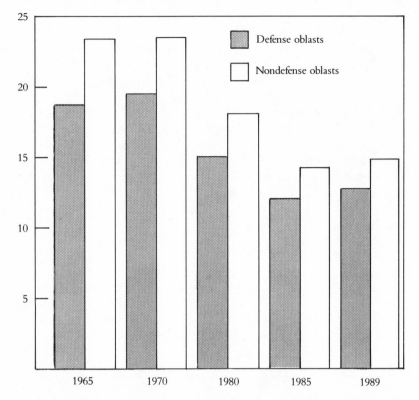

Source: Goskomstat RSFSR, *Pokazateli sotsial'nogo razvitiya respublik, krayev i oblastey RSFSR* [Indicators of social development for republics, territories, and provinces of the RSFSR] (Moscow, 1990), pp. 55–56. Statistics cover blue-collar employees (*rabochiye*) only. For definition of defense and nondefense oblasts see table 9-1 and text and note 1 of chapter 9.

as a whole, the typical defense-industrial region did have a more stable labor force over the twenty-five years covered by the data.[7]

The Net Effect on Defense Enterprises

An intense campaign was waged against labor turnover in the USSR in the 1980s. To repeatedly quit one's job was declared a "social ill" or even a "social anomaly." As a result of the campaign, turnover rates were pushed to a historical low in 1986.[8] But this was artificial containment of a natural phenomenon and probably could not have lasted long in any case. Increased deregulation of the labor market in the late 1980s spurred employee mobility once again. After the more radical reforms of 1992, labor mobility was finally recognized as a normal and desirable feature of a dynamic labor market. Less attention was paid to the phenomenon, and unfortunately, fewer data were collected.

But even if the turnover data were available, they would not reveal many interesting aspects of the labor market picture in recent years. The Soviet-era statistic of turnover did not include movement due to layoffs; nor could it give the net effect on a particular sector of the economy, such as defense industry. Labor turnover only measured movement from one plant to another. A worker who left one defense job for another at a different plant was counted in the turnover statistics the same way as the worker who left the defense sector altogether. A different measure would be to look at the *net* change in the defense-industrial labor force. Based on what appear to be the most authoritative official statements (and some estimates to fill in gaps), the picture that emerges of employment in the defense complex since the mid-1980s looks like figure 7-2.

This is a dramatic picture. By the end of 1994, employment in enterprises of the Russian defense-industrial complex was only about 55 percent of its peak level some six years earlier. Moreover, the rate of decline has accelerated: from 4 percent in 1991 to 9 percent in 1992, 12 percent in 1993, and 19 percent in 1994. Figure 7-2 uses the same definition of defense-complex employee as in chapter 2: employees (blue-collar or white-collar) classified statistically as *promyshlenno-proizvodstvennyy personal* (the so-called PPP, or "industrial production employees"), who work in enterprises subordinated administratively to the State Committee on Defense Branches of Industry (*Goskomoboronprom*), the successor to the Soviet VPK. This category does not include nonindustrial employees of the plants, nor does it include employees of defense research institutes and design bureaus.

The discussion in chapter 2 revealed that this narrow category of "defense employee" may represent only half of those whose jobs were dependent on the defense-industrial complex. However, assuming that overall employment in all categories of defense-related industry has declined at the same rate, as many as 5 million workers may have left the Russian defense-industrial complex since the mid-1980s.[9]

Later in this chapter we need to go beyond the aggregates and ask who these people are, why they left these plants, and where they went. But first there are several questions raised by the data in figure 7-2.

—To what extent do these data take into account so-called hidden unemployment? That is, how many of the workers counted were only nominally employed in defense enterprises but were actually not working for them?

FIGURE 7-2.   *Downsizing of Russian Defense-Industrial Labor Force, 1985–95: The Official Picture*

Millions of industrial employees at beginning of year

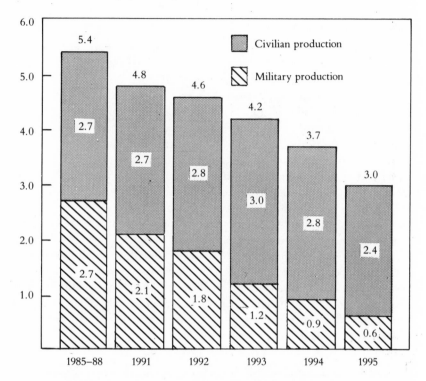

Sources: 1985–88 employment and civilian-military breakdown from table 2-4. 1994 employment from Viktor Glukhikh, "The Defense Industry of Russia: The Situation and Tasks for 1994," *Konversiya*, no. 4 (1994), pp. 3–8, in Joint Publications Research Service, *Military Affairs*, August 17, 1994, pp. 43–49. Rates of change over the period from Tsentr ekonomicheskoy kon"yunktury i prognozirovaniya, *Rossiya—1993: Ekonomicheskaya kon"yunktura* [Russia—1993: Economic situation], no. 1 (Moscow, 1993), pp. 153–60; Center for Economic Analysis, *Russia—1994: Economic situation*, no. 1 (Moscow, 1994), pp. 140–44. 1995 employment computed from data in "Sotsial'no-ekonomicheskoye polozheniye Rossii v 1994 g. [Russia's socioeconomic situation in 1994]," *Voprosy statistiki*, no. 3 (1995), p. 62; and Vitaly Vitebsky, "Voyenno-promyshlennyy kompleks v 1994 godu [The military-industrial complex in 1994], *Krasnaya zvezda*, January 28, 1995, p. 3.

—How reliable is the picture of the internal shift from military to civil production within defense-complex enterprises?

—How does the decline in employment in defense manufacturing compare with the overall trend in the rest of Russia's manufacturing sector, which has also shrunk during the reform period? That is, because there has been a general reduction in manufacturing employment in Russia in recent years, to what extent is defense industry a special case?

These questions merit more discussion and will each be taken in turn.

Hidden Unemployment

The official statistics reflected in figure 7-2 make no attempt to correct for the fact that many workers still formally listed on defense-enterprise payrolls are not working full workweeks. Reductions in working hours are common, whether in the form of shorter hours per day, fewer workdays each week, or simply shutting down the plants for weeks or months at a time. Policy toward workers varies in such cases. Sometimes they are paid; sometimes their leaves are unpaid. In either case, millions of Russian workers have at one point or another clearly operated on what in the West is described as a short-time or labor-sharing regime.[10] That is, the facility does not operate at 100 percent capacity, but work is shared among the current work force rather than laying off some workers.

There are various explanations for this phenomenon of failing to dismiss workers even when there is no work for them. It is variously described as inertia from the old practice of "labor hoarding"; the desire to enhance, or at least preserve, the defense enterprise's political strength derived from employment size; or a sense of paternalism and social responsibility toward the work force. In some cities, legal restrictions are placed on enterprises that account for a large percentage of employment to keep them from laying off workers.[11] Plants even have tax incentives to keep workers. Thanks to the provisions of Russia's so-called excess wage tax law, under certain conditions it can be profitable for enterprises to keep low-paid workers on the payroll even if they do no work at all![12]

Counting such hidden unemployment is important for many purposes. To compute labor productivity, for instance, inputs of labor in the defense complex need to be expressed not in the number of people formally employed but in the number of actual hours of labor they supply. This would almost certainly give a different picture altogether.[13] Yet in the case of Russia today, it may be more important to know the number of people attached to the enterprises of the Russian defense complex—regardless of whether they work full or partial weeks and whether they actually work or not when in the workplace. Indeed, even some people who have formally left defense enterprises still live in plant-owned housing and rely on other services provided by an enterprise. Even if their dependence is reduced substantially when they are no longer formally employees, it is certainly not nonexistent.[14] From this standpoint, figure 7-2 may exaggerate the decline in the number of people dependent on the Russian defense-industrial complex.

Shift from Military to Civil Production

According to figure 7-2, by the beginning of 1995, the number of workers in defense-complex enterprises engaged in military production was down to one-quarter or even less of the peak levels of the mid-1980s. Meanwhile, the number of workers in civilian production had declined only marginally. This is consistent with numerous other statements to the effect that large numbers of workers have been released from military production and reassigned to civilian production within the same plants.

In a study of some 600 defense enterprises in 1992, for example, the Russian state statistics agency reported that 61 percent of workers let go from military production in that year had gone on to work in civilian production within the same enterprises.[15] Despite the seeming precision of the numbers cited, such statements ought to be treated with skepticism. From even the crude data we have on levels of output of defense plants (see figure 6-1), it seems clear that the problem of hidden unemployment affected both military and civilian production. In 1992, civil output dropped by 5 percent; yet enterprises claimed they were adding workers to their civilian production lines. Under those circumstances the reassignment of workers to civilian production clearly must have been a mere formality in many cases. Therefore, the statistical appearance of "demilitarization" of the defense work force is misleading. In reality, it makes no difference whether a worker is nominally listed as a military production worker or as a civilian production worker if that worker is not actually working at all. In other words, though it is undoubtedly true that some workers have been converted from military to civilian activity within the same enterprises, the net effect of this is unclear.[16]

Was the Decline in Defense Employment a Special Case?

While defense-industry employment was undergoing the dramatic reduction shown in figure 7-2, Russian industrial employment as a whole was also shrinking. Was defense industry a special case? To answer that properly requires a look back to the mid-1980s.

It is often not appreciated how much the entire Russian manufacturing labor force shrank during the latter half of the 1980s, even before the dramatic decline in industrial activity that took place beginning in 1992. Part of the labor force reduction reflected shifts in demographics. From the end of World War II through the 1970s, Russian manufacturing enterprises could draw on a steadily growing potential work force. But there was almost no growth at all in the working-age population in Russia in the 1980s.[17] In some regions, including major defense manufacturing regions,

TABLE 7-1. *Estimated Decline in Industrial Employment in Russia, 1985–93*

| | Percent change in number of industrial employees | | |
	1985–91	1991–92	1992–93
All industry	−13	−4	−7
Civil MBMW[a]	−15	−10	−10
Defense complex[b]	−13	−6	−10

Sources: Rates of decline of defense-complex employment calculated from the employment levels for various years given in figure 7-2. (Rates of decline are computed on the basis of estimated average employment for the year.) Data on total industrial employment and data on all MBMW (used together with defense-complex employment to estimate the rates of decline for civilian MBMW) are from Goskomstat Rossii, *Rossiyskaya Federatsiya v 1992 godu. Statisticheskiy yezhegodnik* (The Russian Federation in 1992: Statistical yearbook) (Moscow: Republic Information Publishing Center, 1993), p. 386 (for 1985, 1990, and 1991) and *Russia— 1994: Economic situation*, no. 4, p. 104 (for 1992 and 1993). Employment in all cases is for the category of "industrial production employees," or PPP.

a. MBMW = Machine-building and metalworking industries.

b. Enterprises under Military-Industrial Commission (VPK) and successor institutions.

it showed an absolute decline.[18] As a result, despite efforts to recruit pensioners into the labor force, the total number of workers declined slightly in the 1980s, and manufacturing employment contracted significantly more than the total labor force.[19] Table 7-1 compares post-1985 employment trends in the entire Russian industrial labor force, in the civilian machine-building and metalworking subsector (roughly 50 percent of which was in defense enterprises), and in the defense complex alone.

The data in table 7-1 suggest that the labor outflow from defense enterprises during the early phase of Soviet economic reform (the second half of the 1980s) may simply have been part of the more general pattern of people leaving all types of manufacturing enterprises, not just those in the defense sector. That is, although the defense-industrial labor force was reduced by about 13 percent over this period, this was no more than in the rest of the manufacturing sector. It was not until 1991 that the downsizing in defense industry occurred faster than in the economy as a whole. Not until 1993 could defense enterprises be said to be as badly off as their civilian counterparts in the machine-building and metalworking sector.

An Enterprise Example

Who left the defense sector? Were they old or young, men or women, skilled or unskilled? What were their occupational backgrounds? Did they leave voluntarily or involuntarily? For the future of Russian society and the

TABLE 7-2. *Employment in Tantal (Saratov), 1988–93*

	(1) Total employees	(2) Total workers	(3) Total engineers	(4) Female workers	(5) Female engineers	(6) Total female	(7) Male workers	(8) Male engineers	(9) Total male
1988	17,907	9,631	8,276	4,511	4,603	9,114	5,120	3,673	8,793
1989	17,983	10,178	7,805	4,481	4,843	9,324	5,697	2,962	8,659
1990	18,207	10,182	8,025	4,105	5,004	9,109	6,077	3,021	9,098
1991	17,450	9,246	8,204	4,901	5,195	10,096	4,345	3,009	7,354
1992	12,254	6,176	6,078	2,810	3,058	5,868	3,366	3,020	6,386
1993	12,799	6,728	6,071	3,414	3,192	6,606	3,314	2,879	6,193

Source: Tatyana Krylova, "In-Depth Study of SEPO and Tantal," U.S. National Academy of Sciences, unpublished manuscript, 1993, p. 59.

economy both inside and outside defense enterprises, these are crucial questions.

Such data are not reported for the defense sector, and it is unclear whether they are collected and aggregated. Only recently have Russian statistics authorities begun collecting labor force data by conducting household surveys rather than relying on enterprise censuses. Although the surveys will undoubtedly prove a rich source of data on individual labor market behavior, they do not allow for matching of workers with their enterprises. At the same time, there are data kept by the enterprises themselves. But whether these data are available to authorities at higher levels (quite apart from the question of whether they might be made available to outsiders) is unknown. Individual scholars and business investment analysts have gained access to a few enterprises. So far none of this work has given enough information to allow for rigorous statistical analyses.

Although no defense plant is "typical," data from one large enterprise show the complex evolution of employment during the reform period. (The data also illustrate some of the degree of detail at which employment data are systematically collected at the enterprise level.) Table 7-2 shows the change in employment for Tantal, a large avionics manufacturer in the city of Saratov. The data are broken down into four categories (male and female workers and male and female engineers) for the years before and after the radical cuts made in 1992 in Russian military procurement.

Tantal's data reveal some of the interesting internal dynamics otherwise masked by aggregate figures on employment. For instance, using only the overall employment statistics at Tantal, it would appear that 1991 was a year of little change: Total employment declined by only 4 percent. In fact, more than 1,700 male workers—nearly 30 percent of the total—left this enterprise. At the same time, net hiring totaled almost 1,000 new female staff (800 workers and 200 engineers). Even in the big downsizing of 1992, there was greater variation than any aggregate employment figure alone would convey. In particular, fully 80 percent of the work force reduction that year was accounted for by women.

Many questions are left unanswered even by relatively detailed data such as Tantal's. There is, for instance, the familiar one: How much of the apparent employment in Tantal is fictitious—that is, people who are not actually still working at the plant? Already by the first quarter of 1993 at the latest, Tantal had resorted to substantial unpaid leaves. But the three most interesting questions may simply be who left Tantal, why did they leave, and where did they go? Not even the fairly extensive enterprise data tell the story. Questions of who, why, and where are of course interrelated and important for the entire labor market. Unfortunately, precise data do not exist.

The following sections in this chapter examine only certain aspects of each question. Regarding why people left, the discussion focuses on two issues: layoffs versus voluntary terminations, and the issue of relative wages. For the question of where people went, open unemployment is examined next. Finally, as to who left, the discussion turns to what has become known as the "internal brain drain" from defense industry—that is, the departure of the best educated and most skilled workers.

WHY WORKERS LEFT: VOLUNTARILY OR FORCED OUT?   According to the official records, two-thirds of those who left Tantal in the big downsizing of 1992 quit of their own volition, and one-third were laid off. That any at all lost their jobs because of layoffs was an historical first. Never before had staff reductions been reported as "initiated by management." But in fact, the information on the percentage of voluntary terminations is nearly worthless. It was the workers themselves who decided whether their separation was recorded as a layoff or as a voluntary termination.[20]

In the Soviet system, any separation was frowned on, but involuntary separations for whatever reason were considered especially negative. They were literally a black mark on a worker's record: Each such case was recorded in the mandatory document called the "labor booklet," which each Soviet worker was required to have.[21] To be fired for disciplinary reasons was obviously a stigma. But being laid off was hardly better. The assumption is that the worst workers are laid off first; Soviet (and now Russian) labor legislation required this.[22] By giving workers the chance to have their termination recorded as a voluntary resignation, rather than as a layoff, Tantal's management was doing the workers a favor. Unfortunately, anyone analyzing the data remains ignorant of the real reasons why so many people left the enterprise.[23]

WHY WORKERS LEFT: FOR HIGHER WAGES? Whatever the relative numbers of workers who left the defense sector of their own accord, what were
their motives for leaving? The most obvious answer is that they moved to
higher-paying jobs somewhere else. Although there are apparently no historical data on wages in defense-complex enterprises compared with those
in other economic sectors, it is generally believed that in the Soviet era
average wage levels in defense industry were higher than in nondefense
industries.[24]

Has there then been a decline in defense-industrial wages most recently? And if so, has this mattered? Clearly, relative wage levels within
the Russian economy have shifted substantially. The average wage in those
sectors of the economy traditionally dominated by defense industry has
declined relative to others. The official statistics on relative wage levels
among selected sectors of the economy in 1970, 1988, and 1994 are presented in figure 7-3, which shows sectoral wages measured against the
standard of the average wage of all Russian workers.

A comparison in figure 7-3 of the first two bars in each group (1970
and 1988) shows the high degree of stability in relative wages during the
1970s and 1980s in the Soviet Union. For the eighteen years represented by
the first and second bars in each cluster, there was little change. In the data
for the six years since 1988, however, some dramatic shifts had occurred.
Most noticeable is the rise for the electric power generation and fuels industries
(gas, oil, and coal) and for the finance and government administration sectors.
But significantly, there was also a relative decline in wages for two important
sectors, the machine-building and metalworking industry and science, which
are dominated by defense. They now rank at the same level or below a
traditionally low-paying sector such as health care.

These are the kinds of statistics that provide the basis for claims that
defense-industry employees did indeed lose ground. They are also consistent with figures cited by official representatives of the Russian defense
complex. The Russian State Committee on Statistics reported, for instance, that the average monthly wage in the defense complex for January–
September 1994 was 135,000 rubles, or only 66.5 percent of the 203,000
average wage in all Russian industry for the same period.[25]

Despite the precision of such figures, their implication is far from
unambiguous. These are statistics on cash wages paid to employees and as
such do not capture the full wage. In particular, the various forms of in-
kind (noncash) benefits paid to Russian (Soviet) workers are ignored. Wage
figures also ignore whether or not those wages were actually paid. Since 1992
a large number of Russian enterprises have experienced some long delays in
paying their workers; some paid them only a portion of their wages or simply
not at all.[26] To the extent that defense enterprises differed from others in terms

FIGURE 7-3. *Changes in Relative Wages in Selected Sectors of the Russian Economy, 1970, 1988, and 1994*

Ratio of sector's average monthly wage to average wage in entire economy

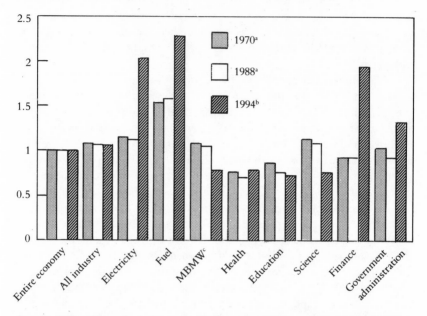

Sources: 1994—*Ekonomika i zhizn*, no. 48 (November 1994), p. S-22. 1970 and 1988—*Narkhoz RSFSR 1988*, pp. 61–62, 363; *Sotsial'no-ekonomicheskoye polozheniye Rossii v 1994 g.* (Goskomstat, 1995), pp. 149–50.

a. Average for year.

b. Average for Jan.–Nov. 1994.

c. MBMW = Machine-building and metalworking industry.

of noncash benefits and in the degree of wage arrears, the comparison in figure 7-3 may not be valid. Moreover, what is shown in figure 7-3 is only the tip of the iceberg as far as relative wages are concerned. The most dramatic change is not shown at all: the growth of a new, legal private economy, in which wages are much higher than in that part of the economy captured by the official statistics on which figure 7-3 is based.

A final point missed by a simple comparison of mean sectoral wages is that the shift in relative wages may reflect a change in the composition of the labor force in the various economic sectors. If defense enterprises did historically have a work force with better and more skilled workers than in the rest of the economy, even in the Soviet system average wages could be expected to be higher there than elsewhere. Similarly, if more highly skilled workers are leaving the defense complex today, average wages might drop for that reason alone. In that case, the causality might be the reverse of what is often cited: Workers are not leaving because wages are declining, but average wages are declining because the best and most highly paid workers are leaving. In short, the issue is complicated, and both processes are likely at play.

But for the study of individual behavior, the real issue is not the average wage being paid to those people who happen to be employed in defense enterprises at any given point. The question is, have relative wages for particular individuals, or at least classes of workers, undergone a shift? Although the precise data needed for such a comparison are unavailable, we do have statements by enterprise managers, who are the ones competing for labor in the market. In numerous anecdotal cases and interviews, managers point to low wages as a main reason why workers have been leaving the defense enterprises. For instance, in a 1993 survey of thirty-eight deputy directors of defense enterprises in Novosibirsk, no fewer than thirty said that the main reason their best workers were leaving was low wages.[27]

WHERE WORKERS WENT: OPEN UNEMPLOYMENT? Presumably, most former defense-industrial employees who left their old jobs voluntarily—whether attracted by higher pay or for other benefits—found new positions quickly. But what of the others—those who faced the prospect of a period of unemployment? How big a problem has this been? From early on in the reform period, various spokesmen for the defense industry, both nationally and locally, assumed that a substantial number of people leaving defense plants would not be able to find work anywhere else. They regularly issued warnings of impending mass unemployment in areas dominated by defense plants. Yet employment figures offered little evidence of the predicted dire consequences in the local labor markets dominated by defense industry.

This is consistent with the earlier picture that defense industry has not lost a greater proportion of its labor force than other industrial sectors (see table 7-1). But what of the number of new jobs? Did the defense-industry regions have the ability to absorb the workers?

Official unemployment figures have not borne out the idea that defense regions should have been harder hit than others. Figure 7-4 shows that by one measure of pressure on the labor market, defense regions were less affected in 1994 than nondefense regions. But this picture is restricted to the official labor market—that is, the jobs that were mediated through the state employment centers. The overwhelming majority of Russians seeking employment appear to search for new jobs by other means than checking with the state employment office—for instance, by using personal contacts or direct applications to enterprises.[28]

The labor market picture in defense regions by the end of 1995 was quite diverse. Although a group of hard-core unemployed workers did

FIGURE 7-4. *Ratio of Job-Seekers to Job Vacancies in Defense and Nondefense Oblasts, 1993 and 1994*

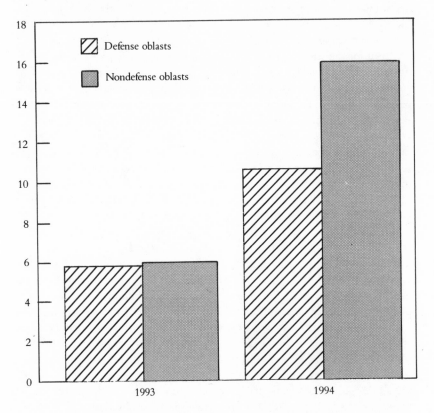

Sources: *Razvitiye ekonomicheskikh reform v regionakh Rossiyskoy Federatsii* (Moscow: Goskomstat, 1994), pp. 125–26, 129–30; *Sotsial'no-ekonomicheskoye polozheniye Rossii v 1994 g.*, pp. 379–89. Data as of November of each year. For definition of defense and nondefense oblasts, see table 9-1 and text and note 1 of chapter 9.

appear to be developing, it was still relatively small, and unemployment was not a critical social issue in most large urban defense centers. The problems were greater in smaller towns and rural areas. City officials in the large capitals had more fear of unemployed workers spilling over from outside the city than from unemployment generated within urban areas.

In general, the pattern is consistent with a picture in which the voluntary movers are the more skilled and educated, who find jobs faster and through their own means. For the economy as a whole, this has the appearance of a dynamic and healthy adjustment, with little social pressure. The defense enterprises viewed the process quite differently. For them, it was extremely negative, because they were losing some of their best workers.

TABLE 7-3. *Russian University Graduates in Defense and Nondefense Fields, 1975–90*

Thousands of graduates per year

Field	1975	1985	1990	Percent change 1985–90
All nondefense fields	297.2	352.8	315.2	−11
All defense-related fields	111.1	123.8	85.9	−31
Technology and machines	18.3	19.2	10.0	−48
MBMW[a]	17.9	21.8	14.0	−36
Radio	12.0	14.8	10.8	−27
Computers	20.7	23.5	17.9	−24

Source: Author's calculations from data in Goskomstat Rossii, *Obrazovaniye i kultura v Rossiyskoy Federatsii, 1992* [Education and culture in the Russian Federation, 1992] (Moscow: Republic Information Publishing Center, 1992), p. 211.

a. MBMW = Machine-building and metalworking industry.

Who Leaves Defense Industry? Or, the Brain Drain

Defense managers and Moscow officials have lamented the loss of skilled workers, describing it as a threat to the individual enterprises, to the defense sector, and to the nation as a whole. Mikhail Malei, for instance, described those leaving the defense sector as "the most dynamic, literate, and skilled people."[29] Much of the concern about the future of the Russian defense industry has been motivated by the threat of losing this human capital. A typical fear was expressed at an early 1993 roundtable of defense industry executives, one of whom declared, "Unless the situation is changed, within half a year all the specialists of any value will have left the defense sector."[30]

The seriousness of this is conveyed by warning of a "brain drain." When Russian defense-industrial representatives use that term, they are not referring to the loss of highly educated specialists to other countries, but to what they call an "internal brain drain." In fact, the actual brain drain out of Russia has not been large. Through 1993 the number of Russian emigrants who had worked in science and science-related occupations never exceeded 2,300 a year.[31] Presumably, out of even that relatively small number, many had never worked in defense enterprises or research institutes.

Although the external brain drain seems not to be a problem of serious magnitude, the same cannot be said of the internal shift of educated Russians away from defense industry into other parts of the economy. Yet once again this is a process that predates the radical reforms in Russia. The internal brain drain increased steadily over the latter part of the 1980s. Table 7-3 presents data on rates of university graduates in engineering professions with application in defense industry. From 1985 to 1990, the number of such graduates declined by nearly one-third. Some of the decline was attributable to a general decrease in university enrollment, and some to the rapid build-up in the numbers of graduates of the past two decades who may have glutted some professions. Still, the attractiveness of defense industry declined early on. During this period the relative share of all university graduates in defense-related fields dropped from 26 to 21 percent. [32]

Women in Defense Industry

The downsizing of the defense-industrial labor force has affected women in specific ways. One is unemployment. In the Russian economy as a whole, evidence suggests that involuntary unemployment is more common among women than men, and women have a harder time finding new jobs. [33]

If women are indeed overrepresented among involuntarily unemployed Russians, this is not unexpected. In any market economy, women tend to bear a disproportionate share of adjustment costs. If layoffs are based on seniority, women lose out. Because women are more likely to interrupt their careers for childbearing, they have less tenure in their jobs. If social factors are taken into account in firing decisions, women fare poorly here as well, for they are generally considered "secondary wage earners." The Russian Labor Code explicitly provides for both social considerations ("principal wage earner") and "uninterrupted tenure" to be given precedence in layoffs. [34] If women have less skilled jobs, they have less firm-specific capital. And finally, if employing women means the enterprise incurs heavier social costs, then women will be the first to go if layoffs are dictated by cost-cutting.

There is no reason to think that these factors would not also apply to women in the defense labor force and, consequently, that women defense workers have borne a disproportionate share of the adjustment costs in that sector as well as in the overall economy. Before concluding that women are paying a greater price for the nation's demilitarization, however, we need to understand some of the costs female defense workers paid in the Soviet era. The first of these features is the extraordinarily high female share of employment in Russian industry in general as well as in defense industry.

Beginning in the 1960s labor force participation rates (that is, the percent of working-age women who were in the labor force) rose dramatically. The rate jumped from 69 percent to 82 percent during the 1960s and continued to rise gradually through the 1970s and early 1980s, reaching what was probably the highest level in the world. [35] There is much evidence that this was an artificially high level, driven by the same problem of "labor shortage" previously discussed.

In general, all Soviet citizens had a constitutional obligation to work. Healthy citizens of working age (ages 16–59 for men and 16–54 for women) had "no right not to work for any length of time, even if [they] had legal means of subsistence." Those who chose not to fell into the category of "persons evading socially useful work," and sanctions could be used to force them back into the labor force. (The first notice from the local office of the Interior Ministry would be sent to an unemployed person after three months of not working.)[36]

In the 1950s and 1960s, the legal obligation to work was not strictly enforced for women. But as the demand for labor grew, so too did the pressure on women to join the labor force. By the late 1970s and 1980s, not only were Soviet women joining the labor force in record numbers, but they were also not allowed to leave. According to one Soviet specialist, women could not stop working "to care full time for their families or just to have a rest."[37]

There are no aggregate statistics for the number of women working in Russian defense enterprises, but in the small number of defense enterprises for which I was able to obtain data on female employment, women made up just under 50 percent of the industrial labor force (not including employees in the enterprises' social sector, which was dominated by women). In an international comparison, this is an extraordinarily high percentage of female workers in a heavy manufacturing sector. It is, however, roughly consistent with the official employment picture in the civilian manufacturing sector in Russia that most closely corresponds to defense industry, namely machine-building and metalworking. In the mid-1980s, women made up about 46 percent of the labor force in that sector. The corresponding figure in the United States was only 26 percent, and in Western Europe it was even lower (figure 7-5).

Having so many women in manufacturing and in the heavy industry of the defense sector had consequences both for Russian society and for the women as individuals. This was connected with the nature of the jobs. Manufacturing jobs in all countries have little flexibility and are rarely part-time. In the USSR the situation was even worse. There was virtually no possibility of part-time employment. Less than 1 percent of employed women had part-time jobs. (The figure rises to about 5 percent if teachers, who had a 33-hour work week, are included.)[38] This can be compared to Sweden in 1986, where 43 percent of all women employed outside the home worked part-time (under 35 hours a week).[39]

In addition, there was the burden of maintaining a household. Women who worked outside the home in the USSR in the mid- to late-1980s— again, these were almost exclusively full-time workers—spent an estimated

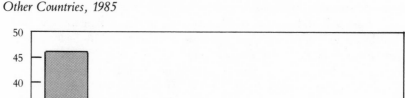

FIGURE 7-5. *Women as a Percentage of Metal Trades Labor Force in Russia and Other Countries, 1985*

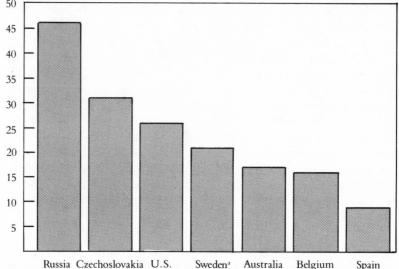

Sources: Calculated from data in International Labour Organization, Metal Trades Committee, *Recent Developments in the Metal Trades* (Geneva, 1994), report 1, pp. 49–54; Goskomstat Rossii, *Narkhoz Rossiyskoy Federatsii, 1992* (Moscow: Republic Information Publishing Center, 1992), p. 123; *Narkhoz RSFSR 1988*, p. 39.

a. Data for 1987.

92 percent as much time on housework (including standing in lines at shops) as on their official jobs.[40]

The lack of opportunities for part-time work, the constitutional obligation to work (and to work full-time), the demands of domestic work, and the priority of defense-manufacturing employment in many regions all meant that the burden on many working women was nearly unbearable.

This picture of the historical conditions of women's work in the defense-industrial sector ought to be kept in mind when evaluating the full effects of Russia's demilitarization on women. Defense downsizing may have affected women more than men, but the effects have not all been negative. Although many women have been discriminated against in firing decisions and have had a harder time holding on to their jobs, others have taken advantage of a new freedom to choose jobs outside the manufacturing sector (including the previously impermissible option of working exclusively in the home). And even for those who remain in defense industry, it is easy to understand why some women might not only tolerate but even welcome the part-time furloughs now prevalent in the defense-industrial sector.

Conclusion

There is no single explanation for why Russians have left defense plants. The shift in labor is a longer-term process that has evolved as people exercised freedom of choice. Without taking into consideration the artificial constraints that governed people's behavior in the old Soviet system, it is impossible to draw valid conclusions about what people are doing and why. The cases of women and young people, in particular, reflect this. Whatever the specific dynamics of the process and motives of the workers at various stages, they all tended to contribute to steadily increasing rates of net labor loss from defense industry.

In the period following the budget cutbacks described in chapter 5, the new opportunity to choose occupations outside defense industry intersected first with the diminished attraction of employment within the defense sector, followed by direct pressure to curtail employment. Even today, with the harsher financial climate in defense industries creating pressure for outright personnel reductions, far from everyone leaving the plants is being laid off against his or her will.

It is never possible to clearly distinguish between "voluntary" and "involuntary" separations in any labor market. As always, it is a matter of weighing alternatives. In the rapidly changing economic climate of Russia today, this is particularly true. New opportunities arise daily that did not exist before. At the same time, it seems reasonable to conclude that following a fairly sudden burst of enthusiasm for testing the waters of a new economy, some of the most dynamic and ambitious individuals left. Now the outflow consists of a mixture of involuntarily laid-off workers who may prove extremely hard to reemploy, and workers who are simultaneously attracted by opportunities outside the defense plants (mostly in the new private economy) and frustrated by the stagnation and deterioration within. So far, the labor turnover has been a gradual one, and for that reason not a threat to social stability in Russia. But it is bound to increase in intensity.

It was estimated that perhaps as many as 5 million people have left defense-industry–related jobs in Russia since 1989. But as dramatic as the downsizing of defense industry has been, at least 6 million Russians still have jobs that depend on defense enterprises—hardly a trivial number. Who are the 6 million people who remain in the Russian defense industry, and why do they stay?

Chapter 8

Defense Enterprises as Company Towns

In Chapter 7 I addressed the issue of mobility within the defense-complex labor force both before and after the economic changes introduced in January 1992. To recruit and keep the workers needed to fulfill its role as a producer of weapons, a Russian defense plant placed strong emphasis on providing social benefits to its employees. In this chapter I examine how the Russian defense enterprise evolved as a supplier of social services and the implications for its role in Russian society and the national economy.

A Russian defense enterprise should not be thought of in terms of an ordinary factory whose employees worked 40 hours a week and then spent the rest of their time elsewhere, living their private lives. In essence, a defense enterprise in Russia resembled a company town in America, such as a West Virginian coal mining town or Southern textile village. Like the workers in those American enclaves of decades past, when Russians decided to become part of the labor force of a defense enterprise they were making a decision not merely to *work* in the plant, but to entrust their entire lives to it.

The scope of social welfare services offered by large Russian enterprises is unlike anything in modern Western market economies. The company-town character of some Russian enterprises was not exclusively a feature of defense industry; it characterized many large civilian enterprises as well. But a much higher percentage of defense enterprises were "superlarge" (having more than 5,000 employees), so the company-town aspect was more typical of defense-industrial entities in general.

A brief case study of one large Russian defense enterprise illustrates the distinctions between many Western firms and Russian enterprises of the company-town type. Although the details of this case distinguish it from all others, the overall picture is similar to that of dozens or even hundreds of other defense enterprises in Russia.

A Case Study of a Defense Company Town

The Saratov Electromechanical Production Organization (SEPO) is located in the city of Saratov, one of a series of major defense-manufacturing centers along the Volga River. In the mid-1980s, SEPO had a labor force of more than 17,000 employees, nearly all of whom worked in a set of colocated plants inside the city. Although in most countries this would have been a uniquely huge manufacturing establishment, in Soviet Russia it was just one of several dozen that size or larger. (The estimate in chapter 2 was that Russian defense industry included at least 100 enterprises employing 10,000 or more workers at a single location.) Even in the city of Saratov, there were two other defense enterprises at least as big as SEPO.[1]

SEPO was typical of large defense plants in that it produced a main military product as well as substantial civilian manufacturing. It made aviation components for Soviet military aircraft. Its civilian product, refrigerators, was sold throughout the Soviet Union and even exported to several foreign countries.

But a third major SEPO "product" was social welfare: a host of goods and services, most intended exclusively for SEPO employees and residents of the community around the plant. SEPO built and operated huge numbers of housing units and was responsible for power generation, street maintenance, sanitation services, and a range of other "municipal" services. It provided education from preschool through postgraduate levels; supplied health services in the forms of preventive care, acute care, and rehabilitation; and grew, processed, and delivered food from its own farms. The list of SEPO services goes on and on. Although it was located in the middle of a city of nearly 1 million, SEPO closely resembled a company town. Figure 8-1 illustrates how extensive some of the so-called social assets associated with this one plant were.

The kind of benefits SEPO supplied to its workers made it a highly attractive place to work in the Soviet Union in the 1980s. But even the partial list of services and social goods does not convey how completely employees' lives were dominated by the plant. By the 1980s, there were thousands of SEPO workers who not only worked in SEPO—they had been *born* there. They had been delivered in SEPO hospitals and raised in SEPO nurseries. They had attended SEPO kindergartens and schools, gone on vacations with SEPO instructors at SEPO-owned camps or resorts, and played on SEPO athletic teams. They may have been sponsored by SEPO for postsecondary and even graduate-level education, returning to take a position in the plant. And of course, their housing, medical care, and continuing education were all provided by SEPO. It was, in short, a world shaped by SEPO and organized by it. SEPO was not merely a firm

FIGURE 8-1. *Profile of a Russian "Defense-Enterprise Community"*

This is a partial list of the nonindustrial infrastructure owned and operated by the Saratov Electromechanical Production Organization (SEPO), a military avionics manufacturer with more than 17,000 employees in the city of Saratov, in the late 1980s.

1. *Housing.* Dozens of high-rise apartment buildings housing some 20,000 people, with 300 new units built each year by SEPO's housing construction division. Separate dormitories were provided for 1,000 workers.

2. *Commercial.* More than 50 shops and stores, including a pharmacy, post office, savings bank branch, clothing and shoe store, self-service laundromat, furniture repair shop, and refrigerator service.

3. *Child care.* Four combined kindergarten–nurseries for several hundred children each. Four kindergartens and two nurseries (6 months to 3 years) for 1,500 children.

4. *Education.* A combined primary and secondary school for 1,136 students cofinanced by SEPO and the Saratov city government. Two vocational secondary schools for 1,000 young workers. A 1,440-student trade school. A branch of the Saratov Polytechnic Institute, a university-level engineering school.

5. *Medical.* Two health centers staffed by 50 physicians and 100 nurses. a 200-bed preventive clinic. A combined health resort and preventive medicine clinic at which 3,000 guests spent a week or more each year.

6. *Sports.* A 78,000-square-meter (840,000-square-foot) indoor and outdoor sports complex. A 7,000-seat stadium. Two competition soccer fields, several outdoor tracks, volleyball and basketball courts, gymnastics halls, indoor track, skating rink, ice hockey arena, three-story aquatic center with swimming pools, dressing rooms, and small hotel. Fourteen sports teams competing in regional and national leagues. Sponsorship of national- and world-class athletes in sports ranging from boxing and fencing to yachting and equestrian sports.

7. *Recreation.* Forty playgrounds; five athletic fields; two summer youth camps for 1,000+ youngsters each; a building solely for the factory chess club.

8. *Culture.* A "palace of culture," including a 1,200-seat auditorium, movie and lecture halls, library, and rooms for arts and crafts. An outdoor summer movie theater for 1,000. A public library. Several choirs, a chamber ensemble, and a drama ensemble. A folk orchestra and a folk dance group that toured the USSR and foreign countries.

9. *Vacation.* Dacha and garden plot communities for workers. A vacation complex on the Volga River with facilities for 6,500 vacationers per summer.

All of this was in addition to cafeterias, cafes, restaurants, butcher shops, bakeries, and vegetable shops inside the plant itself. Breakfast, lunch, and dinner were served to workers from all three shifts. Much of the food served here and that sold in the shops was grown on SEPO's farms, which employed more than 550 workers.

Source: Vladimir I. Lifanov, *SEPO: Smelost', entuziazm, poisk, optimizm! K 50-letiyu Saratovskogo ordena Krasnoy Zvedzy elektroagregatnogo proizvodstvennogo ob"yedineniya* [SEPO: Boldness, enthusiasm, initiative, optimism! In honor of the 50-year anniversary of the Saratov Order of the Red Star Electromechanical Production Organization] (Saratov: Volga Book Publishers, 1989).

for which these people worked; it was the family of which they were all members.

How did all this come to be? As was discussed in chapter 7, one motivating factor for Russian defense enterprises and other enterprises to provide social services was to reduce employee turnover. But the explanation goes back much further than the labor campaign of the 1980s. From the time it was founded, SEPO had never been simply a manufacturing plant. It was always a company town. To truly understand it we must first examine the plant's origins.

The History of SEPO[2]

SEPO's roots date back to just before World War II. In the late 1930s, in an effort to ensure that more of its defense-industrial base was out of range of air attack, the Soviet Union began a build-up of what was termed a "second military-industrial base" in the Volga Valley, the Urals, and Siberia. One project in that campaign was an aviation components factory to be built in Saratov.

Construction began in May 1939. But little happened for more than two years. This changed dramatically in the wake of the German invasion in June 1941, during the legendary evacuation of Soviet industry to the eastern part of the country. From July to November 1941, the equipment and machinery for more than 1,500 industrial enterprises (including 1,360 large defense enterprises) were shipped eastward in 1.5 million train-car loads. To build and then staff the Soviet defense plants, 10 million people— plant workers and their families—were relocated to the East.[3]

The first machinery for what was to become SEPO arrived in Saratov in the first days of that evacuation. It had been shipped in from an evacuated arms factory in the western Soviet Union. Along with the machinery came two men designated by the leadership in Moscow as director and chief designer of a new plant that would be established in Saratov. Carrying Moscow's instructions to the local Communist party offices, the two men announced that they would be taking over the factory site that had been under construction since May 1939. More shipments of machinery would be arriving from Moscow, Leningrad, Poltava, and Rzhev, they said.

The task of the new plant was to produce magnetos (small electric generators used in engine ignition) for military aircraft. According to the orders transmitted to the local leadership, the plant had thirty days from the time of arrival of the last shipment of machinery from the West to get the magneto production up and running. Whether the plant management met that deadline is not reported, but ultimately the task was fulfilled. According to the official company history, every single airplane built by the Soviet Union during World War II—120,800 Ilyushins, Yaks, Tupolevs, and MiGs, among others—contained "a reliably operating Saratov magneto."

A Town in Itself

From the beginning, SEPO was built as a self-contained town, with almost every aspects of the workers' lives connected to the plant. SEPO's responsibility for its workers began with the bare necessities—food and shelter. The thousands of new families that arrived in Saratov in the summer of 1941 were housed in every conceivable form of makeshift shelter, from tents and barracks to earthen dugouts in the open fields surrounding the plant. It was a full year before any of them were able to move out of these primitive lodgings into permanent apartment buildings constructed by SEPO.

Supplying food was also done on an emergency basis. A Department of Workers' Supply was set up immediately to procure food for the workers and their families through the fall and winter of 1941. Early the next spring, the plant took over two nearby state farms and began producing its own food. Thanks to those farms, the plant could provide workers three meals a day. This was an absolute necessity, because for the duration of the war most of the workers would regularly go for days or even weeks without ever leaving the plant. Meanwhile, other services were being established as an integral part of the build-up of SEPO itself—from bathhouses and hairdressers to tailors and shoe repair shops. Soon, there were nurseries, kindergartens, and a health clinic.

The end of the war was a critical turning point in SEPO's history. The draconian labor regime was eased. Demobilized soldiers were added to the labor force. Military output remained the plant's top priority, but diversification of production to civilian goods was under way. In 1951, SEPO was ordered to begin production of refrigerators. This quickly became a major part of its manufacturing activity. Eventually, more than one out of three SEPO employees worked on the refrigerator production lines. By the mid-1980s refrigerator output reached more than 500,000 a year, making SEPO the third biggest refrigerator manufacturer in the USSR.[4]

But despite these postwar changes, one wartime pattern that did not alter was the plant's role in providing a broad array of social and commercial services to its workers. This arrangement, which had been born of necessity in wartime, was now being continued as official policy. The local government in Saratov had its own municipal enterprises for providing housing and social and commercial services to city residents. In principle, SEPO could have turned over many of its social services to the city government of Saratov, but it did not. Instead, as peacetime afforded the opportunity for the Soviet economy to devote more resources to civilian activities, SEPO's "welfare production" role expanded even further.

Although SEPO had already built some housing during the war, in 1945 hundreds of families still lived in the barracks and earthen dugouts built in the early days. The first priority was to move them into more permanent housing. From then on, the plant's responsibility for housing grew unabated. For the next forty years, housing remained the number one instrument for recruiting workers.

By the 1980s, SEPO was building new housing units at the rate of about 300 a year (and it was literally SEPO [through its residential housing construction division], not independent contractors, that did the building). But even at that rate, approximately 2,000 of the plant's workers remained on a waiting list to receive new apartments in 1993.[5] Workers had retired, or died and passed on apartments to relatives. Some workers left the plant but kept the apartments. For all these reasons, the demand for new housing kept rising, as did the number of tenants for whom SEPO was responsible. The result was that from the time of its founding, the plant itself steadily built one high-rise apartment complex after another in the vicinity, thus creating a small city.

City-Enterprise Relationships

SEPO was not alone in this policy. Other large and even medium-size enterprises did the same. In Saratov and other large cities, well over half of all the residential housing was built and managed by manufacturing enterprises like SEPO whose principal activity had nothing to do with the construction and management of real estate. As late as 1993, even after efforts to transfer such housing to municipalities or to private citizens, enterprises of all types still controlled 41 percent of all urban housing stock in Russia. As an especially large city, with huge manufacturing enterprises, Saratov's proportion of enterprise housing was even higher—fully 47 percent of its housing was owned by them.[6]

Plants like SEPO ended up with so much responsibility for welfare services for several reasons. Once established, the practice of letting enterprises provide social services in the post–World War II era may have been continued simply for efficiency. From the standpoint of the central economic planners, production was the first priority. Consumer and social welfare were secondary—important mainly to the extent they served the needs of production. The best way to ensure that these services remained subordinate to manufacturing was to put them under the production manager's aegis. In effect, it made him the residual claimant of any net cost incurred by the social sector of the economy.

This was an efficient solution, whether consciously made or not, and there is little doubt that the approach was endorsed by the Communist party leadership. Much of the system simply evolved, and there was no reason to change what seemed to work. For instance, letting defense enterprises provide benefits for the many nonemployees living in enterprise areas removed a burden from the city administration. But given the constraints of the Soviet economic system, this also suited many ordinary citizens. Housing is a good illustration of the interplay between the public and enterprise sectors in the former Soviet Union.

HOUSING.   In devoting so much attention to housing, SEPO was not only meeting the needs and preferences of its current workers but also preparing to recruit new ones. Saratov, like all major defense cities, was subject to strict residency restrictions. People could not simply decide to move to Saratov and look for a job and a place to live; everything had to be arranged beforehand. It was therefore difficult for the defense enterprise to recruit new workers unless housing could be offered. This was true even of workers who might be recruited from other parts of the city itself.

Saratov was a large city—its population in the 1980s was nearing 1 million—and yet its intracity mobility was low. It was not divided into residential and industrial zones but into separate enterprise zones like SEPO's, which combined manufacturing and housing in the same neighborhood. Saratov was simply not designed to make it easy for people to move around the city itself. As late as 1980, only one family in eight had its own car.[7] Public transport was the only alternative for the vast majority of citizens. Saratov had an extensive public transportation system, but one of the last priorities of public transportation policy was to facilitate travel *between* enterprise housing areas. What transportation there was—buses, trollies, and streetcars—was designed mainly to bring workers from housing areas to nearby factories.

Competing as it did for labor, SEPO benefited from the municipal policy in Saratov of not facilitating transportation between enterprise zones. If good public or private transportation had been available, housing in another part of the city might have been a viable substitute for the apartment provided by SEPO. But because it was not easy to move across the city, the value of housing close to SEPO was enhanced. The employee was thus linked even more closely to the enterprise. This system of enterprise-supplied housing reduced the incentives for workers to accept employment in the enterprise and then quit. Taken together, a job at SEPO and a nearby apartment provided by SEPO were a valuable package, but each component was worth considerably less if taken separately.

The same sort of reinforcing effect between goods and services provided by the enterprise and a municipal policy of not offering competing goods and services existed in nearly all commercial services as well. The stores and service shops in the SEPO residential areas were not exclusively for SEPO employees. But, in practice, to benefit from them a person had to live close by. That meant living in SEPO housing—and working at SEPO.

The Saratov city government also benefited from this arrangement. Every worker who lived in housing close to the plant meant that much less pressure on the city to expand public transportation and other services. This same principle applied to nearly all the benefits provided by the enterprises. It was to the mutual advantage of the city and the enterprise that this arrangement continue.

EDUCATION. Another area that highlights the interaction between the public and enterprise sectors in a different way is education. Like any major industrial city, Saratov had an array of public educational institutions— vocational and trade schools as well as engineering institutes—designed to prepare young people for a career in industry. Saratov had eleven institutions of higher education and more than fifty special vocational schools.[8]

SEPO naturally benefited from having this pool of educated workers on which it could draw. But what would be even better from SEPO's point of view would be to have a competitive edge over other enterprises. Its solution was to set up a system of educating workers that bypassed the general labor market. In pursuing this approach over many years, SEPO built up a system of educational facilities from preschool to university. In addition to its own branch of the Saratov engineering institute, the plant itself ran two vocational secondary schools, offering training for highly skilled technical and clerical occupations. Around 1,000 young SEPO workers were enrolled in these schools.

However, the most important component of the SEPO internal education system may have been its vocational training for workers through a third type of secondary school, the *professional'no-tekhnicheskoye uchilishche*—the PTU or trade school, which focused on occupations for skilled and semiskilled workers that were directly relevant to SEPO's needs. In the view of SEPO management, more advanced education was fine, but it essentially overeducated young people for SEPO. This was a general problem in the Soviet economy in the 1970s and early 1980s. Universal secondary education, including young people from worker backgrounds—a goal set in the 1960s—had led to exaggerated expectations about receiving higher education. In previous decades, a diploma from a standard secondary school had been practically a guarantee of admission to higher education. By the early 1970s, the expectations remained high, but the reality was much more grim. Whereas in the early 1950s 77 percent of secondary school graduates were admitted to universities and other institutions of higher education, in the early 1960s the figure was down to 57 percent and by the early 1970s to only 24 percent.[9]

Soviet labor planners and enterprise managers constantly sought ways to deflate those exaggerated aspirations without demoralizing young people entirely. For enterprise managers, youths trained in PTUs were an advantage. In contrast with many other secondary school students, they did not believe that a factory job was only temporary—they knew what they were being educated for.

Like many other enterprises, SEPO had for many years had its own "base" trade school. PTU-49, which was not located on SEPO territory, sent 400 to 500 graduates each year to SEPO. Not only did this mean that SEPO was getting a significant percentage of all graduates in machine-building and metalworking (MBMW) in the entire oblast,[10] but it was a way of screening applicants. SEPO picked the very best young workers, offered them internships, and then assigned them mentors at recruitment. Of course, to the extent that the training the young people received was tailor-made for SEPO's needs, it made them more valuable to SEPO. It was in effect an apprenticeship program. Perhaps it was only logical that in the late 1980s SEPO decided to build its own PTU inside the plant territory.

All of SEPO's educational facilities were supervised by the enterprise personnel manager (the deputy director for cadres), because the plant's involvement in education was implicitly seen as a way of meeting its personnel needs. Plant management was fond of framing its goal in Marxist terms, stating that it wanted to achieve "self-reproduction of labor power." But though providing education through the defense enterprise suited SEPO management, certain elements of the system of enterprise-provided education were designed to meet employee demand. Formally, all education in Saratov was the responsibility of the Soviet government, which promised free and equal education to all. But here as elsewhere in the Soviet Union, behind the facade of equality and uniformity a demand for goods and services of different types and differentiated quality had produced a system that supplied them informally, despite the official ideology.

So often in the Soviet system, performance criteria in general were based mainly on quantitative measures of resources. This was also true in the case of education: the number of schools and of teachers or the square meters of classroom space were what seemed to matter. But this gave an incentive for low quality; it is always easier to meet a purely quantitative quota by supplying a poorer-quality product. The result was a Soviet educational system that looked much better on paper than in reality.

The state of the physical plant in Soviet schools is illustrative. Some 30 percent of Saratov city schools were substandard construction. Nearly

6 percent of school buildings were condemned, and another 24 percent were in need of major repairs.[11] Enterprises concerned about quality responded by taking matters into their own hands. They adopted existing schools, built new ones, maintained them, and supplied them with equipment. They attracted better teachers by offering them the benefits accorded regular plant employees. In short, the message was if parents wanted a good education for their children, they should come work at SEPO. For SEPO, this effort peaked in the late 1980s when it completed construction of a special ten-year school combining primary and secondary education with an advanced academic curriculum. Through a highly competitive admissions process, the school selected children at the kindergarten level. Foreign language instruction began in the first grade; by the third grade, all subjects were taught entirely in the foreign language.

A similar story could be told about the health care sector of the defense enterprise community. Officially, all Soviet citizens had full and equal access to health and medical care. In practice, access was far from universal, and quality was often low. What SEPO was offering in its resort-level preventive medicine or medical clinics was as close to private quality as could be had in the typical Russian provincial city.

In general, there were three main ways to obtain this higher level of quality of goods and services. One was through the limited channels available only to certain privileged members of the Communist party elite. The second, the so-called shadow economy, was much more broadly accessible but limited in range and often unreliable. The third way for those who wanted something better than what was offered in the "nonpriority" economy—whether working conditions, housing, medical care, or education—was to join the priority enterprise sector. But workers could get it only by taking the entire bundle of job plus benefits.

These sorts of "bundled" choices are not unique to the Soviet system. Even in market economies, a particular good or service is often available only in combination with another. For instance, home buyers cannot generally choose an architecturally attractive and reasonably priced house in one community and the right to send their children to an excellent free public school in another. Homes, public schools, and local municipal services come in bundles. Similarly, most jobs do not permit workers to choose the number of hours they work each week or the level of job safety they want. Different jobs or occupations are bundles of attributes. As long as the number of discrete bundles with different attributes is large enough, people still have a wide range of choices. But in Soviet Russia, few "jobs-services-housing" bundles were available to choose from. The practical limit was the number of large industrial enterprises in the city of Saratov that offered the kinds of benefits SEPO did. There were not many. In 1985, only 151 manufacturing enterprises operated in the entire city of Saratov.[12] Only a handful even came close to SEPO's size.[13]

The system of a small number of huge enterprises providing extensive social welfare services for their employees divided many Russian cities into two worlds. However, the dividing line was not always clear. For instance, many of the benefits provided by SEPO extended to more people than just its own employees. In the first place, the definition of who actually was a SEPO employee was vague.

Take, for instance, the teachers in the schools listed in figure 8-1. Although the school buildings may have been built by SEPO and the plant was responsible for a considerable part of their operating and maintenance costs, the teachers were not SEPO employees and their salaries were paid directly by the city government, not by SEPO. Yet those teachers enjoyed most of the fringe benefits associated with SEPO employment: housing, medical care, vacation facilities, and so on.

Many services provided by SEPO were not and could not be exclusively for SEPO employees. They were available to anyone who lived in the territory around SEPO, whether or not they were SEPO employees, even in the liberal sense of people like the schoolteachers and school staff. In SEPO's case, some 70,000 people lived on its territory, although the plant employed only 17,000. In other words, for every current employee living on the territory of a large enterprise, typically two or three more nonemployees lived there. Some were family members, others former employees. But many were neither. Yet, simply by virtue of living near SEPO, they enjoyed the right to certain services provided by the plant, and SEPO had obligations to them. The heat in their buildings may have been supplied from a SEPO-owned local power station, the streets outside their apartments repaired, swept clean, or kept free of snow by SEPO road repair crews, and so on. Depending on how large the enterprise was and whether there were other sizable plants nearby, the influence of the defense enterprise could extend beyond its immediate housing area to bigger sections of the city. Large Soviet cities were administratively subdivided into boroughs, or rayons. Averaging 100,000 to 200,000 residents, each borough had its own government and Communist party apparatus. Because of its size, history, and priority status, there was little doubt that SEPO dominated its rayon, one of six in Saratov. The degree to which SEPO regarded itself not simply as a powerful force within its borough, but very nearly as its proprietor, is reflected in a statement in the official SEPO history: "To say that SEPO is the largest enterprise in the Lenin rayon of the city of Saratov says nothing at all. After all, that rayon came into being, and developed, thanks to SEPO, and on the basis of SEPO."[14] The people who lived in the Lenin borough were part of the world of SEPO, like it or not.

"Like a Family"

Given the picture painted here, it is no surprise to hear the Soviet-style defense enterprise compared to a town, its workers to subjects, and its manager to mayor or even regent. Although he was not specifically referring to a defense enterprise and its manager, the description given by a Russian economist makes the point: "The director of an enterprise of the Soviet type is the president of a ministate who is responsible for his 'subjects': for years he was responsible for their educational levels, their living conditions, their social behavior, their diets, their physical development and their performance in sports. . . . Today, he is the mayor of a small town, a hired manager, a quasi-owner, a travelling salesman, and a supply agent all rolled into one."[15]

The one word that might be added to make the picture complete is *patriarch.* The notion of the enterprise community as family is one that recurs constantly. In the official SEPO history, one chapter is entitled *"Kak odna sem'ya"*—"Like a Family." On the chapter's opening page the author quotes a sociologist who had studied the plant and its employees: "My meetings and conversations with workers, specialists, and managers of the production departments of SEPO convinced me: a fine moral and psychological climate has been created in this collective; people value the reputation of their enterprise and strive to live like a family. . . ."[16]

The idea of enterprise as family was even reinforced by the official terminology of the Soviet bureaucracy. The housing area surrounding a big plant was called a *posyelok*—literally, a settlement or community. The term had a specific meaning: a population area attached to a large factory, mine, hydroelectric project, or the like, with more than 3,000 residents, of whom at least 85 percent were blue- or white-collar employees and their family members. But *posyelok* had another connotation. Historically, a *posyelok* was a group of peasants, usually linked by familial ties and headed by a patriarch, who left the main village and settled on idle communal land nearby, thereby founding a new community.[17] In fact, that patriarchal association is sometimes explicit. Older residents of large cities even today refer to the *posyelok* around an enterprise not by the name of the plant but by the name of its first director. Hence, they refer to *posyelok Antonova*—"Antonov's village."

Paternalism and the Labor-Management Relationship

The cradle-to-grave welfarism described here is often referred to as paternalism. One of the best definitions of it is the near-literal one given by Janos Kornai: the economic relationship between parent and child. That relationship evolves as the child matures, but it is always characterized by the child's dependence on the parent and the parent's assumption of responsibility for the child.[18] Kornai defines the concept in relation to the paternalistic state, where the relationship is between the government and its citizens. But the concept of paternalism suits the labor-management relationship that prevailed in Russian defense enterprises. Just as a parent decides what is best for the child, the paternalistic enterprise director protected his workers and gave them security, but also in many cases dictated what goods and services they should have. To that degree, the employees of these defense enterprises gave up freedom of choice.

SELF-SELECTION OF WORKERS.   It took a particular kind of person to work in this system. Some people were literally born into the "families" of enterprises like SEPO. But each year, many others voluntarily chose to join them. Earlier I stressed some of the constraints on labor market choice in Soviet Russia. Certainly not every employee of a Russian defense plant had an ideal range of choices for his or her career or city of residence. But labor mobility was not particularly low in Russia. People could and did change jobs. What the preceding argument says is that those who chose to work in the defense plants were making that choice based (among other things) on a preference for the paternalistic benefits offered. These workers were also more prepared to pay for that bundle of services by submitting to a dependent relationship. Every new worker who chose to join the enterprise "family" was choosing this way of life, and it was something that inevitably shaped them and their own lives as well.[19]

THE MANAGERS.   And what of the enterprise management? Just as it took a special kind of person to work in a large paternalistic enterprise, not every otherwise competent manager was suited to head an enterprise responsible for tens of thousands of people. Andrei Neshchadin, author of the quote describing the Russian enterprise director as "the president of a ministate," also emphasized how different that role is from that of a Western manager. The responsibilities and tasks that befall a Russian manager are things no Western manager would dream of doing "in his worst nightmares."[20] Why, indeed, did the Russian managers do them? It is understandable only in the context of the selection process that brought these people into their jobs.

More than 2.5 million persons served in top and middle management positions in the Russian economy in the late Soviet years.[21] Of those, only a few hundred were directors of large defense enterprises. They were at the pinnacle of a process that had successively weeded people out until only an elite was left. They attained their positions because they were good at the duties outlined by Neshchadin and wanted to perform those duties.

Apparently, despite the difficulties, the overwhelming majority of managers still want to (or perhaps feel obligated to) meet these responsibilities. The best evidence available points to a remarkably low turnover rate among defense-complex directors in the post-Soviet era.[22] Even in cases where a plant's work force has been substantially reduced, top managers remain.[23]

Paternalism and Reform

This system of enterprise paternalism reached its historic peak in the late 1980s. Well before that, the paternalistic benefits had become regarded as a right by most workers (and a duty by management), quite apart from any directives from central planners. But the reforms of the post-1985 period of *perestroika* served as a crucial experiment. The reforms granted defense enterprises more autonomy in many ways, including their ability to use financial resources directly, without approval or allocation from the Soviet administrative center. Previously, many of the paternalistic benefits had been centrally funded. Would these enterprises have devoted so much attention to the benefits if they had had a choice between cash wages and benefits, for example? Enterprise housing provided a test case.

In 1988, the Soviet state changed its policy on financing of enterprise housing. Around 80 percent of the housing built by enterprises had been financed by funds earmarked from the Soviet state. That shifted radically in 1988, when enterprises were permitted to retain more profits and decide how to use their own funds.[24] Like other enterprises with housing programs, SEPO had to make a critical decision: would it continue its housing program, or would it scale back and use disposable funds for other purposes?

SEPO's housing program was particularly ambitious. In 1980–85, it had been building apartments at a very high rate—"several times higher than called for in the plan."[25] Before the state decision to stop giving earmarked funds, plans had been made to push that rate even higher in the next five-year period. SEPO decided not to cut back. Rather, it committed itself to keep the same rate of housing construction or to raise it. Management stated that it would do so even if this meant reducing some of the cash bonuses ordinarily paid to the workers.[26]

SEPO also bent *perestroika* measures to suit its own pro-paternalism agenda in the way it dealt with the 1988 Law on Cooperatives, a key piece of early reform legislation designed to introduce limited competition into the Soviet economic system. In the minds of some reformers, that legislation had been intended to facilitate competition with precisely those giant enterprises such as SEPO, by allowing small groups of individuals to provide goods and services in a quasi-private enterprise setting.[27]

SEPO seized the opportunity to create new mechanisms for paternalism. It initiated a competition down to the department and shop levels to see who could come up with the best ideas for using cooperatives to provide social services to SEPO employees. The goal was to "increase the . . . quantity of such services, . . . to better [use] labor resources, equipment, materials, and more fully satisfy the demand by employees." Management canvassed the employees and discovered that what they wanted most of all were cooperatives for apartment maintenance, gardening, auto repair, and furniture production, plus cooperative cafés and service shops. Enterprise-sponsored and -controlled cooperatives were set up for this purpose. Everything was under the "direct control of management, the [Communist] party committee, and the trade union committee" of SEPO.[28]

In another decision, SEPO bought out a poorly performing collective farm near Saratov, declaring its intention to provide the resources needed to turn it into a model farm. Apparently understanding that this use of enterprise resources might seem questionable, SEPO's management issued a statement: "Having our own meat, milk, and vegetables will not deplete but will enrich the plant's finances."[29]

SEPO continually developed new ideas on how to spend funds to improve the lives of its workers. In one example reported in the official SEPO history, plant representatives returned from a trip to Riga, Latvia, where they had been impressed by one enterprise's automated cafeteria system. The system had dispensed food and then collected and washed trays and dishes. When they returned to Saratov, the SEPO representatives decided that they too needed this convenience. SEPO engineers were given orders to develop and test an entire new cafeteria facility of their own design, which was then built from scratch in SEPO shops.

SEPO Post-Reform

In 1992 SEPO's defense business was almost obliterated overnight by procurement cuts. Avionics sales had accounted for 56 percent of its revenues in 1987; by 1992, this share was down to 3 percent.[30] The plant fulfilled its entire avionics order for 1992 by the end of the first quarter. Several hundred employees were shifted to refrigerator production, but that was considerably more than output warranted. In real terms, nearly half of SEPO's work force had no work to do. Yet the enterprise continued to hire new workers, paying them the highest average wages of any enterprise in the city. Only 200 employees were fired in 1992. The credit pumped into defense enterprises beginning in the summer of 1992 allowed SEPO to continue paying wages and to maintain its social services.

In the fall of 1992, SEPO was given permission to "privatize"—that is, to be converted into a joint-stock company. (It had not formally been a state-owned enterprise since a government decision in January 1991 recognizing its status as a "collective enterprise.") In the spring of 1993, at the first meeting of the board of directors after privatization, the board issued a statement of the five main principles of the company's policy for the future:

—To avoid layoffs.
—To preserve the comparatively high level of wages.
—To continue housing construction.
—To maintain the social and cultural infrastructure.
—To develop and implement a pension plan.[31]

The Consequences for the Enterprises Today

Neither SEPO nor any of Russia's large enterprises can continue to afford the plans they proposed in 1993. Across the country, enterprises have had to cut back on social benefits and have had to reduce spending in all areas—including wages. How are these decisions being made?

One trend is that communities become more self-contained and their benefits more exclusive. The enterprises are less and less inclined to allow outsiders—nonemployees—to benefit free of charge from the goods and services they provide. Housing, medical care, and day care are all examples. Even some public goods provided by the enterprises—street maintenance, for example—have become much lower priorities.

One of the major conclusions in chapter 7 was that many people have left Russia's defense enterprises in the past few years. The unanswered question remains: Who leaves and who stays? The role of paternalism can also help clarify this issue. One explanation consistent with the paternalism model is that people who have left the defense enterprises are those for whom the paternalistic benefits were relatively less important than cash. In other words, the original self-selection of "paternalism-loving" workers toward defense enterprises has been intensified by a reverse process. Those who are really interested in cash incomes and have the best alternatives are leaving.

A filtering process is under way in which those who stay behind care less and less about cash relative to paternalism. For whatever reason—perhaps because they are better at coping in a cashless world or may prefer the work and living environment of the enterprise, or simply because it is the only world they know—some workers are more tolerant of an enterprise manager who fails to pay wages as long as he provides paternalistic benefits. In the extreme case, they are the workers like those who in 1994 continued day after day to report for work in the giant Perm Motors aircraft engine plant though they received no pay at all. When asked why people continue to go to work at an enterprise when they are not being paid, one employee retorted: "Where [else] should they go? It's their home."[32]

Conclusion

Russia's defense-industrial enterprises had multiple roles and functions in society. We have analyzed their roles as manufacturers of military and civilian goods. In this chapter we have attempted to show that these plants were more than technical production facilities. In its Soviet-era heyday, a plant like SEPO represented a combination of four roles in society.

First and foremost, SEPO was a priority manufacturing facility that produced an essential component of Soviet national defense. Second, it produced civilian goods. Third, through its own history it became a part of the greater history of Russian cities, regions, and the Soviet Union. Many similar plants were built during World War II or in other periods Soviet history deemed heroic. Descriptions of the accomplishments of the enterprises, recorded in plant histories or plant museums, bring to mind the histories of military units. Almost all the elements are there: the glorious origins under fire; the commanders (directors); and the human interest stories (child soldiers or, in the case of enterprises, child laborers). (Of course, the vocabulary of such history is that of combat and patriotism.)

SEPO's fourth role was that it was an institution for the production and delivery of social welfare, and one whose responsibilities extended beyond its own work force. That role was truly a significant one. By the mid-1980s, social services at SEPO formally employed as many people as the civilian manufacturing divisions (roughly 25 percent).[33] Even in this enterprise, which (in addition to its main role as arms producer) was one of Russia's largest manufacturers of refrigerators, providing social welfare services for its own employees was arguably as big a business as building consumer goods for the nation!

Today, all four roles characteristic of SEPO have diminished. Military production has been hardest hit. As early as the spring of 1993, only 20 percent of SEPO's labor force was officially engaged in military production.[34] Output of its main civilian product, refrigerators, is down. The plant's history and traditions remain important for the identity of SEPO and its directors and workers, as they do at similar enterprises across Russia. But without the active campaigns of the government and the Communist party, the history of enterprises like SEPO is no longer as important. Measured in rubles spent, even SEPO's welfare production has been scaled back. But relatively speaking, that role as provider of social services is probably more central than ever in the lives of those employees who remain. More than ever, these employees look to SEPO as their safety net.

In the past, the importance of the social function within the Soviet-style enterprise's identity was often not fully appreciated. Today, in the effort to restructure defense enterprises as capitalist firms, outside advisers tend to ask how much the social assets cost an enterprise. The implicit assumption is that social services are distinct from the defense enterprise and a burden on it. The argument presented here challenges that view and suggests that there is no such thing as a separate, identifiable entity called a production enterprise that "has" social assets or a welfare sphere. The enterprise *is* these assets as much as it is or, indeed, more than it is anything else. A defense enterprise and its work force and management have all evolved together within this social role. Changing this is a momentous decision. "Converting" from the production of welfare services and paternalism is probably a bigger undertaking and one of greater import than conversion from arms manufacturing to civilian production.

What are the prospects for making such a conversion? If a reverse-selection process has truly been at work recently when so many have left defense enterprises, then the prospects for converting Russian defense industry may be worse than most have imagined. The enterprises are left with a work force more committed to paternalism than ever before. These workers are satisfied with *less* paternalism; ironically, to them it is less important that an enterprise becomes less paternalistic as long as more is still offered within the plant than in the society outside it. In that sense, the cost of paternalism can be reduced.

But the real problem of paternalism is not its cost but the culture it represents. If the paternalistic environment is antagonistic to development of a market-oriented business—a true capitalist *firm*—then the prospects for change from within this system are poor indeed. The pressure will have to come from the outside. The key is the development of the market economy in Russia outside the defense enterprises, regardless of what happens within them.

The rise of a market economy in defense-industrial cities cannot help but affect the defense *posyelki*. Defense enterprises enjoyed a monopoly on providing services in their regions, and a privileged position as providers of *quality* in their cities as a whole. The development of the market has already brought forth alternatives for obtaining quality goods, medical services, housing, and education. A small but growing private sector provides all this. These services can now be acquired with money, not exclusively as part of a package deal with a job. This is precisely what has lured many of the best and most ambitious defense employees away. As the monetization of the Russian economy increases, this process will continue, but it will not encompass every worker. There is a core of the old work force for whom money has little value. Many of them will remain with their defense enterprises until what may be the bitter end.

Chapter 9

Regional Legacy and Prospects

I have described Russia's large defense enterprises as company towns because of the way they shaped the economic and social lives of entire communities. Although there were examples of defense-industry company towns that were literally that—separate towns—most of the huge defense plants were located within the limits of cities with populations up to 1 million or more. There, the territory dominated by an enterprise functioned almost as a separate village within the larger city.

In the old Soviet system, because so much of the public life of many cities was dominated by defense enterprises, the role of the nominal local government was correspondingly diminished. Today, those municipal and provincial governments face a new situation. As the financial resources allocated to defense enterprises by the central government are reduced, the enterprises cannot perform all the functions they once did. In particular, many of the social responsibilities previously assumed by the enterprises now fall by default to local governments.

At the same time, decentralization and devolution of authority throughout Russia have meant that the regions are being left to solve their own problems to a greater extent than ever before and must rely on their own resources. How can the governments in defense regions cope? In this environment, is the legacy of defense industry a boon or a bane to the regions where these enterprises operated?

I begin to answer this question by reviewing some statistical evidence on how defense regions—oblasts and cities—compared with other regions in economic structure, demographics, and living standards. I then discuss some important issues regarding the future development of the regions, with special emphasis on the defense-industrial cities.

Comparing Defense and Nondefense Oblasts

In chapter 2 I showed how Russia's defense industry was concentrated geographically in certain oblasts, mainly in the European part of the country. All but one of the most heavily militarized oblasts were located in or west of the Urals, and there appeared to be less defense-industrial activity in the extreme northern and southern areas (see figures 2-5A and 2-5B). This means that there tend to be strong geographical and climatic differences between defense and nondefense oblasts. I am less interested in such differences, however, than in what can be interpreted as the result of the presence or absence of defense industry. Therefore, to compare oblasts with more similar natural conditions, I excluded from the analysis the oblasts of the Far North, the Caucasus, eastern Siberia, and the Far East. The remaining forty-nine oblasts were then divided into "defense" and "nondefense" regions on the basis of a composite measure of both absolute and relative defense employment.[1]

Size and Structure

Because the criterion for classification of the oblasts is based on both total defense-industry employment and the relative weight of defense industry in the region, we would expect the two groups to differ in both size and economic structure. The question is, by how much?

Table 9-1 shows that the defense oblasts are on average nearly one and a half times more populous than the others. Moreover, that population difference is concentrated overwhelmingly in urban areas. More than 90 percent of the discrepancy is accounted for by people living in the defense oblast's capital city or in other cities and towns. The size of the rural populations in the two groups is fairly close. This is reflected in the economic structure. Not only civilian (non-VPK) industry but also non-industrial activity in particular accounted for a substantially larger proportion of total employment in the nondefense regions.

Demographics

Although the structure and size of their economies differed sharply, the defense regions were virtually indistinguishable from the others in terms of their demographics. Age ranges—that is, the relative numbers of young, old, and working-age people—and the ratio of men to women were nearly identical (table 9-1). The percentage of ethnic Russians in each was about the same as well.

The latter point is worth noting, as it was observed in chapter 2 that a disproportionate amount of the defense industry of the USSR was located in the Russian Republic. However, the data indicate that within Russia itself, defense industry was by no means located exclusively in areas dominated by ethnic Russians. In two of Russia's leading defense-industry regions, the republics of Tatarstan and Bashkortostan, non-Russian

TABLE 9-1. *Population and Employment Characteristics in Defense and Nondefense Oblasts in Russia, 1985*
Mean value per oblast

Characteristic	Defense oblasts	Nondefense oblasts
Population	2,468,000	1,706,000
Share in urban areas	71.8%	62.7%
Industrial employment[a]	440,000	236,000
As share of total labor force	37.6%	30.7%
Industrial employment in defense complex enterprises[b]	144,000	36,000
As share of total industrial employment	35.2%	16.5%
Total employment in defense complex enterprises[c]	192,000	49,000
As share of total labor force	17.5%	6.6%
Share of population		
Below working age	23.3%	23.4%
Working age	57.8%	57.0%
Above working age	19.0%	19.5%
Female	53.8%	53.7%
Ethnic Russian	82.5%	84.2%

Note: Based on a sample of forty-nine oblasts categorized according to a combined ranking of total defense-industrial employment and defense-industrial employment as a percentage of the population. There are twenty-three "defense" oblasts and twenty-six "nondefense" oblasts in this sample. Northern regions, the Caucasus, eastern Siberia and the Far East, and the cities of Moscow and St. Petersburg are excluded. See text and endnote 1 of chapter 9.

Sources: Author's database. Employment data on the Russian defense complex from the source discussed in appendix, note 1. Population data from Goskomstat Rossii, *Narodnoye khozyaystvo SSSR v 1984 g. Statisticheskiy yezhegodnik* [The national economy of the USSR in 1984: Statistical yearbook] (Moscow: Finances and Statistics, 1985), pp. 14–16 (hereafter *Narkhoz*); and *Narkhoz SSSR 1985*, pp. 12–14. Population data are the average of population on January 1, 1985, and on January 1, 1986. Labor force data from *Narkhoz SSSR 1988*, pp. 34–36; labor force data exclude *kolkhozniki* (collective farmers). Urbanization data as of January 1, 1985, from *Narkhoz SSSR 1984*, pp. 14–16. Age data from Goskomstat RSFSR, *Pokazateli sotsial'nogo razvitiya avtonomnykh respublik, krayev i oblastey RSFSR* [Indicators of the social development of autonomous republics, krays, and oblasts of the RSFSR] (Moscow, 1990), pp. 11–14; additional age data from Goskomstat RF, *Pokazateli sotsial'nogo razvitiya respublik, krayev i oblastey Rossiyskoy Federatsii* [Indicators of the social development of autonomous republics, krays, and oblasts of the Russian Federation) (Moscow: Republic Information Publishing Center, 1992), pp. 13–14; gender and ethnicity data are from 1989 census as reported in *Natsional'nyy sostav naseleniya SSSR* [National composition of the population of the USSR] (Moscow: Finances and Statistics, 1991).

a. Industrial employment = *promyshlenno-proizvodstvennyy personal (PPP)* (industrial production employees).

b. Enterprises subordinate to the Military-Industrial Commission (VPK).

c. *PPP* * 1.333 to account for nonindustrial employees.

nationalities constitute the majority of the population. The region with the highest concentration of defense industry (employment in defense enterprises as a share of total industrial employment) was another ethnically based republic, Udmurtia, which is 40 percent non-Russian.

Living Standards

The indicators used to compare social welfare and living standards in defense and nondefense oblasts are shown in table 9-2. They were grouped into five categories: personal incomes, food consumption, durable consumer goods consumption, housing, and health. Where possible, I tried to select measures of outputs as well as pure inputs, and indexes that suggest quality as well as quantity. For instance, in the case of health care, infant mortality tells more about the actual outcome of health services than does a measurement such as the number of physicians or hospital beds. Similarly, in housing the purely quantitative measure of housing space per capita should be viewed in combination with data on the percentage of housing units with amenities such as baths and indoor plumbing.

The comparison suggests that average living standards were remarkably equal in the two groups of oblasts. Although the average wage and per capita income were higher in the defense oblasts, the difference was slight indeed. In the case of food consumption, only with meat is there a real gap: People ate slightly more meat annually per capita in regions with high levels of defense industry. The other measures of goods consumption reflect only minor differences.

Housing presents a somewhat more interesting picture. The urban residents of defense regions had less housing space per capita, but their housing was better equipped with amenities such as indoor baths, plumbing, and hot water. In the area of health services, though the numbers of physicians and hospital beds per 10,000 residents were similar, infant mortality (the death rate for infants in their first year of life) was actually higher in defense regions.[2]

Education

One area where significant differences might be expected between defense and nondefense oblasts is in the quality of the labor force. Many important components of labor quality are not directly measurable, but table 9-3 presents some data on one criterion that is: education. There are data on both the educational infrastructure in an oblast (number of institutions and number of people trained) and also on how well educated the labor force is. The distinction is important, because opportunities for post-

TABLE 9-2. *Living Standards in Defense and Nondefense Oblasts in Russia, 1985*
Mean value per oblast

Characteristic	Oblasts	
	Defense	Nondefense
Income (rubles)		
Monthly wages	185.7	181.2
Annual per capita	1,595.1	1,587.1
Food consumption (annual per capita)		
Meat (kg)	63.2	60.5
Milk (kg)	333.6	332.5
Eggs	307.7	307.5
Bread (kg)	125.1	127.3
Durable goods		
Vacuum cleaners (per 100 urban households)[a]	57.0	56.8
Washing machines (per 100 urban households)[a]	79.7	77.5
Cars (per 1,000 people)	39.8	41.9
Housing[b]		
Square meters per capita[c]	9.29	9.55
Urban units		
With bath	81.3%	77.8%
With hot water	67.3%	63.4%
With indoor plumbing	88.2%	85.3%
Health care		
Physicians (per 10,000 people)	38.5	37.8
Hospital beds (per 10,000 people)	135.2	138.6
Infant mortality (per 1,000 births)	19.4	18.9

Sources: Monthly wage data from Goskomstat RF, *Pokazateli sotsial'nogo razvitiya respublik, krayev i oblastey Rossiyskoy Federatsii* (1992), pp. 67–68. All other data from Goskomstat RSFSR, *Pokazateli sotsial'nogo razvitiya avtonomnykh respublik, krayev i oblastey RSFSR* (1990), pp. 19–20, 83–84, 151–152, 153–156, 161–62, 189–192, 305–306, 335–36, 391–92, 395–96, 399–400, 433–434, 437–38.

a. 1984 data.

b. Data as of January 1, 1986.

c. "Living space" (*zhilaya ploshchad'*).

For definitions of defense and nondefense oblasts, see table 9-1.

TABLE 9-3. *Vocational and Higher Education Levels in Defense and Nondefense Oblasts in Russia, 1991–92*

Mean value per oblast

	Oblasts	
	Defense	Nondefense
Education[a]		
Universities	7.6	5.0
University students, total	40,600	24,600
(per 10,000 people)	157.1	143.4
Vocational school students		
(per 10,000 people)	151.6	149.2
Trade school graduates		
(per 10,000 people)	80.4	80.0
Share of labor force[b]		
With university or vocational		
education	28.5%	27.5%
Under age 30		
With higher education	11.7%	11.1%
With specialized secondary		
education	21.7%	22.3%

Sources: Data on share of labor force with university or vocational education from Goskomstat RSFSR, *Pokazateli sotsial'nogo razvitiya avtonomnykh respublik, krayev i oblastey RSFSR* (1990), pp. 39–40. All other data from Goskomstat Rossii, *Obrazovaniye i kultura v Rossiyskoy Federatsii, 1992* [Education and culture in the Russian Federation, 1992] (Moscow: Republic Information Publishing Center, 1992), pp. 21–22, 170–71, 181–82, 202–205.

a. 1991 data.

b. 1989 data.

For definitions of defense and nondefense oblasts, see table 9-1.

secondary education in a region have little value for the local economy if they are not eventually reflected in the level of education of the people who work there.

The data show that defense oblasts had on average a greater number of universities and other higher educational institutions. This is to be expected because they had larger populations. In the case of higher education, there was also a *denser* network; the defense oblasts had roughly 10 percent more university students per 10,000 people. This, however, is where the differences end.

The relative number of students in the more vocationally oriented institutions—specialized vocational schools and trade schools—was about the same in the two groups of regions. Most important of all, there was virtually no difference in the level of education of the labor force. The typical defense oblast's share of its labor force who had either attended an institution of higher education or graduated from a specialized vocational training institute was less than 1 percentage point higher than in a typical nondefense region. Among the younger members of the labor force—workers in their teens and twenties—the defense regions had no advantage at all. In both cases, the percentage with some higher or specialized vocational education in the late 1980s was 33.4 percent.

A Trickle-Down Effect?

In all of these analyses, the choices of indicators were limited by the data available, and they are highly imperfect. As such, they should be considered more suggestive than conclusive. Nevertheless, taken as a whole, a consistent pattern does emerge, and it may be surprising.

It appears that in oblasts dominated by defense industry in Soviet-era Russia, residents as a whole—as distinct from workers in the defense enterprises—did *not* enjoy higher living standards than residents of nondefense oblasts. That is, the average Russian citizen of a defense region was not paid a higher wage, did not consume more goods, did not have better access to health care, and was not better educated than his or her counterpart in a nondefense region.

This has interesting implications. If the employees of defense *enterprises* did indeed have higher standards of living and were better educated than people employed in other sectors of the Russian economy, then these advantages to defense-industry workers were balanced by correspondingly lower than average levels in the rest of the population. In this sense at least, there was no positive trickle-down effect from the defense industry to the rest of its region. In fact, the opposite appears to be the case—that is, on the whole the development and well-being of defense industry was at the expense of the rest of the local economy. From previous discussions, this should not be a surprise: Defense industry parasitized the rest of the economy and society. What the analysis suggests here, though, is that the parasitical effect may not have been so much a national one—that is, one in which certain regions of the country were given priority over others—as it was an effect *within* oblasts. But how local was the effect? If defense oblasts did not seem to differ from nondefense oblasts, would the picture be different if cities were compared instead?

Cities

There are fewer data available on Russian cities than on oblasts.[3] Most seriously, there is no convenient source from which to derive systematic estimates of defense-industrial employment at the city level, as was done

TABLE 9-4. *Top Russian Defense-Industrial Cities, Late 1980s*
Employment in defense industry

Thousands of employees	As percentage of total civilian labor force	City	Population (1989 census, in thousands)	Rank (of all cities)
> 300	10–15	St. Petersburg (Leningrad)	5,024	2
200–250	5–10	Moscow	8,972	1
	20–30	Nizhny Novgorod (Gorky)	1,438	3
150–200	25–35	Perm	1,091	10
	20–30	Samara (Kuybyshev)	1,254	6
	20–30	Yekaterinburg (Sverdlovsk)	1,365	5
	25–35	Kazan	1,094	9
	20–30	Novosibirsk	1,437	4
100–150	30–40	Izhevsk	635	17
	20–30	Voronezh	887	16
	30–40	Tula	540	29
	15–25	Ufa	1,078	11
50–100	10–20	Saratov	905	15
	10–20	Omsk	1,148	7
	10–20	Krasnoyarsk	913	14
	10–20	Chelyabinsk	1,142	8
	10–20	Rostov-na-Donu	1,019	12

Sources: Defense employment from author's estimates. Size of civilian labor force from Goskomstat Rossii, *Sotsial'no-ekonomicheskoye razvitiye stolits respublik, krayevykh i oblastnykh tsentrov Rossiyskoy Federatsii. 1992* [Socioeconomic development of republic capitals and kray and oblast centers of the Russian Federation, 1992] (Moscow: Republic Information Publishing Center, 1992), pp. 37–38. Data on 1989 city populations and ranks from *Narkhoz RSFSR 1990*, pp. 81–84.

earlier for the oblasts. I have been forced to use a variety of information sources to identify the cities that have the biggest defense employment and to classify as many of the oblast capitals as possible into defense and nondefense cities. Table 9-4 identifies Russia's seventeen leading defense-industry cities, listed in five groups by estimated range of defense-industry employment.[4] The table also indicates the relative weight of defense industry in the city's total labor force and gives each city's population and population rank among all Russian cities according to the 1989 census.

Table 9-5 presents the results of a comparison between living standards in the top defense cities and in other Russian cities similar to the one made earlier for the oblasts. For this comparison, I did not include Moscow and St. Petersburg, because they differ in so many other ways from all other Russian cities, defense or nondefense. And again, because the biggest defense cities are all in the western half of Russia, I restricted the comparison to other cities in that part of the country as well. These other cities were categorized as "medium-defense" (fifteen cities with 25,000–50,000 defense-industry employees) and "low-defense" cities (twenty-six cities with fewer than 25,000 defense-industry employees).

Owing to data limitations, the comparison of the cities covers fewer categories than for the oblasts. But in general, the picture for cities is quite similar to that observed earlier. Only in the quality of housing (measured by various amenities) do defense-industry cities have a consistent advantage. Unfortunately, the data for education allow only a comparison of the educational infrastructure, not the impact of education on the educational level of the work force. But they follow the pattern for the regions as well: "high-defense" cities with somewhat more university-level students per 1,000 population than the other cities and an equal or lower percentage of students in vocational education.

To sum up, in measures of living standards, defense and nondefense regions—whether defined as oblasts or as cities—differ little in outcomes. Even where there is an advantage in defense regions, it is slight and may in fact be explained by features other than the concentration of defense employment.[5] Similar outcomes in health and education suggest that the defense regions as a whole have not emerged from the Soviet era with a positive legacy of human capital. If such a legacy exists, it has to be sought at the enterprise level—in differences between defense-enterprise employees and the rest of the local population. But even this advantage is likely to be a diminishing one, as defense workers—especially some of the best ones—leave the plants and go to work elsewhere in the economy.

In the end, then, in the search for differences between defense and nondefense regions, we are left to a large extent only with the structure of the economy, rather than its content. The defense cities were much larger than other urban areas and were dominated by much bigger industrial enterprises. The implications of these differences are great.

Dominance of Large Enterprises

In chapter 2, I commented on the huge average size of Russian manufacturing enterprises. The scale of these enterprises distinguished Russia from other countries—certainly, from the United States, with its multitude

TABLE 9-5. *Living Standards and Education Levels in Russian Cities with High, Medium, and Low Levels of Defense Industry, 1985*
Mean value per city

| Characteristic | *Level of defense industry* | | |
	High	*Medium*	*Low*
Monthly wages (rubles)	197.2	198.0	196.1
Housing			
Square meters per capita[a]	13.9	14.2	13.9
Units			
With bath	79%	77%	74%
With hot water	71%	68%	65%
With indoor plumbing	85%	83%	81%
Health care			
Physicians (per 10,000 people)	65.6	61.8	66.0
Hospital beds (per 10,000 people)	145.9	165.9	171.2
Infant mortality (per 1,000 births)	21.0	18.4	21.5
Consumer goods (per 1,000 people)			
Cars	44.9	43.3	44.7
Telephones	120.5	116.6	124.2
Education (students per 1,000 people)			
University	51.3	47.9	45.7
Vocational school	27.0	28.4	30.4
Trade school[b]	14.6	13.9	15.7

Sources: 1985 population data from *Narkhoz SSSR 1984*, pp. 21–25. All other data from Goskomstat Rossii, *Stolitsy respublik, krayevyye i oblastnyye tsentry Rossiyskoy Federatsii v 1992 godu* [Republic capitals and kray and oblast centers of the Russian Federation in 1992] (Moscow: Republic Information Publishing Center, 1994), pp. 30–31, 38–39, 42–43, 88–89, 96–99, 102–103, 142–45, 160–61, 166–67, 251–52, 272–73.

a. Total space (*obshchaya ploshchad'*).

b. Figures as of the beginning of 1986.

Note: Based on a sample of fifty-six capital cities, categorized according to estimated number of defense-industrial employees. High level = fifteen cities with more than 50,000 defense-industrial employees (Moscow and St. Petersburg not included); medium level = fifteen cities with 25,000 to 50,000 defense-industrial employees; low level = twenty-six cities with fewer than 25,000 defense-industrial employees.

TABLE 9-6. *Large Enterprise Dominance in Russian Defense-Industrial Cities, 1985 and 1992*

Characteristic	City type (level of defense industry)		
	High	Medium	Low
Number of industrial enterprises			
1985	143	94	79
1992	142	95	74
Total industrial employment (PPP)			
1985	247,000	123,000	77,000
1992	189,000	95,000	59,000
Average size of industrial enterprises			
1985	1,741	1,316	965
1992	1,396	1,027	813
Share of housing owned by enterprises (as of January 1, 1993)	42%	35%	33%

Sources: 1985 data from *Sotsial'no-ekonomicheskoye razvitiye stolits respublik, krayevykh i oblastnykh tsentrov Rossiyskoy Federatsii 1992*, pp. 217–18, 231–32. 1992 and 1993 data from *Stolitsy respublik, krayevyye i oblastnyye tsentry Rossiyskoy Federatsii v 1992 godu*, pp. 86–87, 180–81, 192–93.

For definitions of cities with high, medium, and low levels of defense industry, see table 9-5.

of small firms. Almost equally remarkable is the way the average enterprise size in Russia grows as the size of the city grows. It is hard to avoid the conclusion that this pattern is the result of defense industry. In Russia's fifteen largest provincial defense-industry cities—a list that is nearly the same as a list of the fifteen largest cities by population—the average industrial enterprise in 1985 had nearly 80 percent more employees than in cities that were smaller and had little or no defense industry (table 9-6). By 1992, official industrial employment had declined considerably in all Russian cities, but the average enterprise size in cities with high levels of defense industry remained much larger than in other urban areas.

This positive association between the Russian city's population and the average size of its manufacturing enterprises is yet another way in which Russia differs from the United States. In the United States today, smaller cities and towns tend to have larger establishments than large cities.[6]

One of the consequences of the relationship between enterprise size and city size in Russia is that large cities tend to be more dominated by a few giant enterprises than medium-sized cities. Or, in terms of the theme of chapter 8, Russia's biggest cities are more like "company towns" than the others. More of their social services are delivered by enterprises, their economies are less diverse, and their populations are more rigidly divided into separate worlds. Table 9-6 offers partial confirmation of this point as well. In the fifteen high-defense cities, 42 percent of housing was owned by enterprises in 1993; in the low-defense cities, only 33 percent was.

A comparison of average enterprise size is persuasive enough. But averages conceal details. A look at one city's development—that of Perm in the Urals—better illustrates how extreme the dominance of large defense enterprises could be and how it got to be that way. Perm epitomizes the phenomenon of large enterprise dominance. In the mid-1980s, the ten largest enterprises in this city of 1 million were all in defense industry. The average size of the defense plants (including two smaller ones in addition to the ten giants) was more than 15,000 employees. The average size of the remaining 130 manufacturing enterprises in the city was only 500 employees. Figure 9-1 provides further details on the case of Perm.

Growth of the Defense Cities

One of the many striking features of Perm's development is its dramatic growth in the 1930s. This was not atypical of the defense-industry cities. In 1926–39, urban areas all over Russia were growing at extremely high rates of more than 6 percent a year—enough to more than double the total urban population in those thirteen years. Most of the top defense cities had even higher rates of growth in that period.[7]

The cities that were to become large defense-industrial centers naturally had different starting points. A few of the biggest defense cities were already large urban areas when the defense build-up began. In the mid-1920s, Rostov and Saratov were the third and fourth largest cities in Russia. Their relative growth has therefore been less dramatic than that of some others. On the other hand, Nizhny Novgorod, Russia's fifth largest city in 1926, continued to grow fast in later decades, despite its initial size. But the most dramatic growth was in those cities that were relatively obscure before the Soviet period. Perm was one example; Chelyabinsk was another. In 1926, with only 59,000 residents, Chelyabinsk ranked forty-first among Russia's cities; by the end of the 1930s, it had more than 273,000 people and had climbed to seventeenth place.

FIGURE 9-1. *Defense Industry and City Growth: The Case of Perm*

HISTORY. Perm—one of the half-dozen largest defense-industrial cities in Russia—began as a company town in the early eighteenth century. On the orders of Peter the Great, a copper processing plant was built on the banks of the Kama River in 1723. In 1781 the town was made the administrative seat of the newly created *gubernia* (province) of Perm and renamed for the province.

For the next 150 years, Perm remained in relative obscurity. In 1923, with a population of 67,000, it was Russia's thirty-first largest city. Modern Perm dates from 1929, for in the next ten years, Perm tripled in size. By 1939, it was the thirteenth largest city in the country.

DEFENSE INDUSTRY. Perm's explosive growth was almost perfectly correlated with the development of defense industry in the city. A dozen huge enterprises were located in Perm in three fairly well-defined phases. During the first phase—the 1930s—five plants were built. Phase II began in 1941. Two new defense plants were built in Perm in the first months of World War II; the others were expanded as more of the nation's military production was evacuated from the western part of the country into the heartland. Phase III for Perm began in the late 1950s. The missile race of the 1950s and 1960s brought five more giant plants, including a couple of the city's most important and most secretive plants.

By 1970, when that third defense build-up phase ended, the city was essentially what it is today. For the next two decades, growth slowed to barely 1 percent a year—a slower rate of growth than it had had on average during the 200 years from the time the copper plant was founded until the Bolshevik Revolution. Since 1992, population has declined.

CITY AND OBLAST. The population of the province of Perm never grew as fast as that of the city. The city's rapid growth meant that it increasingly dominated the oblast. Before 1926, less than 5 percent of the total population of the oblast resided in the city. By 1959, more than 20 percent did. The oblast population stopped growing in the 1950s. To an increasing extent, the addition to the labor force and the population of Perm City that continued during the 1950s and 1960s was thus drawn from within the oblast (from the rural areas and smaller towns). In 1989, more than one in every three Perm oblast residents lived in the capital city.

COMPARISON WITH U.S. CITIES. Today, Perm is the tenth largest city in Russia. Its population of 1.1 million would make it the seventh largest city in the United States, slightly bigger than Detroit. And yet such comparisons with American cities—indeed, the very use of the word "city"—are ambiguous when it comes to Perm. It sprawls for 76 kilometers (50 miles) along the Kama River. Its population density is only half that of Detroit. In some ways it is more like an American metropolitan area. Yet that, too, is not a particularly good reference point. It is far more densely populated than a U.S. multicounty metropolitan area of comparable population. U.S. Statistical Metropolitan Areas (SMAs) in roughly the range of 1 million residents cover five to ten times the land area of Perm.

But the feature of Perm that really distinguishes it from American cities is the legacy of the large enterprises. An American city of Perm's size would have easily a couple of thousand manufacturing establishments; in 1985 Perm had 144. The twelve defense enterprises accounted for 65 to 80 percent of all industrial employment in Perm. They averaged more than 15,000 employees each. The other 130 industrial enterprises averaged fewer than 500 employees each.

ROLE OF GOVERNMENT. In the old Soviet system, the ultimate mediator among these separate company towns was the Communist party. From the economic side, there was little need of local coordination. The twelve defense plants were subordinate to six different defense industry ministries in Moscow. At the local level, there was little or no interaction among most of them. The general directors knew each other, but more as rivals than collaborators. Below the level of director, the enterprises were almost hermetically sealed from one another.

To city government fell the task of coordinating the social services of the enterprises. This was done first of all at the level of the city borough, or rayon. In the Soviet era, each borough had its own Communist party apparatus, legislature (soviet), and executive administration. Today, the party and the soviet are gone. The executive bodies of the rayons live on, with the chief executive appointed by the mayor of the city.

Perm is divided into seven rayons. Five of them are named for the defense plants that dominate them.

Name of rayon	Population	Number of defense enterprises	Estimated percentage of industrial labor force employed in defense enterprises in 1985
1. Sverdlov	232,800	4	89
2. Motovilikhi	187,000	2	86
3. Industrial	169,500	1	29
4. Dzerzhinsky	164,900	1	75
5. Kirov	138,400	2	63
6. Ordzhonikidze	122,900	1	40
7. Lenin	70,600	1	43
	1,086,100	12	75

Sources: Historical background from V. S. Verkholantsev, Gorod Perm, ego proshloye i nastoyashcheye [The city of Perm, its past and present] (Perm: "Pushka" Publications, 1994); Vsya Perm, 1993 [The complete Perm, 1993]; statistics from Narodnoye khozyaystvo permskoy oblasti: Statisticheskiy sbornik (various years) [The economy of Perm oblast: Statistical handbook] (Perm: Goskomstat RSFSR, Perm Oblast Statistical Administration); Sotsial'no-ekonomicheskoye polozheniye gorodov i rayonov permskoy oblasti [Socioeconomic situation of the cities and rayons of Perm oblast] (Perm, 1994); Permskaya oblast v tsifrakh: Statisticheskiy sbornik [Perm oblast in numbers: Statistical handbook] (Perm, Goskomstat, Perm Oblast Statistical Administration, 1994); Komitet ekonomiki i sotsial'nogo razvitiya, "Pokazateli sotsial'no-ekonomicheskogo razvitiya goroda Permi" [Indicators of the socioeconomic development of the city of Perm] (Perm: RIA, 1993).

The history of growth for all of these cities is a reflection of the development of Soviet defense industry. All were built up through defense manufacturing. In fact, without defense industry, the major Russian cities compared here would have had a much more similar economic structure, because their civilian manufacturing bases are fairly similar, at least in size. Figure 9-2 makes this point. The defense-industry city was not just generally bigger; it was bigger specifically because it had defense industry superimposed on what otherwise would have been a fairly typical industrial base.

Growth by Compulsion and Control

The key to the development of these cities in which a huge percentage of the labor force worked in just a few plants was the dual policy of residence restrictions and labor control. The few designated arms manufacturing plants grew larger and larger. The demand for labor by other sectors of the local economy was kept artificially low. Once a city was closed off because of the presence of sensitive defense-industry projects, a big cost was incurred in maintaining not only political power but also economic control over the city (through a lack of labor market competition and other factors). Everything was designed to control the flow of labor into and out of the defense-industry cities.

The Propiska

The policy of strict residence restrictions and obligatory internal passports carried over from the Tsarist era. This system, known as the *propiska,* was first instituted during the early seventeenth century, and its use became firmly established under Peter the Great. The Bolsheviks abolished the passport system soon after taking power. But only a few years later, Joseph Stalin reintroduced the *propiska* system in an effort to stop the soaring rates of labor turnover in Soviet industry.[8] At the end of 1932, a decree was issued requiring a nationwide system of passports and obligatory residency registration.

The combination of the labor booklet (the *trudovaya knizhka* described in chapter 7) and the residence permit implied that the amount and quality of labor coming into the city was regulated. Unplanned entry of firms of course, was excluded. We have seen how labor was regulated within the city—the policy of a dual labor market for defense industries and others. But the growth of the defense industries required labor from outside. The permit system ensured that labor came from the entire oblast and larger region.

In the early phases of construction of Soviet defense industry, achieving this goal may have been easier. In the 1930s many Russians wanted badly to get out their small towns and rural areas. There was explosive

FIGURE 9-2. *Industrial Labor Force in Defense-Industrial and Other Enterprises in Russian Cities with High, Medium, and Low Levels of Defense Industry, 1985*

Thousands of employees

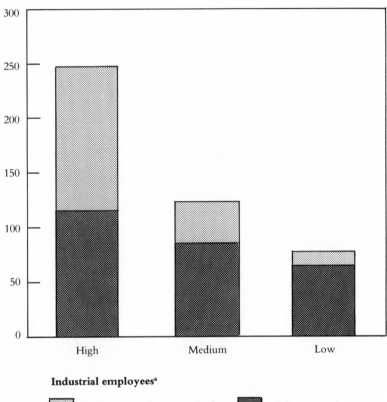

Industrial employees[a]

Defense-complex enterprises[b]   Other enterprises

Source: Author's calculations based on data in Goskomstat Rossii, *Stolitsy respublik, krayev-yye i oblastnyye tsentry Rossiyskoy Federatsii v 1992 godu*, pp. 34–41.

a. Industrial employees = industrial production employees (PPP).

b. Defense-complex enterprises = enterprises subordinate to the Military-Industrial Commission (VPK).

For definitions of cities with high, medium, and low levels of defense industry, see table 9-5.

growth in the big cities before World War II and then again in the 1960s. But beginning in 1966, the growth rates of the large defense cities were slower than the average for Russia's urban areas. This growth slowdown had major psychological effects on the people already living there. These cities had once represented opportunity and upward mobility. A generation of Soviet citizens had striven to move to the cities to free themselves from the near-serfdom of the Soviet countryside. But things were quite different for the children of those internal immigrants. It was one thing when individuals moved to a city to improve their lot in life, but quite another to be born in it. Many of the children of those who had migrated to the cities felt more like prisoners than a privileged elite. The regulated labor market and residence permit system that had represented a way for their parents to escape the countryside and have a better life were viewed by the children of emigrants as chains binding them to their cities.

These feelings of repression were unexpressed for most of the Soviet period. It was not until *glasnost'* that they burst forth, occasionally surfacing in unprecedented ways. The feeling was eloquently summed up by a resident of one of the defense cities we have encountered earlier—Nizhny Tagil in Sverdlovsk oblast. At a 1990 meeting between Soviet President Mikhail Gorbachev and worker representatives, one of the locals bitterly demanded of Gorbachev: "For how long will all of us, the inhabitants of the Soviet Union, be slaves to the system of passports and registration which often condemns a person to live or, more frequently, live out his entire life, from birth onward, in the ecologically or socially deprived region where he had the misfortune to be born?"[9]

Nizhny Tagil was home to the largest tank factory in the world. But it was not so much its character as a defense-industry outpost that made Nizhny Tagil so oppressive as it was its status as the so-called second city in its oblast. As such, its citizens were denied the right to freely move not only to Moscow or St. Petersburg, but even to the oblast capital of Sverdlovsk (now Yekaterinburg).[10]

The system of restrictions on residence in Russia lasted for more than sixty years. Not until 1993 were Russian citizens granted the right to move freely within the country and to live where they liked.[11] One commentator compared the decision to abolish the *propiska* to the abolition of serfdom in Russia 130 years before.[12]

Free to Move . . . But Where?

What will happen now as the forces that brought people into these cities and kept them there are breaking down? Workers have left the defense plants in large numbers. Will they also leave the defense-industrial cities?

So far, there is no sign of this. The large cities still appear to offer the better alternative locally. Within the regions, life in the big city—as difficult as it may seem—is still what many want.

In the past, as long as the goal was to make living in the defense-industrial city more attractive, Soviet planners had few incentives to narrow the gap between living standards in the defense-industrial centers and those of the rural areas and small towns in those regions. Today this gap persists and may even be widening. Certainly, the faster growth of the new private economy in the larger cities, and all that this new economy has to offer in terms of opportunities to both earn and spend income, is a powerful draw.[13] Not surprisingly, government officials in some large Russian defense cities are more concerned that people will move to their urban areas from the rest of their regions than that city residents will leave. In that situation, the desire to preserve social stability has even led to talk of limiting immigration by resurrecting the system of residence permits.

Development without Growth?

In contrast to enterprises, cities cannot successfully restructure by "downsizing," that is, by shedding their least productive members. Nor can they expect to develop by raising protective barriers against the influx of people from the outside. On the contrary, historical experience throughout the world has shown that positive change in cities is nearly impossible without growth. The quickest way to raise the average level of productivity and, above all, to introduce a psychology of development is to welcome new residents who have the ability and the desire to engage in new forms of economic activity.

There are limits to this, of course. If the influx of new residents is overwhelmingly of people simply fleeing poverty, the result for the city will not be a positive one. But as long as newcomers seek opportunities to work and even create jobs for others, their movement should be tolerated and even encouraged.

Making the Russian defense-industry cities larger may seem exactly the opposite of what needs to be done. They are already huge relative to the population of their regions. (On average, a Russian oblast's capital city accounts for one-third of its population; in the case of these large defense-industry–dominated capitals, the percentage is even higher.) Yet the needs of these cities for new economic activity are also enormous. A great amount of development has yet to happen within Russian cities. A comparison between a Russian defense city and almost any American city of the same size illustrates this point. In table 9-7 I compare the size, popu-

TABLE 9-7. *Comparison of Cities with 1 Million Inhabitants, Russia and the United States: Perm, Detroit, Louisville, and Nashville*

	Perm	Detroit (central city)	Louisville (metro area)	Nashville (metro area)
Population (thousands)	1,035	1,012	953	985
Land area (square miles)	278	139	2,266	4,073
Population density (persons per square mile)	3,723	7,297	420	242
Manufacturing				
Total number of establishments	144	1,255	1,223	1,506
Average size of establishments (employees)	1,471	81	70	59
Retail				
Total number of establishments	759	3,847	5,618	5,840
Food stores	372	n.a.	788	740
Auto dealers	n.a.	n.a.	381	440
Gas and service stations	12	n.a.	435	445
Restaurants	110	n.a.	1,391	1,371
Service				
Total number of establishments	230	3,734	6,091	7,107
Hotels	12	n.a.	89	195
Auto repair shops	20	n.a.	657	611
Laundries and dry cleaners	24	n.a.	n.a.	n.a.
Hairdressers and barbershops	88	n.a.	n.a.	n.a.

Sources: U.S. data: Bureau of the Census, *State and Metropolitan Data Book, 1991* (Government Printing Office, 1991), pp. 30, 38–44, 52–55, 758, 766–68. Perm population and area data from Komitet ekonomiki i sotsial'nogo razvitiya, "Pokazateli sotsial'no-ekonomicheskogo razvitiya goroda Permi"; see also *Vsya Perm*.

n.a. = Not available.

Perm data for 1993; population and land data for U.S. cities for 1990; manufacturing, retail, and service data for U.S. cities for 1987.

lation density, and economic structure of Perm with three very different types of American cities: the central city of Detroit, Michigan, and the metropolitan areas of Louisville, Kentucky, and Nashville, Tennessee—all of which have populations of around 1 million.[14]

The table shows the vast gap between the Russian city and its American counterparts, especially in the provision of services. When it comes to the basic infrastructure required to meet the everyday needs of its citizens, Perm is closer to the level of a small American city of 50,000 than an urban center of more than 1 million. Yet it may be this very level of underdevelopment in Russia that gives grounds for the greatest optimism about the future of the large defense-industry cities. There is ample opportunity for people to choose differently how they will work and where; there will be rich and immediate rewards for anyone, whether a current resident or new immigrant, who can find the right goods and services for this undersupplied market. Right now, that is being done by traders. They are providing eager customers with goods that are much in demand. Most of the goods are foreign, but there must still be a huge potential market for decent Russian-made goods. The need for services is even more acute than the market for goods in Russian cities.

Finally, there is another reason for optimism. In many ways Russian defense-industrial cities have far to go to reach living standards comparable to those of the United States. But it is equally true that in other aspects of urban life they would have to seriously decline before being in as bad a way as American cities. For all the difficulties they may face, and as poor as they may appear in comparison with their American metropolitan counterparts, the picture still appears considerably brighter for the Russian cities when compared with some inner cities in the United States.

The Future of the Russian Defense-Industrial City

In the future, all of Russia's subnational units—both regions and cities—will increasingly find themselves forced to find solutions to their problems on their own, without the intercession of "the Center," the national government in Moscow. This means, quite simply, that costs and benefits will be calculated locally in a new way. For the defense regions, this signifies a particularly great change. Under the regime of militarization in the old USSR, most of the benefits the defense-industrial complex enjoyed were taken for granted. They were not perceived as costing anything, usually because the net cost of these benefits was borne elsewhere. Entitlements were subsidized from the Center in Moscow, but this was never readily understood. The fact that the burden of benefits could be

borne at all had depended on the *entire* Soviet system. This was the ration-
alization: Any one subsidy could be absorbed by an all-encompassing
system of extraction of taxes from the Russian people. There was never a
notion of identifiable costs associated with any one part or project—it was
all so intertwined.

For instance, once the defense-industrial cities and related industries
were built, agriculture had to be adapted accordingly to support them.
Planners and politicians may have been aware of the huge volume of some
of the subsidies to agriculture. But there was not (nor could there be) any
specific accounting of what portion of those subsidies arose because much
of the agriculture sector was artificially developed to service this particular
industrial and geographical structure. The same argument holds true for
all other aspects of Soviet infrastructure—roads, railways, health services,
and so on.

Today, the farms are still there, often in places where farms should
not be. In the past, the net cost of farming in these nonviable areas—the
difference between the costs of locating agriculture there and the benefits—
was borne ultimately by the national budget, spread throughout the economy and across the entire Soviet Union. Today, the federal government is
increasingly less able and willing to pay for such local costs, no matter
what their origin. The burden of payment will most likely end up, by
default, being a local one.

It is here that the defense-industry regions face a critical choice. Arguing that militarization was a policy imposed upon them from above,
from the Center in Moscow, they can continue to define themselves as
regions linked to the Center and dependent on it, based on those policies
of the Soviet past. They can demand to be treated "fairly" and to be
compensated for the new costs they will incur.

There is, however, another path that can be taken. The defense regions
can recognize that the best way to escape the burden of the past is to
abandon it as completely as they can. They can seek a different identity as
"new regions," ones which offer their own citizens as well as outside
investors a chance to escape the regulation and rigidities of the old. This
is undoubtedly the more difficult choice.

A vital part of a new identity for the defense regions is their openness. Most of Russia's defense-industrial cities have stagnated since the
1970s. What they are now experiencing is not totally new, although they
face some major problems of a different kind. There is a risk that some
might react by only looking inward and closing themselves off from the
greater society and the market economy. This would be dangerous. The
fundamental change that has to happen must come from within, and
the cities that can prove themselves to be real and viable will need to

not simply transform themselves, but to grow. These cities must therefore be open.

The conditions are right in Russia for an aggressive regional or city leadership to take advantage of the opportunity to distinguish its region by creating the best climate for investment. It is here, rather than through any inherent physical advantages, that the defense-industry regions must seek to define themselves.

Chapter 10

The Future

I f progress in demilitarization were measured by the volume of arms produced in an economy, Russia in the past five years would have demilitarized to an extent that is hard to grasp. Figure 10-1 presents the official picture. According to these data, the military output of the country's defense complex in 1995 was barely one-ninth what it had been in 1990.[1]

Russia's arms industry is producing weapons at levels far below those in its Soviet-era past. But what is more signficant for the focus of this book is that it is *consuming* much less of the nation's resources. For several years, defense enterprises (like other plants) continued to invest in the construction of already planned facilities as long as funding was available, regardless of the market outlook for the production initially envisioned. But anecdotal evidence suggests that by late 1994 and early 1995 even these inertial trends of construction and investment in defense plants had finally come to a halt. And, as reported in chapter 7, labor employed in military production showed the same steady, deep decline as output. According to figure 7-2, at the beginning of 1995, as few as 600,000 people (down from 2.7 million in the mid-1980s) remained on military production lines. It is also likely that a large percentage of them were not fully employed.

However, the decline in military production is only part of the picture. Figure 10-1 also shows the trends for civilian production by defense plants in 1990–95. Through 1993, civilian output remained relatively stable, thus providing a basis for some continuing activity in defense enterprises. But a disturbing tendency emerged in 1994 as civilian output declined at the same rate as military output. The same trend held in 1995.

The aggregate data do not reveal the extent of decline in individual enterprises. Many plants have seen their orders for military production vanish altogether. This picture of output collapse is reflected in the financial state of the enterprises. Already by the spring of 1995, Russian federal authorities had declared more than 200 defense complex enterprises or institutes financially insolvent.[2] Many more were on the verge of insolvency.

FIGURE 10-1. *Decline in Output by Enterprises of Russia's Defense-Industrial Complex, 1990–95*

Annual output as percentage of 1990

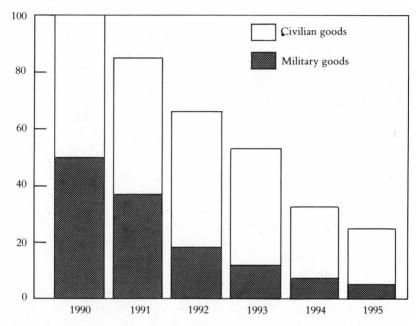

Source: Computed by the author on the basis of data in Tsentr ekonomicheskoy kon"yunktury i prognozirovaniya, *Rossiya—1992. Ekonomicheskaya kon"yunktura* [Russia—1992: Economic situation] (Moscow, November 1992), p. 114 (decline 1990–91); "Voyenno-promyshlennyy kompleks v 1994 godu [The military-industrial complex in 1994]" *Krasnaya zvezda,* January 28, 1995, p. 3 (year-by-year decline, 1991–94); "Predpriyatiya VPK prodol-zhayut sokrashchat' proizvodstvo [VPK enterprises continue to cut production]" *Izvestiya,* January 25, 1996 [on-line version] (decline from 1994–95).

But what will happen next is unclear. The Russian government has yet to take the step of declaring the enterprises formally bankrupt. Lacking paying customers, incapable of paying their debts, and with no real prospects of improvement, these enterprises—including some of Russia's largest manufacturing plants—nevertheless continue to exist as legal entities and (more importantly) as social institutions. As we saw in chapters 7 and 8, the enterprises have still retained their roles in the social functioning of their communities. Though the allocation of society's resources into military production has declined radically, the ultimate fate of Russia's defense enterprises still hangs in the balance—and with them, the fate of the people and the communities that depended on them, directly and indirectly.

To a large extent, Russia's record in demilitarizing, and its prospects for further progress, should rightly be measured not so much in aggregates of military spending, investment, or output but in these three dimensions: the enterprises, the communities, and the people. In this chapter I examine each dimension in turn to assess Russia's progress in overcoming its legacy of hypermilitarization, the prospects for further demilitarization and the policies needed to ensure it continues, and how and to what extent the West might play a role.

The Enterprises

The record of performance of the enterprises that once made up Russia's defense-industrial complex is poor and their outlook bleak. They have been unable to adjust to the conditions of a market economy. But should they realistically have been expected to?

Especially in the West, Russian defense enterprises are often compared to corporations undergoing major crises. But almost everything about the Russian enterprises distinguishes them from even the worst cases of firms in crisis in modern capitalist economies. Whatever its ultimate condition, the capitalist firm in crisis did originally evolve along natural, market-driven lines. At some point, the firm must have passed the test of competing in the market; otherwise, it would never have been viable. But the Russian defense enterprise has bigger problems. From the market standpoint—from which it is now viewed—there was nothing natural about it from the beginning.

As has been stressed in earlier chapters, many of the advantages defense enterprises enjoyed under the old system—skilled and disciplined workers, up-to-date technology, and reliable supplies of other high-quality inputs—have not lasted, nor could they have under the new market system. When administrative allocation of resources was abandoned, the defense enterprise lost its right to prized raw materials. When Soviet citizens were given the freedom to choose their occupations and places of work, the defense enterprise was deprived of what had been considered *its* skilled labor. The further along the path toward market reform Russia has moved, the more intense these trends have become. Today Russia's defense enterprises are, on the whole, organizations ill suited for transformation into capitalist firms. For many of them, no realistic degree of "adjustment" will accomplish the task.

The Criterion of the World Market

There have been some exceptions to this bleak picture: defense enterprises that, though not yet prosperous, at least have the potential to survive. In examining such cases, the most important conclusion is that for most the real test has been acceptance in the world market, as a competitor or as a partner.

By the criterion of the world market, the enterprises that made up the Russian defense-industrial complex can be grouped into three broad categories. Two of the three groups consist of enterprises that are passing the market test. Some enterprises produce arms that sell successfully on the world market. Others have proved capable of winning the approval of established Western firms by successfully participating in joint ventures.

The distribution of Russian defense enterprises can be imagined as a curve taking the shape of the letter U. The two successful groups of defense enterprises—the weapons exporters and the joint venture partners—form the arms of the U, as they have managed to lift themselves up. Unfortunately, the middle of the U consists of many enterprises whose futures are not so promising. Let us look at each of the three groups in turn. We can also analyze the survival prospects for defense enterprises in the middle of the U: Can they, too, join the world market, or if not, is there any hope they can insulate themselves from it?

Exporting Arms

In a sense, of course, the performance criterion for Soviet arms manufacturers was always international competitiveness. But in today's world, the competition is principally in the business arena rather than in combat. Earlier we saw how exaggerated expectations about the success of Russian arms exports early in the post-Soviet era had a negative effect on decision-making in many defense enterprises (see chapter 6). Measured against these exaggerated hopes year after year, arms sales have been disappointing. Today, there is more realism and even grounds for cautious optimism about future exports from Russian defense industry. There does seem to be a market for Russian weapons, typified by nations such as China, South Korea, Malaysia, and India. These countries want serviceable weapons at a low price, and all have recently concluded arms deals with Russia.

In 1994 Russia's arms sales overseas totaled $1.71 billion; sales for 1995 were probably more than $2 billion and perhaps as high as $2.5 billion.[3] Against the baseline of post-Soviet Russia's early performance, this should be deemed a success. If the upward trend continues, it will mean more orders for a number of defense plants.

Some cautionary notes should be made, however. The first is that it still may be too early to forecast success. The verdict is not yet in on the real potential and performance of Russian arms manufacturers (either individually or as a group) in the international market. Much of what has been sold by these defense enterprises in recent years has come from inventory and reflects only previous production. It has not yet been proven that Russian arms can be produced as well (that is, can be simple but durable) and as cheaply under the new market conditions as they once were.

A second note of caution in judging the export situation is that it is a relative judgment. Compared with the overall performance of the Russian economy recently, today's arms export levels are quite significant. Weapons are already the country's largest manufactured export item. If Russia were to export arms for $4 billion a year, that would bring sales of arms up to the level of its aluminum or timber exports, and sales would be exceeded only by oil and gas and ferrous metals.[4]

But as to the effects on the enterprises, the situation is far different from what it was the 1980s. In those years, the Soviet Union may have suffered a net loss in arms exports. Yet arms shipments abroad accounted for a huge volume of production in the defense plants and kept large numbers of workers busy producing those weapons. Today, even in the best scenario (perhaps of foreign arms sales totaling $4 billion a year), the arms export business would employ roughly only one-fifth of the previous production capacity.

Foreign Partnerships and Investment

The enterprises of Russia's defense-industrial complex continue to attract the interest of foreign business circles. Though some is encouraged by conscious efforts by Western governments as part of their assistance programs for Russian defense conversion, there is also business interest that is purely privately financed. Major corporations worldwide assay the potential of high-technology products of the Russian defense sector. When it comes about, this cooperation between Western and Russian partners is ideal for Russian enterprises that want to become competitive in the world market. A Western partner can provide investment capital, specific technology, and management and marketing expertise. Some of these deals, especially in electronics and aerospace, have garnered much publicity. But how substantial has this foreign investment been, and what are the chances that more enterprises will be involved?

Despite the publicity, the real volume of foreign investment has been quite modest. Summary data on Western funds invested in Russian defense enterprises are not available. Attempting to account for the volume of direct investment by tracking published reports on deals is tricky also, because many intended ventures never get off the ground. But one crude measure can be obtained by taking the total amount of foreign direct investment in *all* sectors of the Russian economy and then using a process of elimination. In 1994, foreigners invested $1.3 billion in Russia. Roughly $1 billion of that total was in fuels—mainly oil and gas. The other leading recipients of foreign capital were the timber, paper and pulp, retail trade, and construction industries.[5] By implication, other manufacturing branches received very little foreign investment. The defense-enterprise share may have been no more than $10 million to $20 million.

There are good reasons to think this amount will increase, however, as the level of total foreign investment in the Russian economy increases. The volume and direction this investment in Russian defense enterprises will take will depend on the overall investment climate in the Russian economy and on specific government policies permitting foreign investment and management influence. The latter point is especially unclear at the moment. Until foreign firms can be sure that their investment is safe from the vagaries of policy shifts, they will remain reluctant to make long-term strategic commitments. What investment is made will have more limited, short-term goals: for instance, to gain access to a specific technology (which may not even then be put into production inside Russia), or to take advantage of the political influence of the particular Russian enterprise.

In many cases, the main motivation for Westerners to choose a defense enterprise as their partner will be to acquire a powerful and influential Russian friend. Those ventures will be designed to buy influence.[6] This motive for cooperation can have pernicious results. To the extent that the legal environment in Russia remains fuzzy, Western firms themselves may encourage their Russian partners to rely more on their political connections. Although this may temporarily benefit some Russian enterprises, it is unlikely to be the foundation for sustainable competitive positions in a market economy.

Domestic Strategies

After examining successful arms exporters and the defense enterprises participating in joint ventures, it seems that both groups may expand, but only marginally. In any event, many former defense enterprises will still be left. What are their prospects? If they cannot compete internationally, as the enterprises in the first two groups have, can they simply ignore the world market and stick to the market in Russia?

PRODUCING CIVILIAN GOODS IN RUSSIA, FOR RUSSIA.   The strongest argument against whether most of Russia's defense enterprises could successfully pursue a policy of strictly "domestic conversion" from military to civilian production is their own record. Even when defense enterprises have produced major consumer goods for decades, they have been unable to withstand foreign competition. The kinds of civilian products Russian defense-complex plants traditionally produced—refrigerators, washing machines, and the like—do have a market, but defense enterprises have lost those markets to foreign imports.

The defense enterprises have not come up with any new and original ways of manufacturing their traditional products better, faster, or cheaper than they once did—certainly not better and cheaper than the foreign producers that can now sell to the Russian market. Even an apparent advantage such as the local presence of the defense plants—which should have offered these plants thorough knowledge of the Russian market and a better position to provide service and maintenance—has not helped. Russian defense enterprises that produced civilian goods in the Soviet era knew little about their markets and cared even less, because distribution to consumers was centrally administered and outside their control. Today's independent distributors and sellers are stocking the products consumers want, regardless of where they were manufactured.

The failure to meet the challenge of foreign competition in the Russian market has not left defense-industry representatives with much faith in the future of conversion. Consider the following statement from Aleksei Shulunov, the president of the prominent lobbying group, the League of Assistance to Defense Enterprises:

> There has been a fall in demand for durable consumer goods, the main producers of which are enterprises of the military-industrial complex. Such goods are affordable only for a thin stratum of wealthy individuals, who prefer imported items. We need a policy of state protectionism of our domestic manufacturers, but we do not have one. As a result, Russian goods are proving to be noncompetitive on the domestic market. It is not surprising that in the past three and a half years, the output of television sets has dropped by three-fourths, and production of tape recorders and vacuum cleaners by more than 80 percent. The same fate awaits washing machines and other goods in the near future. So why then should anyone invest money in conversion?[7]

PRODUCING WEAPONS FOR RUSSIA.   One market that could be expected to be truly protected in Russia is weapons procurement for the Russian armed forces. It is also a market that can be expected to grow. Under almost any realistic scenario of Russia's future development, if it is to survive as a nation it will need more arms than it is currently producing. Russia will keep more than 1 million people in its active forces. Its territory spans eleven times zones and is bordered by fifteen nations of varying and highly uncertain degrees of friendliness and reliability. Although Russia may never spend more than a fraction of what the Soviet Union did on its defense establishment, future spending will increase significantly.

This means that many defense enterprises that currently have few orders for defense products or none at all may see an increase in the coming years. Exactly which enterprises will benefit from increased procurement remains unknown. The volume of arms Russia needs can be efficiently produced by an industrial establishment much smaller than its current size. From early on, observers inside and outside Russia's arms industry have argued that only a small percentage of the former arms manufacturers should be retained as true producers of arms. In addition, those arms-makers ought to be just that: specialists in arms production unsaddled by manufacturing civilian lines.

It is not difficult to suggest some basic efficiency principles for the Russian defense industry of the future. Sensibly, the government would ensure that the best facilities are maintained in a manufacturing core. In some cases, resources from several defense enterprises would be pooled, regardless of past bureaucratic subordination. Managers of the new enterprises would be chosen on the basis of ability. Most managers would probably still come from the old defense enterprises, but not necessarily from among current directors; some might be brought up from middle management. As exports become more important, some new managers would even come from outside the defense complex, having proven themselves in new market-oriented civilian firms.

That said, the Russian government will probably be unable to adhere strictly to such a policy. Political, social, and even geographic considerations will certainly enter into the choice of enterprises supported through defense orders. No matter what the level of affordable spending, there will be constant pressure to dilute the procurement budget and spread the orders over more enterprises than would be ideal.

But the countervailing pressure from the world market will also be strong. Russia will ultimately have to shape its domestic procurement policy in light of the success of its exporters. In the long run, it will be difficult to defend a policy of having one set of defense enterprises that successfully meet world competition by selling weapons on the international market and another group of defense plants that cannot export but can produce arms only for Russia. The pressure to abandon the weakest plants inside Russia will grow even stronger if Russia joins in cooperative agreements in arms production. As a condition for coproduction and subcontracting agreements with foreign countries, Russia may be required to purchase some of its arms abroad.

More Radical Changes?

Counting on a purely domestic market as a shield against the pressure of international competition is unlikely to succeed—except to the extent that the defense enterprises' political power wins them the kinds of demands that Aleksei Shulunov makes (protectionist foreign trade policies, direct subsidies, and the like). Thus far, however, I have been examining the prospects for defense enterprises to survive in close to their traditional structure. Some enterprises could survive (at least in a formal, legal sense) if they underwent substantially more radical changes. This might mean entire lines of production abandoned, either by shutting them down or by spinning off viable lines into separate companies and letting the rest die.

But the most important change would be to reduce costs. The number one measure would be to cut the labor force—specifically, to fire the least productive workers rather than continue to allow them to stay while the most productive leave. Downsizing the work force would be accompanied by an even greater reduction in social services. However, under current management, few enterprises will take this path. Large enterprises will be especially reluctant to do so, for they would risk losing their special status as social institutions and being cut off from subsidies and other special treatment. But above all, the old managers, whose personal identities were shaped by the traditional paternalism of the "enterprise community," would find it unthinkable to tear down the very structures they spent their lives building up. Only new management brought in from the outside could attempt it. Is such a takeover even possible?

Ownership and Control of Defense Enterprises

As of mid-1995, slightly more than one-third of all former defense enterprises in Russia had been fully privatized with no state ownership.[8] About one-quarter remain fully state owned. The Russian state has partial ownership of the remaining defense enterprises.

The status of most of the entities that are partially state owned is unclear and likely to remain so. In some cases, the state actually owns a controlling package of shares. In others, it retains what is called a "golden share"—an ownership portion that, independent of size, conveys the right to veto certain management decisions. But a focus on formal ownership is misleading. In practice, the state, through the agency of *Goskomoboronprom*, has other levers of control, even in fully privatized companies. The requirement that *Goskomoboronprom* must approve the appointment of any director of a public or private enterprise that produces weapons is certainly one such lever.[9]

Other control mechanisms relate to secrecy requirements and are more subtle.[10] So far the state has generally not attempted to exercise continuous hands-on control over day-to-day business within the enterprises. The Moscow bureaucracy is simply too small and too far away for that. The state's role has instead been a passive one.[11] But some recent cases suggest that *Goskomoboronprom*'s representatives will not allow critical decisions to be made on strategic issues (such as ownership or partnerships with outside investors) without their approval. This illustrates the confluence of interests between the "insiders"—management and workers—and the Moscow defense bureaucracy. To the extent that *Goskomoboronprom* does play an active role, its bias is clearly against "outside" investor control, especially foreign investment.[12]

The takeover battles in the Russian economy have just begun. One of the effects of the macroeconomic stabilization that characterized Russia in 1995 is that manufacturing has begun to attract financial capital. Some defense enterprises are targets: priced low but with valuable assets (including prime real estate in large urban centers), these entities *could* be made profitable. The difficulty is not so much knowing how to do this but getting the social and political acceptance to let it happen. For the defense enterprises the issue is more than mere survival—it is survival at what cost and at whose expense. The key to what happens with the defense enterprises is what happens within their communities.

The Communities

The ultimate arbiters in the fate of many defense enterprises may not be in Moscow but in the defense regions. City and regional governments in general will almost certainly weigh in against downsizing of the labor force and shedding of social assets. This is especially true if such policies were applied to large defense enterprises, or to several in one location. Even if an individual plant succeeds in the marketplace, the community may not see it as a success. Downsizing means that the city will be burdened with those individuals fired from a plant who are hard to employ (and who are potentially among the hard-core jobless). Similarly, divestiture of a plant's social services leaves the city government with the responsibility for providing vital social services the defense enterprise had once supplied.[13] Enterprise insiders and city officials will join forces to maintain the status quo.

This undirected tendency to muddle through may appear to be a poor outcome. Enterprises will still exist; but they will become less and less viable as better workers move elsewhere, leaving behind the least productive members of the original labor force. Despite these valid concerns, the muddling-through approach is not entirely without merit. In the short and medium term, it will work insofar as it preserves tranquility. The outflow of labor will be voluntary; there will be less social tension. Those who leave the defense plants will be gradually absorbed into the labor force elsewhere (although that will become increasingly difficult).

The defense enterprises will continue to be a cost to Russia. Part of the cost will be the direct drain on the national budget, although perhaps not as great as some suggest. The alternative would also have a cost, because developing a separate social safety net would entail major expenses. The bigger economic cost of continued support for defense enterprises is the failure to use these resources. These plants will not divest productive infrastructure, real estate, or other assets at the same pace as they downsize their labor forces. This has been a major negative result of demilitarization so far: Workers from the defense sector, ready and willing to engage in new and economically viable work, lack the tools to realize their potential. If more of the physical assets are not released from the control of the defense enterprises, there is little hope of success in building up a vibrant alternative local economy.

Ultimately, the fate of those who made up the defense complex is the yardstick of demilitarization policy. Russia's people are its biggest potential asset. But realizing that potential raises other problems.

The People

Russians and foreigners alike often refer to Russia's vast human capital. The country has a huge number of educated citizens with professional experience in an industrial economy. Such individuals are of great value to a nation's economic development; as a result, the great stock of educated Russians is assumed to represent immense wealth.

In general, this is true. But it is important to be aware of some points generally taken for granted in Western market economies. When a nation's stock of education or educated individuals is measured, it is assumed that the education suits the individual in his or her abilities and tastes. Different types of education can have varying effects on people in a range of economic settings. Years of legal training may have little benefit for someone who is otherwise ill suited to be a lawyer, and a vocational course in plumbing would be time wasted for a person with no mechanical aptitude.

In a market economy, the match between abilities and education is taken for granted. Many alternatives are offered, people are well informed about their choices, and—above all—they are free to make those choices themselves.

A second point is even more important in Russia's case. Even the "right" kind of education—training that suits a person's aptitudes and preferences—has no economic value in itself. Its value is determined by the market. Assuming that education contributes economic value is reasonable in a market economy. In the long run people would not have educated themselves as scientists or engineers, say, if it had not been the best thing for them to do. But even if people make mistakes in a market economy, they correct them. (It is essential to understand how a "mistake" is defined and determined here: by the market.) Similarly, most new occupations spread gradually, in evolutionary fashion, with adequate time for adjustment throughout the entire working population. But none of this is true if this optimizing mechanism has not been at play.

In short, just as with physical capital, adding up human capital in this way by merely totaling numbers of people or years of education is nothing more than a hypothetical estimate of the nation's potential. It is more correct to say that for a large part of its stock of education, Russia has the *inputs* required to produce human capital but not necessarily the human capital itself yet.

Russia's problem today is not to *preserve* the value of *existing* human capital as much as it is to *give* value to its *potential* human capital. That value comes when people are allowed to find better matches between their preferences and their professions and when they are able to find rewards in the market. This poses a dilemma. Russia needs individuals who can help establish the market by transforming its current economic structures and creating and organizing new ones. It needs entrepreneurs—people who, by finding new products and new markets, can create job opportunities that employ both the nation's human capital and domestic and imported physical capital. It needs bankers, marketing specialists, accountants, insurance agents, financial planners, public relations experts, tax and corporate lawyers, and practitioners of hundreds of other occupations that did not exist in Russia before.

The dilemma is that many of these people will come from the ranks of those having skilled scientific-technical human capital. They will be part of a so-called brain drain from industry, including the defense-industrial complex. To the extent that policymakers continue their well-meaning efforts to prevent a brain drain from science or defense industries by subsidizing the status quo in the form of continued employment in the "wrong" occupations, they will not be preserving the nation's human capital but impeding the realization of its potential.

The hardest thing will be to pursue a humane policy toward those people most affected by demilitarization, while avoiding doing anything that in the long run may harm them and succeeding generations of Russians, especially in regions so dominated by defense industry. Every step of the way policymakers will confront the dilemma of efficiency versus equity, change versus stability. The temptation to introduce regulations aimed at slowing down painful change is understandable. But if there is one lesson to be learned from demilitarization, it is that continued constraints on the market are dangerous. These constraints take hidden as well as overt forms. Privileges and exemptions for defense industry in general as well as for particular enterprises restrict the free play of market forces so vital to normalization of the Russian economy. The goal of normality is not a state that anyone in Russia now knows. Only the freedom of Russia's people to choose what is most important for them—what they want to do or to buy, and what futures they want for themselves and their loved ones—is what will lead to normality.

Every continued restriction does not merely distort allocation of economic resources in some abstract and technical sense but also distorts the most personal decisions people make. Interference through restrictions encourages people to make the wrong choices about their education, their occupations, and their places of work. In so doing, it reduces the value of their economic activity. In the past, the militarization of Russia's economy did this in the extreme, wasting not only the nation's physical resources but also the lifework of generations of its citizens. Russians deserve to know that what they choose to do will have meaning and value today and tomorrow.

What Can the West Do?

In all of the complex and difficult tasks Russia must face in overcoming its legacy of hypermilitarization, what role is there for the United States (and the West in general) to play? So far, efforts to render foreign assistance have been largely judged by the goal of successful conversion in the classic sense: using former military production facilities for civilian production. I have argued that conversion by that definition is unrealistic for most former defense enterprises in Russia and is therefore not a viable goal for foreign assistance efforts.

The fact remains that the West has focused much of its effort on such conversion. Individually and through multilateral institutions, Western nations have developed programs related to defense conversion for Russia. Wisely, the U.S. programs have in general *not* followed the principle of conversion for its own sake but have linked conversion to other objectives.

Some have targeted areas of immediate and acute concern to Americans, including funds to Russian enterprises engaged in dismantling of nuclear arms and other weapons of mass destruction. Other programs have enlisted the aid of former Russian defense enterprises in tasks that could help integrate Russia into the world economy—for example, development of air traffic control networks. Finally, efforts have been made to facilitate partnerships between American firms and former Russian defense enterprises. Most of this assistance has been administered by the U.S. Department of Defense through the Cooperative Threat Reduction Programs, known as Nunn-Lugar programs.[14]

These programs have not cost the United States much money. Even at maximum projected levels, spending on projects involving Russian defense enterprises will remain well under $200 million spread out over several years, with much of that ultimately accruing to American partners. I believe this has been about what the Russian defense sector and its American partners could absorb. The United States should continue to provide funds for enterprise development and joint ventures. However, this is best done through more general enterprise funds such as the U.S. Russia Investment Fund (TUSRIF)—funds for loans and equity investments available to defense enterprises on the same terms as others.[15]

Beyond Conversion

Are these the only ways the United States can assist Russia in demilitarization? To answer that question, we need to return to the broad definition of demilitarization and to one of the themes of this book: that for Russia, the most important factor in demilitarization has been market reform itself. It was the introduction of market pricing and removal of constraints on individuals and firms that undermined the special status of the Russian defense industry. The market reforms thereby made it obvious that market-economy Russia could not afford the military establishment Soviet Russia had borne. A precondition to make a return to hypermilitarization impossible is continued progress on the road to a market economy.

Of course, market reform alone will not ensure that Russia's demilitarization will take care of itself. New problems will arise, and negative social consequences will necessarily be an increasingly important part of the economic transition. They will take a special form in the defense regions, especially the large defense cities. To the extent that the United States—alone or in multilateral efforts—engages in assisting Russian economic transition in general, Americans may be involved in the Russian defense regions. There are numerous needs at the regional level that the U.S. could help meet, especially for technical assistance dealing with problems of federal-regional relations or of managing large cities and the like. But even in this case, it hardly makes sense for the United States to earmark aid to particular Russian regions merely because they have had a heavy concentration of defense industry. As our discussion in chapter 9 suggests, these defense cities may turn out to have fewer problems than some other important regions of Russia. Here, too, the United States should be guided by a *general* approach to reform and transition in Russia as a whole.

Russian policymakers have important decisions to make on economic issues relating to the legacy of Soviet militarization. Most boil down to establishing priorities and striking a balance between conflicting social goals. These are issues that properly must be left to the Russians themselves. The American or foreign contribution could be marginal at best; meanwhile, they represent a political minefield no less explosive than some of our own domestic debates on American economic priorities. The sensitivity and pride that often encumber the U.S.-Russian relationship are especially acute regarding the defense industry. For Americans, it is of course particularly frustrating, because the stakes are higher but the ability to influence is quite small.

Looking to the Future

There is one final point to be made on how the United States relates to Russian demilitarization. In looking at the connection between economic reform and politics, the United States has so far been concerned mainly with the possible consequences of the *failure* of Russian economic reform. Less attention has been paid to the way in which *success* in economic reform will surely complicate relations between the United States and Russia politically, especially regarding security issues.

From the standpoint of Western security policy, Russia's current economic weakness has been an unexpected benefit. Although economic troubles have accentuated the focus on certain issues—the brain drain of nuclear scientists, exports of arms and other militarily sensitive technology to rogue nations, and corruption in the arms industry, all allegedly made worse by economic weakness—they have taken the edge off the urgency of politics. Since the demise of the Soviet Union, Russia has been restrained (indeed, passive) on the international scene. To some extent, the reasons for that passivity have been misinterpreted. Some have attributed it to the success of our own Western policy toward Russia. Others view it as a fundamental shift in Russian foreign policy and security thinking away from the outlook of the Soviet era. Although both explanations may have some validity, a more significant cause of Russia's relative docility has been its simple inability to act—to do things it might otherwise have attempted.

But Russia is growing economically stronger, owing in part to economic reform and in part to the country simply recovering its balance after a period of sudden and wrenching dislocation after the breakup of the Soviet Union. As Russia gains economic strength, it will be capable of more assertive postures in many areas. Barring a radical reversal of current trends, post-Soviet Russia will in the next few years have many options it has not yet had in its brief existence as a nation—options in international relations vis-à-vis the developed West, the third world, and, most immediately, its neighbors from the former Soviet Union (the so-called Near Abroad).

An economically stronger Russia will also be able to spend more on its defense. Undoubtedly, this alone will be enough for some in the West to warn of resurgent militarism in Russia. To react reflexively in this way would be a mistake. Just as the goal of *demilitarizing* Russia must not be understood as one of *disarming* it or of taking away its ability to provide for legitimate security needs, so too we must distinguish between increased arms spending and remilitarization. In coming years, various political forces in Russia may advocate different degrees of emphasis on national security—specifically, on different levels of spending on arms. To the extent that Russia remains a democratic society, those debates will be resolved as its citizens choose among various societal priorities, just as we do. We need to remain confident that as long as both the economy and politics remain free and open, there is no possibility of a return to the hypermilitarized society of the past, regardless of the rhetoric regarding restoring Russia's superpower status and the like. A market economy will make clear the true cost of a return to militarization; freedom of political expression will ensure that that cost be made known to the citizenry.

But what both Russians and Westerners alike need to take much more seriously is any attempt to abolish democratic freedoms and reintroduce the economic policies of coercion, secrecy, heavy regulation, and administered prices that helped conceal the true cost of militarization. If instituted today, they would make it much more likely that the mistakes of the past would be repeated. The consequences would be dire, but not so much in the first instance for the United States as for Russia itself. Before today's Russia could ever come close to mounting a conventional military challenge to the United States the way the old Soviet Union did, it would undermine the integrity of the nation and its economy first. But it is, of course, the prospect of that unstable and possibly disintegrating Russia, still armed with nuclear weapons, that is scarier than the old USSR.

Continued support for Russia's market reform, democratization, and openness is the best thing the United States can do to help create a climate in which the Russians themselves consider demilitarization the natural and most desirable option. It is important to realize that helping create favorable conditions for the Russians' own choice is realistically all we can hope to do. To actively push a policy of demilitarization on the Russians would almost certainly be counterproductive.

Russia's big decisions about its military industry may not be made for another five to ten years. Few things about the Russia of the twenty-first century are more than marginally in our hands. But on this particular issue, there are ways in which American action will prove significant. Our influence on Russian defense industry will not be primarily through economics, but rather through politics. It will be exerted through the way we help shape the political relationship between the United States and Russia, as well as Russia's world outlook in general. More important than any individual American program directed toward defense industry is how the United States is perceived as treating Russia.

As much as anything else, success in dealing with Russia as it continues to overcome the legacy of hypermilitarization will require patience. The road to economic conversion and demilitarization in Russia will be long and twisting. Our goal should be to help foster understanding of the difficulties the Russians face as they travel that road. We must look beyond the inevitable day-to-day problems in our evolving relationship with the new Russia (even if these difficulties should reach crisis stage) and keep sight of Russia's overall transition to a normalized society.

Appendix

Sources of Data and Derivation of Estimates

Note 1. Data on 1985 VPK Industrial Employment

My estimates of industrial employment in the enterprises subordinate to the Soviet Military-Industrial Commission, or VPK, were derived from data in an unpublished document of the USSR State Committee on Statistics [*Goskomstat*]. The *Goskomstat* document does not explicitly give defense employment. Rather, for each of the administrative regions of the Soviet Union (the republics and, where applicable, the provinces within them), it gives the total number of so-called industrial production employees (*promyshlenno-proizvodstvennyy personal*, or *PPP*), along with separate totals for fourteen identified industrial sectors and one sector labeled "other." However, when the sum of the employees in those fifteen sectors is subtracted from the total for each region, an unaccounted-for residual is left. It is this residual that is assumed to represent the people who worked in the VPK enterprises.

This procedure can be illustrated with the example of Perm oblast. The total number of industrial employees reported for Perm is 563,566. However, when the number of employees reported for each individual sector (92,479 in the wood and paper industry, 72,695 in machine-building and metalworking [MBMW], 44,538 in textiles and clothing, 33,549 in fuels, and so on down the list, including 3,717 in the category of "other") are added up, the sum turns out to be only 350,864. In other words, a huge number of industrial employees—212,802—appear to be missing. Perm oblast, therefore, is assumed to have had around 213,000 defense-industry employees in 1985, or about 38 percent of its total industrial labor force.

The data from the unpublished *Goskomstat* document were first used to estimate defense employment in this way by Brenda Horrigan in a study of the regional distribution of Soviet defense industry ("How Many People Worked in the Soviet Defense Industry?", *RFE/RL Research Report*, vol. 1 [August 21, 1992], pp. 33–39). On the basis of her article, or through direct access to the data, many Western and Russian specialists have come to take the number of persons in this "hidden sector" as the most accurate estimate of Russian defense employment in the mid-1980s before reform. My own comparison of the estimates obtained from the *Goskomstat* data with information I have on defense-industrial employment regionally also lead me to accept the hidden sector employment as the basis for my estimates, albeit with some qualifications and reservations.

The first question to raise about the data is that the totals for some regions are suspiciously round numbers. For instance, after going through the procedure described here, one ends up with precisely 300,000 defense employees for the city of Moscow and exactly 350,000 for Sverdlovsk oblast. Whether these figures have merely been mildly rounded off or intentionally distorted in more serious fashion is not known.

A second criticism of the *Goskomstat* data is that the hidden sector that results from using the residual approach seems to include not only defense industry. Certain other industries (notably gold mining, diamond mining, and uranium mining and processing) were considered so secret by the Soviet authorities that they were also not included in normal regional breakdowns of employment. The residual method shows relatively large hidden sector employment in the regions of Sakha (Yakutia) and Magadan—territories not known to have defense industry, but which are centers of gold and diamond mining.

The argument about hidden industries other than defense is made in two other articles that used the *Goskomstat* data: Matthew J. Sagers, "Regional Industrial Structures and Economic Prospects in the Former USSR," *Post-Soviet Geography*, vol. 33, no. 8 (October 1992), pp. 487–515; and Ilya Bass and Leslie Dienes, "Defense Industry Legacies and Conversion in the Post-Soviet Realm," *Post-Soviet Geography*, vol. 34 (May 1993), pp. 302–17. Bass and Dienes put the number of gold and diamond workers in Russia at approximately 50,000. Removing these workers from the Russian total of hidden employees would not have a significant effect, because they still represent less than 1 percent of the total. But it would alter the picture considerably for Sakha (Yakutia) and Magadan.

Horrigan's article (the only one of the three cited above that lists the defense employment estimates for each oblast) did not correct for employment in gold and diamond mining. Nor was any such adjustment made when her data were later used in the authoritative report of the World Bank on the Russian economy, World Bank, *Russian Economic Reform: Crossing the Threshold of Structural Change* (Washington, September 1992), table 9-1, p. 152. (In addition, the World Bank's table presenting the data contains an unfortunate typographical error, attributing to Saratov oblast the total for Samara. This gives the false impression that Saratov is the second most

TABLE A-1. *Sectoral Distribution of Industrial Employment in the Russian Defense Complex (VPK), 1985*

Industry sector	Number of VPK employees in sector[a] (thousands)	Sector share of all VPK employment (percent)	VPK share of all employment in sector (percent)
MBMW[b]	4,582	84.6	45.7
Chemicals	483	8.9	40.9
Nonferrous metallurgy	204	3.8	41.0
All others	148	2.7	1.5
Total VPK	5,417	100.0	24.8[c]

a. Estimated as the difference between official data on total employment in the sector and the total given for the sector in the unpublished *Goskomstat* document.

b. MBMW = Machine-building and metalworking.

c. VPK's share of employment in all industrial sectors.

Note: Employment in all cases is industrial production employees (PPP).

heavily militarized region in Russia in terms of defense employment as a percentage of total industrial employment. It actually ranks twentieth.)

SECTORAL DISTRIBUTION OF DEFENSE–INDUSTRY EMPLOYMENT.   In addition to allowing for a regional breakdown of VPK industrial employment, as is done in the text of this book, the *Goskomstat* data also allow us to infer what the sectoral distribution of employment in VPK enterprises was. Most of the VPK enterprises are what in the civilian economy would be classed as machine-building and metalworking (MBMW). But significant industrial facilities in other branches were also run by the VPK ministries. By looking at the difference between the totals in the unpublished *Goskomstat* data for various Russian industrial sectors and the published employment totals for those same sectors, the sectors to which the VPK enterprises belong can be inferred (see table A-1). The dominance of MBMW is confirmed: Roughly 85 percent of all VPK employees worked in such plants. Employment in the chemical industry (nearly half a million, or about 9 percent of all VPK employees) is accounted for in part by workers engaged in producing nuclear, chemical, and biological weapons. The third large branch with heavy VPK employment was nonferrous metallurgy: Some 200,000 workers (about 4 percent of VPK employees), mainly in the aluminum industry, worked there.

The table also shows the relative importance of VPK enterprises for the economic sectors. About 41 percent of all chemical and nonferrous metallurgy workers and 46 percent of MBMW workers were in enterprises run by the VPK ministries.

Note 2. Data on Military R&D

NUMBER OF MILITARY R&D INSTITUTES.   Russia had an estimated 750 to 800 military R&D institutes in the mid-1980s. See Note 4 below.

TOTAL EMPLOYMENT IN MILITARY R&D.   Yevgeny Kuznetsov states that military R&D employed 1.2 million people in Russia. "Adjustment of Russian Defence-Related Enterprises in 1992–94: Macroeconomic Implications," *Communist Economies and Economic Transformation*, vol. 6, no. 4 (1994), pp. 473–513 [Table 1, p. 476]. This is consistent with a statement by the chairman of the VPK, Viktor Glukhikh, who gave figures for the number of defense-industry workers and scientists in December 1993. His figure for the number of workers (3.674 million) was about 68 percent of the mid-1980s estimate of 5.417 million. If the figure he cited for scientific workers in 1993 (813,500) also was 68 percent of the mid-1980s total, that would imply a prereduction figure of 1.2 million. Viktor Glukhikh, "The Defense Industry of Russia: The Situation and Tasks for 1994," *Konversiya*, no. 4 (1994), pp. 3–8, translated in Joint Publications Research Service, *Military Affairs,* August 17, 1994, p. 43.

REGIONAL DISTRIBUTION OF MILITARY R&D.   Military R&D was overwhelmingly concentrated in and near Moscow and St. Petersburg. I estimate that these two regions alone accounted for 70 to 80 percent of total R&D employment and research facilities. My own database of the Russian defense complex includes the names, location, and employment of 149 research institutes. By number of institutes, Moscow City leads with 42.3 percent, Moscow oblast has 11.4 percent, and St. Petersburg has 15.4 percent—a total of 69.1 percent for the Moscow and St. Petersburg regions combined. Measured by employment, the dominance of these regions is even greater: 42.6 percent of employees worked in the city of Moscow, 16.3 percent in Moscow oblast, and 20.1 percent in St. Petersburg—a total of 79.0 percent.

The rest of the country ranks far below the metropolises. By employment, next after Moscow oblast are the cities of Nizhny Novgorod and Penza (3.5 to 3.6 percent), Novosibirsk (2.7 percent), and Kazan (2.0 percent).

These conclusions are generally supported by other sources. In a 1994 report, two Russian scholars estimated that 50 to 75 percent of the R&D resources of the Russian military complex were located in Moscow and St. Petersburg. They do not specify how they define "resources"—whether persons employed, assets, or number of institutes. Galina A. Kitova and Tatyana E. Kuznetsova, "Russia's Science Policy: National and Regional Dimensions," Occasional Paper No. 7 of the Georgetown University Russian Area Studies Program, Washington, September 1994, p. 4.

A table presented in another report by Kuznetsova shows the geographical distribution of 277 military R&D institutes: 98 (or 35.4 percent) were located in the city of Moscow, 13 (4.7 percent) in "Moscow Region," and 95 (34.3 percent) in the "Leningrad Region" (which presumably includes the city of Leningrad, now St. Petersburg). Unfortunately, the report does not indicate the sources of these data nor the year to which they apply. Tatyana E. Kuznetsova, "Conditions and Features for the Development of Russia's Science Resources in the 1990s," Occasional Paper No. 2 of the Georgetown University Russian Area Studies Program, Washington, September 1994, table entitled "Distribution of R&D Organizations by Sector and Region."

Note 3. Indirect Employment Effects of Defense-Industrial Activity

INDIRECT EMPLOYMENT EFFECTS IN THE UNITED STATES. The indirect-to-direct employment effects ratio of 0.66 cited in the text for the United States can be calculated from the Congressional Budget Office (CBO) estimate that "defense-related jobs totaled some 2.9 million in 1991, including 1.75 million directly attributable to defense spending and another 1.15 million indirectly attributed to it." See Congressional Budget Office, *The Economic Effects of Reduced Defense Spending* (Government Printing Office, February 1992), p. 23.

The same CBO study cites a different coefficient used by the Missouri Division of Employment Security in its estimates of the effects of defense spending in the St. Louis area. Each civilian defense job was assumed to generate an additional 1.16 jobs [p. 39, fn. 20]. Defense employment in St. Louis, however, was dominated by the McDonnell Douglas Corporation; the aerospace industry probably generated more indirect jobs than defense industry in general.

All of the U.S. estimates of indirect employment effects are based on the results of input-output models of the economy. Without going into the technical details of how input-output models work, the essence of this technique is to capture both the direct and indirect effects of all production activity in the economy. Precisely because of the indirect effects, many sectors of the economy not commonly considered defense industries end up as highly significant in terms of defense purchases. One U.S. estimate based on input-output models shows that the leading "defense industry" sectors include wholesale trade (where the indirect purchases are 88 percent of total defense purchases from that sector), real estate operators (90 percent indirect effect), eating and drinking establishments (88 percent indirect), and banking (100 percent indirect). The analysts responsible for those estimates sum up the phenomenon of the indirect effect with the following illustration: "A dollar's worth of a B-1 bomber includes not only the airframe, landing gear, and avionics, but also indirect expenses such as building rents and maintenance, electric utilities, business travel, communications, banking, and insurance services." Earl R. Wingrove III, Donna J. S. Peterson, and Scott E. Dahne, "Impacts of Defense Spending Cuts on Industry Sectors, Occupational Groups, and Localities," LMI Report DC201R2 (Logistics Management Institute, February 1993), Annex F to *Adjusting to the Drawdown, Report of the Defense Conversion Commission*, p. 2-2.

INDIRECT EMPLOYMENT EFFECTS IN RUSSIA.   I argue in this book that the high degree of vertical integration of Soviet-style defense enterprises is the main reason why one would expect lower indirect effects from defense production in Russia than in the United States. Because of that integration, a relatively much smaller part of key industries remains outside the core of defense industry in Russia than in the United States. Table A-1 shows that more than 40 percent of all employment in entire sectors of the economy such as nonferrous metallurgy, chemicals, and MBMW was *inside* the VPK.

Most of the rest of the Russian labor force was in sectors that probably did not supply much to defense (agriculture, for instance). As I have mentioned, some of the biggest indirect suppliers to defense contractors in the United States are in the service sector—financial services, real estate, and so on. Many of these were minor parts of the Soviet economy.

There is one counterargument. Given the inefficiences in the planned Soviet economy in terms of turning inputs into outputs, one Russian arms worker may have needed more metalworkers than his or her American counterpart. This is true; however, it is not a question of the absolute number of metalworkers needed, but rather the relative number. It is not clear that the Russian ratio of metalworkers to defense workers would have been higher.

Note 4. The Number of Defense Enterprises

This is another question for which there are nearly as many answers as there are people offering them. Not only do different authorities in Russia offer widely different figures; there are also numerous cases of inconsistencies by the same individual. Viktor Glukhikh, head of the

Russian Committee for the Defense Sectors of Industry (*Roskomoboron-prom*), the successor to the old Soviet VPK, may hold the record. In April 1993 he wrote, "The military-industrial complex comprises more than 1,700 enterprises and organizations, including about 200 research centers, and a labor force of 6 million." ("Viktor Glukhikh: Still an Arms Race," *Delovyie lyudi* [Business in the Ex-USSR], no. 32 (April 1993), pp. 22–23.) In June 1993, his numbers were smaller: "What exactly is the Russian military-industrial complex today? It encompasses over 1,200 enterprises and organizations, at which several million people work." (Viktor Glukhikh, "Can a Tank Plant Be Privatized?," *Rossiyskiye vesti*, June 17, 1993, p. 7, translated in Foreign Broadcast Information Service, *Daily Report: Central Eurasia*, June 22, 1993, pp. 27–28.) Then in September 1993, Glukhikh wrote: "As of January 1, 1992, the defense complex encompasses more than 1,500 production and scientific-production associations, industrial serial enterprises, and scientific organizations (NIIs and KBs)." "Nekotoryye aspekty promyshlennoy politiki v oboronnykh otraslyakh promyshlennosti" [Some aspects of industrial policy in the defense branches of industry], *Voprosy ekonomiki*, no. 9 (September 1993), pp. 100–104.

The highest of Glukhikh's three different 1993 numbers is close to the number cited by other sources. Yakovleva wrote that *Roskomoboronprom* in 1993 had supervision over 1,750 enterprises and organizations. See I. Yakovleva, "Privatizatsiya VPK: chto zhdet tekh, kto stoit na ee poroge, i tekh, kto uspel ego pereshagnut'" [Privatization of the VPK: what awaits those standing on its threshold and those who have managed to cross it], *Ekonomika i zhizn'*, no. 21 (May 1993), pp. 1–2.

One could also proceed from information about the size of the defense complex of the USSR and what proportion was inherited by Russia. In the summer of 1992, the Russian government presented an economic program to the parliament that stated that the defense complex of the former USSR had consisted of "more than 1,100 industrial enterprises and about 920 scientific-research and experimental design organizations." See "Programma uglubleniya ekonomicheskikh reform Pravitel'stva Rossiyskoy Federatsii [Program for deepening the economic reforms of the Government of the Russian Federation]," *Voprosy ekonomiki*, no. 8 (August 1992), p. 96.

Yevgeny Kuznetsov cites those same figures and writes that 82 percent of the production enterprises and R&D facilities are in Russia. If the 82 percent applies to both categories equally, this implies $(1{,}100 \times 0.82) = 902$ enterprises and $(920 \times 0.82) = 754$ R&D institutes, or a total of 1,656, in Russia. See Kuznetsov, "Adjustment of Russian Defence-Related Enterprises in 1992–94." pp. 473–513 [Table 1, p. 476].

It therefore seems that a figure of about 900 production enterprises and 750–800 R&D institutes is fairly consistent with numerous statements.

Note 5. The Size Distribution of Russian Civilian Industrial Enterprises

In 1985 Russia had 23,095,000 industrial employees (PPP) and 26,300 industrial enterprises, implying (23.095 − 5.417) = 17.678 million employees and (26,300 − 900) = 25,400 enterprises in civilian industry. This gives a mean enterprise size of 696 employees in the civilian industrial sector. Data from Goskomstat RSFSR, *Narodnoye khozyaystvo RSFSR v 1988 g. Statisticheskiy yezhegodnik* [The national economy of the RSFSR in 1988: Statistical yearbook] (hereafter *Narkhoz*), p. 321.

In 1991 the figures were 20,117,000 industrial production employees (PPP) and 28,023 industrial enterprises, implying 14.7 million employees and about 27,100 enterprises in civilian industry, or a mean civilian enterprise size of 542. Data from *Narkhoz Rossiyskoy Federatsii 1992*, pp. 346–47.

The above estimates only take into account the industrial personnel (PPP). If for both years one were to assume that nonindustrial employees account for 15 percent of total employment at the civilian enterprises (in other words, the PPP estimates are only 85 percent of total employment), the mean size for 1985, including nonindustrial employees, would be (696 ÷ 0.85) = 819, and for 1991 it would be (542 ÷ 0.85) = 638.

For both years, the means may be overstated, however. Soviet industry employment statistics also included persons engaged in industrial activities of nonindustrial organizations—in other words, people who did not work in enterprises in industry. See Murray Feshbach, "Soviet Industrial Labor and Productivity Statistics," in Vladimir G. Treml and John P. Hardt, eds., *Soviet Economic Statistics* (Duke University Press, 1972), pp. 195–233 [p. 211].

Note 6. The Size Distribution of Russian Defense Enterprises

The data on size distribution were presented in *Rossiya—1992. Ekonomicheskaya kon"yunktura* (Moscow, November 1992), table VI.5, p. 114. This publication is by the *Tsentr ekonomicheskoy kon"yunktury i prognozirovaniya*, which is attached to the Russian Ministry of Economics.

A less precise description of the size distribution of Russian defense enterprises is in *Voprosy ekonomiki i konversii,* 1992, special issue, pp. 70–71, cited in Julian Cooper, *The Conversion of the Former Soviet Defence Industry* (London: Royal Institute of International Affairs, 1993), p. 2. That source reports that the defense enterprises could be broken down into three groups. The first was a core group of enterprises, comprising half the total number, which had an average of 10,000 workers each. A second group, which engaged in a combination of military and civilian work, represented about one-quarter of the total number and averaged 8,000 employees each. Finally, a third group, engaged mainly in civilian manufacturing, accounted for another one-quarter of the total and had about 2,000 workers per plant.

If one assumes that the total number of defense enterprises is 900, these data on the number and average size of enterprises allow one to also compute the total number of employees in all enterprises. The resulting sum of 6.75 million [(450 × 10,000) + (225 × 8,000) + (225 × 2,000)] is larger than the figure of 5.4 million cited in the text on the basis of the unpublished *Goskomstat* data. If, on the other hand, one assumes that nonmanufacturing employees are being included as well, the estimates are roughly consistent.

Finally, I have a database that includes about 450 Russian VPK enterprises, with data on total employment (in other words, PPP plus nonindustrial employees). The mean size of enterprises in this sample is 9,600 employees. There are 154 enterprises with more than 10,000 employees and another 138 with 5,001 to 10,000 employees.

Note 7. Comparing Russian Enterprises and U.S. Firms

The U.S. size distribution data in table 2-5 are by "establishment." An establishment is defined as "a single physical location at which business is conducted or where services or industrial operations are performed." The employees counted are everyone who is on the payroll, including management. Bureau of the Census, *County Business Patterns, 1991* (Government Printing Office, February 1994), p. v.

If one were to use data on firm size, the results would be different. U.S. corporations can be vastly larger than establishments, because they may encompass many different companies, not to mention separate manufacturing facilities. Thus, though the current downsizing trend may have reduced average U.S. *establishment* size, many *corporations* have grown much larger. This is partly due to the recent wave of mergers and acquisitions, including some important ones in the defense sector. The new Lockheed Martin Corporation, for instance, began its operations with roughly 170,000 employees. But this corporation has manufacturing facilities scattered over at least fifty different sites, and it reportedly has employees in every state in the United States. John Mintz, "Taking a Painful Plunge," *Washington Post*, April 16, 1995, p. H1.

Although a Russian enterprise may operate at more than one location, most do not. Hence the Russian data on enterprise size are more comparable to the U.S. data on establishment size than to data on firm size. For a discussion of this point, see Paul L. Joskow, Richard Schmalensee, and Natalia Tsukanova, "Competition Policy in Russia during and after Privatization," *Brookings Papers on Economic Activity: Microeconomics, 1994,* pp. 301–81 [p. 314].

Notes

Chapter 2

1. Aleksei Izyumov, "Konversiya? Konversiya! Konversiya . . . [Conversion? Conversion! Conversion . . .]," *Literaturnaya gazeta*, no. 28 (July 12, 1989), p. 11.

2. "Razoruzheniye i razvitiya na mezhdunarodnoy konferentsii v N'yu York [Disarmament and development at the international conference in New York]," *Pravda*, August 27, 1987, p. 4, cited in Bruce Parrott, "Political Change and Civil-Military Relations," in Timothy J. Colton and Thane Gustafson, eds., *Soldiers and the Soviet State: Civil-Military Relations from Brezhnev to Gorbachev* (Princeton University Press, 1990), pp. 44–92 [p. 88, footnote 204].

3. In addition to the fact that the "budget" did not express the true costs of the Soviet military sector, it is important to remember that the budget was not the way military or any other expenditures were controlled in the Soviet Union. Physical plans always came first. In the apt words of an American expert on Soviet defense matters, budgets were an "after-the-fact accounting device." Arthur J. Alexander, *Perestroika and Change in Soviet Weapons Acquisition,* RAND Corporation Report R-3821-USDP (Santa Monica, Calif.: RAND Corporation, June 1990), p. 60.

4. A good example is Sergei Rogov, "Zagadki voyennogo byudzheta [Mysteries of the defense budget]," *Novoye vremya*, no. 11 (March 1991), pp. 18–20. Rogov concluded that the newly published (and allegedly complete) Soviet defense budgets for 1989 and 1990 still vastly underestimated true spending. According to Rogov, 60 to 70 percent of expenditures remained hidden.

5. Vasily Selyunin, "Konversiya po-general'ski [Conversion in the generals' style]," *Ogonyok*, no. 36 (August 31–September 7, 1991), pp. 15–18 [p. 16]. Selyunin followed this statement with a joke about Poland. "[Polish Communist leader Stanislaw] Gomulka, when he came to power, also wanted to know how much his country was spending on defense. The experts gave him widely divergent figures, so finally the exasperated leader remarked with gallows humor: 'Well, you'd better go out and catch an American spy and find out from him.'"

6. The last time I heard such public references to CIA authority by Soviet officials was in July 1991 at conferences in Washington, D.C., and at Stanford University. The 6 to 8 percent figures appeared frequently in the Soviet media, with or without reference to the CIA. Consider, for instance, the statement by Oleg Baklanov, at that time the first deputy chair of the USSR Defense Council, a former Communist Party Central Committee secretary in charge of defense matters, and soon to be a member of the group of men who attempted a coup in August 1991. Protesting against critics of the military-industrial complex and its burden on the economy, he insisted: "The myth of a militarized economy is being created, but this doesn't correspond to reality: we spend around seven percent of our material resources on arms production. This is no more than others do." Quoted in Selyunin, "Konversiya po-general'ski," p. 16.

7. Before 1976, the CIA had indeed concluded that Soviet defense spending was about 6 to 8 percent of GNP. However, in 1976, citing new information about Soviet prices, the CIA revised its estimates of Soviet defense spending (for those same years) to 11 to 13 percent of GNP. The revisions did not stop there. A 1983 report declared that defense as a percentage of GNP had "remained roughly constant at 13 to 14 percent through the 1970s." In 1986, the estimate for the 1970s was raised to 15 to 17 percent.

For a summary and criticism of the CIA's estimates by a panel of outside economists, see Daniel M. Berkowitz and others, "An Evaluation of the CIA's Analysis of Soviet Economic Performance, 1970–90," *Comparative Economic Studies*, vol. 35 (Summer 1993), pp. 33–57.

8. In reality, there *are* distortions in U.S. defense pricing. But most of them—at least, the most highly publicized of them—work in the opposite direction, that is, to inflate the defense budget. Rather than forcing defense contractors to accept below-market prices, the U.S. procurement system is accused of overpaying them. In that case, the notorious $1,000 hammers and $600 toilet seats represent a subsidy, not a tax.

9. Selyunin, "Konversiya po-general'ski," p. 16.

10. In Soviet economic statistics, machine-building and metalworking is one of roughly a dozen major subsectors of industry (with industry in turn being one of some fifteen broad divisions of the economy). In terms of employment, MBMW was the biggest branch of Soviet industry, with 43 percent of all workers in industry in 1988. Goskomstat SSSR, *Narodnoye khozyaystvo SSSR v 1988 g. Statisticheskiy yezhegodnik* [The national economy of the USSR in 1988. Statistical yearbook], (Moscow: Finances and Statistics, 1989), p. 366 [hereafter *Narkhoz*].

MBMW has no direct counterpart in U.S. practice, but it would correspond most closely to industries in the following two-digit groups of the Standard Industrial Classification (SIC): fabricated metal products (34), industrial machinery and equipment (35), electronic and other electric equipment (36), transportation equipment (37), and instruments and related products (38). See the *Standard Industrial Classification Manual*, Executive Office of the President, Office of Management and Budget, Washington, D.C., 1987.

11. Aleksandr Ozhegov, Yevgeny Rogovsky, and Yury Yaryemenko, "Konversiya oboronnoy promyshlennosti i preobrazovaniye ekonomiki SSSR [Conversion of defense industry and transformation of the USSR economy]," *Kommunist*,

no. 1 (January 1991), pp. 54–64 [p. 54]. This article offers no indication of the data used for the computation nor the methodology used.

12. Vasily Selyunin, the Soviet economic journalist cited earlier, carried the logic of Ozhegov and his colleagues one step further. What, Selyunin asked, are these "investment goods"? They are machines and equipment used to expand or upgrade existing facilities in the machine-building sector itself. Let us be quite conservative, he said, and assume that half of these new machines would be going to the arms-producing sector. In other words, half of the 32 percent of investment goods would need to be added to the 62 to 63 percent of the MBMW output that was directly in the form of weapons. The result would be that nearly 80 percent of the output of the MBMW sector each year was dedicated to military ends! Selyunin, "Konversiya po-general'ski," p. 16.

13. In fact, prodigious efforts were made by Western intelligence agencies and scholars to compute the size of Soviet GNP, its rate of growth, and the share of GNP attributable to defense. Perhaps because so much was invested in the effort, the issue of the size of Soviet GNP, not to mention the defense share of GNP, is a minefield of controversy among Western analysts. Although I have no desire to enter that debate, it appears to be impossible to avoid. My position is that although the Western exercises to compute Soviet GNP yielded both useful information and valuable insights into the Soviet economy, what was being estimated was *not* GNP. It was not comparable to Western GNP and did not in a meaningful way indicate either the size of the economy or the well-being of its citizens. Most important for the theme of this book, it could not be used to reflect the true cost of defense.

For those interested in the debate over Western estimates of Soviet defense spending, the best place to begin is James H. Noren, "The Controversy over Western Measures of Soviet Defense Expenditures," *Post-Soviet Affairs*, vol. 11, no. 3 (1995), pp. 238–76.

14. See Logistics Management Institute, "Impacts of Defense Spending Cuts on Industry Sectors, Occupational Groups, and Localities," *Adjusting to the Drawdown, Report of the Defense Conversion Commission*, LMI Report DC201R2 (February 1993), Annex F to p. 4-1.

15. Vyacheslav Shchepotkin, "Oboronnyy kompleks mozhet ne razoryat' a kormit' [The defense complex is capable not of destroying but of feeding]," *Izvestiya*, March 31, 1992, p. 2. Yablokov's figures are in *Izvestiya*, April 24, 1992, p. 2.

16. For details on this data source and the way in which the defense employment figures were derived, see Note 1 in the appendix on data sources and estimation methods.

17. Russia's share of employment in all sectors of Soviet industry (60.6 percent in 1985) was also disproportionately high in relation to its population share, but not as high as for defense industry. See Goskomstat SSSR, *Trud v SSSR, Statisticheskiy sbornik* [Labor in the USSR: Statistical handbook] (Moscow: Finances and Statistics, 1988), p. 51.

18. PPP stands for *promyshlenno-proizvodstvennyy personal*. It consists of six categories of employees: wage workers [*rabochiye*], apprentices [*ucheniki*], engineering and technical personnel [*inzhenerno-tekhnicheskiye rabotniki*, or *ITR*], salaried employees [*sluzhashchiye*], junior service personnel [*mladshiy obsluzhivayushchiy personal*], and guards [*rabotniki okhrany*]. In the Soviet economy of the 1980s, wage

workers made up about 80 percent of the total number of PPP, engineering and technical staff another 14 to 15 percent, and white-collar employees about 3.5 percent. *Narkhoz SSSR 1984*, p. 143.

PPP was the single largest employee category in the labor force. In Russia in 1985, 23.1 million people—more than one of every three people in the civilian labor force—were so classified. *Narkhoz RSFSR 1988*, p. 32.

19. The nonindustrial activities of defense enterprises are discussed in greater detail in chapter 8.

20. My estimated proportion of 25 percent of total employment in the social sector may appear high and deserves comment. I base my estimate above all on direct observation of the Russian defense enterprises I have studied, but there is a more general argument as well. In the early 1970s, Murray Feshbach estimated that roughly 10 percent of total employment in Soviet industrial enterprises was allocated statistically to other branches. Murray Feshbach, "Soviet Industrial Labor and Productivity Statistics," in Vladimir G. Treml and John P. Hardt, eds., *Soviet Economic Statistics* (Duke University Press, 1972), p. 211. This percentage probably rose for all Soviet enterprises in the 1970s and early 1980s, as more resources were devoted to enterprise social programs. Defense enterprises, I argue, had an even higher ratio than the rest. The percentage of additional employment in the social sector attached to Soviet enterprises was positively correlated with enterprise size, and as is evident later in this chapter, Russian defense enterprises were extremely large—on average more than ten times larger than civilian manufacturing plants.

21. See Note 2 of appendix.

22. I base my estimate of 200,000 on the assumption that the R&D institutes had a lower ratio of social sector employment than the enterprises—15 percent of total employment versus 25 percent.

23. Andrei Kokoshin, "Defense Industry Conversion in the Russian Federation," in Teresa Pelton Johnson and Steven E. Miller, eds., *Russian Security after the Cold War: Seven Views from Moscow* (Washington: Brassey's, 1994), p. 45.

24. The 50 percent figure remains constant through 1990. Thereafter, the percentage of the labor force engaged in civilian production rises steadily each year, reaching around 80 percent by the beginning of 1995. The 1988 figure is from Tsentr ekonomicheskoy kon"yunktury i prognozirovaniya, *Rossiya—1993. Ekonomicheskaya kon"yunktura* [Russia—1993: Economic situation] (Moscow, February 1993), figure VI.2, p. 156. (For subsequent years, see figure 7-2 on p. 115 in this book.)

25. For the source of this estimate of the indirect effects of U.S. defense spending, see Note 3 of appendix.

26. The number of enterprises involved in Soviet tank production was given by Air Force Marshal Yevgeny Shaposhnikov, commander-in-chief of the CIS Armed Forces, as reported by Moscow INTERFAX News Service in English, "Shaposhnikov on Declining Military Production," February 28, 1993; quoted in Foreign Broadcast Information Service, *Daily Report: Central Eurasia* [hereafter FBIS, *Central Eurasia*], March 1, 1993, p. 2. Shaposhnikov noted also that one-third of the enterprises were located outside Russia.

Information on the U.S. tank base is from Congressional Budget Office, *Alternatives for the U.S. Tank Industrial Base* (Washington, February 1993), p. 10.

27. It should also be remembered that these 1.8 to 3.6 million indirect jobs would have to be divided between jobs generated by the military production side of the VPK enterprises and the civilian production side. It is likely that the military production generated more.

For further discussion of indirect employment effects, see Note 3 of appendix.

28. The principal U.S. agencies that estimate defense employment are the Department of Defense (DoD) and the Congressional Budget Office (CBO). For DoD methods, see Logistics Management Institute, "Impacts of Defense Spending Cuts," p. 4-1; for CBO's methods, see Congressional Budget Office, "The Economic Effects of Reduced Defense Spending" (Government Printing Office, February 1992).

As applied to the year 1991, the two models differ (sometimes significantly) in the sectoral breakdown of defense-industry employment but are fairly close in their overall estimates of employment. CBO estimates defense industry employment at 2.908 million in 1991; "The Economic Effects of Reduced Defense Spending," table 7, p. 25. A DoD-commissioned report gives a figure of 3.243 million; Logistics Management Institute, "Impacts of Defense Spending Cuts," table 2-4, p. 2-9.

29. Office of the Comptroller of the Department of Defense, "National Defense Budget Estimates for FY 1994" (Department of Defense, May 1993), table 7-7, p. 158. U.S. defense-related industry employment was at its post–Korean War high from 1986 to 1989, ranging from 3.3 million to 3.7 million.

30. The civilian labor force in the U.S. from 1986 to 1988 was 90 to 95 million people. Bureau of the Census, *Statistical Abstract of the United States 1990*, 110th ed. (Department of Commerce, 1990), table 627, p. 379.

31. *Trud v SSSR*, p. 43.

32. See Note 4 of appendix for a discussion of sources on the numbers of enterprises and institutes.

33. See figure 2-3. The total number of VPK industrial production employees (PPP) was 5.4 million; including nonindustrial employees, employment in VPK industrial enterprises rises to 7.2 million. Dividing those totals by the 900 enterprises in Russia yields the averages of 6,000 PPP and 8,000 total employees per enterprise.

34. See Note 5 of appendix on the average size of Russian civilian-industrial enterprises.

35. Like the names of some of the secret defense industry ministries under the VPK (see figure 2-2), Soviet arms plants and research institutes frequently had "civilian-sounding" names. In contrast with some other cases, the name "Urals Railway Car Factory" does convey some information, because the *Uralvagonzavod* actually did produce train cars—about two-thirds of all the freight cars in the USSR. See Marcus A. Kuiper, "From War Economy to De-Militarized Economy," *Journal of Soviet Military Studies*, vol. 4, no. 4 (December 1991), pp. 649–73 [p. 662].

36. The number of *Uralvagonzavod* employees is from my database of 450 Russian defense plants, and from information in the Soviet press during the time of a visit by Mikhail Gorbachev to the plant in April 1990. See, for instance, a Moscow television program of April 27, 1990, as reported in "Views Coopera-

tives," Moscow Television Service, April 27, 1990, in FBIS, *Soviet Union,* FBIS-SOV-90-083 (April 30, 1990), p. 104.

As impressive as the number of workers are the sheer physical dimensions of the plant: 827,000 square meters (200 acres) of floor space—about eight times as much as the average for its U.S. counterparts. In 1981, a publication of the U.S. Department of Defense included a map showing the floor space of *Uralvagonzavod* superimposed on a map of downtown Washington, D.C. It extends from the Lincoln Memorial to the Capitol building. See the "Military Resource Allocation" section of *Soviet Military Power* (U.S. Department of Defense, 1981), p. 11.

37. See Note 6 of appendix on the size distribution of Russian defense enterprises.

38. See Note 6 of appendix.

39. See Note 7 of appendix on issues involved in the comparison of U.S. firms and Russian enterprises.

40. The ratios would likely be even larger if the size distribution classes on the lower end were more finely disaggregated, something the Russian data do not permit. Of the 390,000 U.S. establishments in the "under 250 employees" group, 335,000 establishments had fewer than 50 employees, and 140,000 had fewer than five employees. U.S. Bureau of the Census, *County Business Patterns, 1991* (GPO, 1994), tables 1b and 1c.

41. U.S. data do not report the number of establishments with more than 10,000 employees. Whatever the number is, it is small and (in the current era of corporate downsizing) shrinking fast. Among the few remaining giants, there are some notable cases of defense industries, especially in shipbuilding. The sole builder of America's nuclear-powered aircraft carriers, the Newport News (Virginia) Shipbuilding and Drydock Co., has 18,000 employees. The Electric Boat Co. in Groton, Connecticut, a submarine builder, has 11,900. Personal communication with public affairs offices of these companies, March 26, 1996.

42. The claim that there are at least 150 defense enterprises with more than 10,000 employees is based on my own database of Russian defense enterprises and counts not only industrial production employees (PPP) but nonindustrial employees as well. The 97 enterprises in table 2-3 listed in that class are based only on PPP employees.

43. This number is computed by dividing the number of manufacturing employees (18,383,368) by the number of establishments (373,999) reported in Bureau of the Census, *County Business Patterns 1991*, table 1b. Mining establishments were even smaller: 23.5 employees on average.

44. See Note 5 of appendix.

45. In this and in later chapters I will for convenience use the term "oblasts" to refer to all of the so-called second-tier subnational units in Russia. In fact, there are four distinct kinds of these units: oblasts, krays, republics, and okrugs. In addition, the cities of Moscow and St. Petersburg are often reported separately in statistical tables. Present-day Russia has eighty-nine of these subnational units, or "subjects of the federation." But for reasons of consistency with certain data from the Soviet period, my analysis in this book is based on consolidation of all data into seventy-three units that correspond to the forty-nine oblasts, sixteen republics, six krays, and two cities of the Soviet era.

46. This procedure amounts to ranking the regions on the basis of an index for each region that is equal to the sum of two scores:

$$INDEX_i = (VPKTOT_i/(VPKTOT_{max}) +$$
$$(VPKPOP_i/(VPKPOP_{max}),$$

where $VPKTOT_i$ is the absolute number of VPK industrial employees in oblast i, $VPKPOP_i$ is VPK industrial employment as a percentage of the population in oblast i, and the "max" subscripts for those variables represent the extreme high values among all the oblasts.

Chapter 3

1. *KPSS v rezolyutsiyakh i resheniyakh s"yezdov, konferentsiy i plenumov TsK* [CPSU in resolutions and decisions of congresses, conferences, and plenums of the CC] (Moscow, 1970), vol. 3, p. 507, cited in Aleksandr I. Pozharov, *Ekonomicheskiye osnovy oboronnogo mogushchestva sotsialisticheskogo gosudarstva* [The economic foundations of the military power of the socialist state] (Moscow: Military Publishing House of the Ministry of Defense of the USSR, 1981), p. 43.

2. Andrei Nikolayevich Lagovsky, *Strategiya i ekonomika. Kratkiy ocherk ikh svyazi i vzaimnogo vliyaniya* [Strategy and economics: A brief outline of their relationship and mutual influence] (Moscow: Military Publishing House of the Ministry of Defense of the USSR, 1957). A second revised edition of this work was published by the same publishing house in 1961. All citations in this book are from the 1957 edition.

I was introduced to the writings of Lagovsky by the works of Michael Checinski, who has written numerous articles on the Soviet war economy, from its birth in the 1920s through the 1980s. See especially "Kriegs- und Kriegswirtschaftsdoktrin der Sowjetunion. Entwicklungen und Tendenzen 1946–1983," *Osteuropa-Wirtschaft*, vol. 34 (March 1984), pp. 177–92, and "The Legacy of the Soviet War-Economy and Implications for Gorbachev's *Perestroika*," *Journal of Soviet Military Studies*, vol. 2 (June 1989), pp. 206–40.

3. Lagovsky, *Strategiya i ekonomika*, p. 57.

4. Ibid., pp. 87–88.

5. Ibid., p. 98.

6. Ibid., pp. 87–99.

7. Ibid., p. 100.

8. Ibid., p. 71.

9. Ibid., p. 72.

10. Ibid., p. 108.

11. Ibid., p. 73. The recommendation is repeated on page 112: "Under contemporary conditions, one-of-a-kind industrial enterprises are impermissible, even if they were to be located in remote regions of the country, well camouflaged, and even hidden underground."

12. Ibid., p. 74.

13. Mikhail V. Frunze, "The Front and Rear in a Future War" [1925], in *Izbrannyye proizvedeniya*, vol. II, pp. 140–41. Cited in Checinski, "The Legacy of the Soviet War-Economy and Implications for Gorbachev's *Perestroika*," p. 215.

14. The United States currently has two types of strategic reserves. In addition to the self-explanatory Strategic Petroleum Reserve, there is the National Defense Stockpile, established in 1939. It is composed primarily of stocks of four strategic minerals—chromium, cobalt, manganese, and platinum—for which the United States is 100 percent dependent on foreign imports. Kent Hughes Butts, "Strategic Minerals in the New World Order," pamphlet, Strategic Studies Institute, U.S. Army War College, November 30, 1993.

15. Vitaly Shlykov, "The Defense Industry and Democracy in Russia: The Interplay," paper presented to the Conference on Russo-Ukrainian Security Issues, Monterey, California, November 15–17, 1993, pp. 11–12.

16. Shlykov, "The Defense Industry and Democracy in Russia," p. 12. During the Soviet era, Shlykov had a career in the General Staff's directorate for military intelligence (GRU). He briefly served as deputy defense minister of Russia in 1991–92. *Kto est' kto v Rossii i v blizhem zarubezh'ye* [Who's who in Russia and the Near Abroad] (Moscow: Novoye vremya, 1993), pp. 738–39.

17. Lagovsky, *Strategiya i ekonomika*, p. 110.

18. Ibid., p. 109.

19. Ibid., p. 108.

20. The failure to take into account the cost of locating industries in remote regions also explains in part why Soviets (and today, Russians) often had an exaggerated notion of the value of their mineral and other natural resources. Since the distinction was rarely made between the concepts of "physical deposits" of a resource and "economic reserves" (those which made sense to exploit once costs are taken into account), Russians talked frequently about "inexhaustible" reserves. David Humphreys points out that this misconception dates back at least to Peter the Great. "Mining and Metals in the CIS: Between Autarky and Integration," paper prepared for the Post-Soviet Business Forum, Royal Institute of International Affairs, November 23, 1993, draft version, p. 26.

21. Andrei Kokoshin, "Defense Industry Conversion in the Russian Federation," in Teresa Pelton Johnson and Steven E. Miller, eds., *Russian Security after the Cold War: Seven Views from Moscow* (Washington: Brassey's, 1994), p. 52. It is not clear how many of the new plants in new regions referred to by Kokoshin were duplicates of old facilities. But that the Soviet Union actually followed the costly proposal of Lagovsky (and others) to build multiple plants for the same product was confirmed in the following statement issued by the Russian defense lobby group, the League of Assistance to Defense Enterprises, at a spring 1993 conference: "It is clear . . . that with the collapse of the USSR, the unity of the MIC [the military-industrial complex] was disrupted to the same degree as the unity of the economic complex. The MIC faces . . . three acute problems . . . , [including] the problem of establishing duplicate production facilities and plants." "Mekhanizm konversii: problemy i perspektivy [The mechanism of conversion: problems and prospects]," *Ekonomist*, no. 7 (July 1993), pp. 50–61 [p. 50].

22. Ibid., p. 130.

23. Viktor D. Belkin, "Parallel'naya valyuta dlya rynochnoy reformy miltarizovannoy ekonomiki [A parallel currency for market reform of a militarized econ-

omy]," *Ekonomika i matematicheskiyye metody,* vol. 28, no. 4 (July–August 1992), pp. 293–500 [p. 493].

24. Yevgeny Kuznetsov, "Adjustment of the Russian Defence-Related Enterprises: Macroeconomic Implications," *Communist Economies and Economic Transformation,* vol. 6, no. 4 (1994), p. 474.

The case of tractor production and its close relationship to tank manufacturing is also cited by Michael Checinski. He calls the tractor industry the "stepson" of tank production and says that the build-up of massive tractor production in the Soviet Union in the 1950s and 1960s was primarily intended as a way of keeping excess capacity for tank production. "Structural Causes of Soviet Arms Exports," *Osteuropa-Wirtschaft,* vol. 22 (September 1977), pp. 169–84. Checinski also states that the initial diversification of defense industry to produce civilian goods was in precisely this sense actually intended to strengthen the military-industrial sector. Michael Checinski, "The Conversion of the Soviet Arms Industry: Plans, Reality and Prospects," *Osteuropa-Wirtschaft,* vol. 22 (January 1991), pp. 15–34.

25. Hedrick Smith, *The Russians* (London: Sphere Books Limited, 1976), p. 291.

26. Personal communication from Jerry Paner, October 6, 1992.

27. Kuznetsov, "Adjustment of the Russian Defence-Related Enterprises," p. 21; Yevgeny Kuznetsov and Feliks Shirokov, "Naukoyemkiye proizvodstva i konversiya oboronnoy promyshlennosti [High-tech production and conversion of defense industry]," *Kommunist,* no. 10 (July 1989), pp. 15–22.

28. Author's interview in Chelyabinsk, January 5, 1993.

29. Author's interview in Izhevsk, July 1995. An article about the institute had expressed the same idea earlier when it was reported that "only a tiny number of graduates were sent into civilian production—according to the residual principle." V. Krasnova, "Rynok ne lyubit slabykh [The market does not like the weak]," *Inzhenernaya gazeta,* nos. 147–48 (December 1992), p. 3.

30. Kuznetsov and Shirokov, "Naukoyemkiye proizvodstva i konversiya oboronnoy promyshlennosti," p. 17.

31. The dual nature of the Soviet economy in terms of priority (military) and nonpriority sectors was formalized in a groundbreaking paper by Richard E. Ericson, "Priority, Duality, and Penetration in the Soviet Command Economy," RAND Note N-2643-NA (Santa Monica, Calif: RAND Corporation, December 1988).

32. Pozharov, *Ekonomicheskiye osnovy.*

33. Ibid., p. 120.

34. Ibid.

35. Ibid.

Chapter 4

1. "Korennoy vopros ekonomicheskoy politiki partii. Doklad tovarishcha M. S. Gorbacheva [The fundamental issue of the Party's economic policy: Report of comrade M. S. Gorbachev]," *Pravda,* June 12, 1985, p. 1.

Andropov had used the phrase in his first major speech when he assumed the leadership of the Soviet Union in November 1982. "Rech' General'nogo sekretarya

TsK KPSS Yu. V. Andropova na plenume TsK KPSS 22 noyabrya 1982 goda [Speech of the CC CPSU General Secretary Yury V. Andropov to the Plenum of the CC CPSU, November 22, 1982]," *Pravda,* November 23, 1982, p. 1.

2.   Quoted in Dusko Doder and Louise Branson, *Gorbachev: Heretic in the Kremlin* (Viking, 1990), p. 207.

3.   Speech to a group 'of veterans of the Stakhanovite movement. "Nemer-knushchiye traditsii trudovogo podviga. Rech' M. S. Gorbacheva [The unfading traditions of heroic labor exploits: Speech of M. S. Gorbachev]," *Pravda,* September 21, 1985.

4.   Bruce Parrott, "Political Change and Civil-Military Relations," in Timothy J. Colton and Thane Gustafson, eds., *Soldiers and the Soviet State: Civil-Military Relations from Brezhnev to Gorbachev* (Princeton University Press, 1990), p. 55.

5.   "Korennoy vopros ekonomicheskoy politiki partii," *Pravda,* June 12, 1985.

6.   "Korennoy vopros ekonomicheskoy politiki partii," *Pravda,* June 12, 1985.

7.   Nikolai Ogarkov, "Na strazhe mirnogo truda [On guard over peaceful labor]," *Kommunist,* no. 10 (July 1981), p. 86.

8.   For his part, Gorbachev reportedly once remarked to an aide that of all the military leaders in the Soviet Union, Ogarkov was the only one who impressed him. Doder and Branson, *Gorbachev,* p. 108.

9.   Ogarkov, "Na strazhe mirnogo truda," p. 89. The same demand in virtually identical language was also incorporated in his booklet for publication in December 1981, *Vsegda v gotovnosti k zashchite otechestva* [Always in readiness to defend the fatherland] (Moscow: Military Publishers, 1982), p. 60.

10.   See Parrott, "Political Change and Civil-Military Relations," especially the section "The Consolidation of Civilian Dominance, 1985–1988," pp. 75–89.

11.   Ibid., p. 81.

12.   The *Uralmash* Production Association (*PO Uralmash*) consisted of six manufacturing plants and one large research institute. The group's main plant, *Uralmashzavod,* employed about two-thirds of the 50,000 *Uralmash* workers. Bureau of Export Administration, *Russian Defense Business Directory, 1995,* PB95-949400 (Department of Commerce, May 1995), pp. 1–230; and *Biznes-Karta Rossii 92. Ural. Promymshlennost'* [Business map of Russia 92: Urals, industry] (Moscow: NIK, 1992), p. 76.

13.   See Anders Åslund, *Gorbachev's Struggle for Economic Reform: The Soviet Reform Process, 1985–88* (Cornell University Press, 1989), pp. 37–41, on Ryzhkov.

14.   Ibid., pp. 44–47.

15.   Julian Cooper, "The Defense Industry and Civil-Military Relations," in Timothy J. Colton and Thane Gustafson, eds., *Soldiers and the Soviet State: Civil-Military Relations from Brezhnev to Gorbachev* (Princeton University Press, 1990), pp. 177–79.

16.   Some reports have stressed that the power of the military inspectors was tempered by their dependence on the plant for material benefits such as housing. Even the testimonials of the plant director or general designer were said to be important in promotions of the inspectors. See, for example, V. Zhilyakov, "Voyenpred pod dvoynym kontrolem. Chto zastavlyayet ego zakryvat' glaza na brak? [The military representative under dual control: What makes him turn a blind eye to junk?]" *Izvestiya* (Moscow evening edition), January 23, 1990, or Anatoly Kravtsov, "Kontroler na povodke: zametki voyenpreda [Inspector under the thumb:

Notes of a military representative]," *Ogonyok*, no. 43 (October 1990), pp. 7–8. The authors of these articles served as *voyenpredy* for 20 and 30 years, respectively. On the other hand, the Defense Ministry would have been aware of this and had ways of minimizing the "capture" of their representatives by the plants they were supposed to monitor. In any event, there is ample evidence of the authority of the military representatives, even over powerful industry figures. The memoirs of Mikhail Kalashnikov, *Zapiski konstruktora-oruzheynika* [Memoirs of a weapons designer) (Moscow: Military Publishers, 1992), are an example.

17. Åslund, *Gorbachev's Struggle for Economic Reform*, p. 77.

18. Ibid., p. 80.

19. "Rech' tovarishcha Gorbacheva M. S. [Speech of Comrade M. S. Gorbachev]," *Pravda*, October 2, 1987.

20. Andrei Kokoshin, "Defense Industry Conversion in the Russian Federation," in Teresa Pelton Johnson and Steven E. Miller, eds., *Russian Security after the Cold War: Seven Views from Moscow* (Washington: Brassey's, 1994).

21. "O gosudarstvennom plane ekonomicheskogo i sotsial'nogo razvitiya SSSR na 1986–1990 godu. Doklad Predsedatelya Soveta Ministrov SSSR deputata Ryzhkova N. I. [On the state plan for economic and social development of the USSR for 1986–1990: Report of the chairman of the USSR Council of Ministers, Deputy N. I. Ryzhkov]," *Pravda*, June 19, 1986.

22. "Nagrada rodiny—stimul dlya novykh sversheniy [The motherland's award: incentive for new achievements]," *Pravda*, June 29, 1986.

23. Julian Cooper, *The Soviet Defence Industry: Conversion and Economic Reform* (London: Royal Institute of International Affairs, 1991), pp. 31–33.

24. "Vystupleniye M.S. Gorbacheva v Organizatsii Ob"yedinennykh Natsiy [M. S. Gorbachev's address to the United Nations]," *Pravda*, December 8, 1988, pp. 1–2.

25. Ibid.

26. John Tedstrom, "Glasnost' and the Soviet Defense Budget," *RFE/RL Institute Report on the USSR*, vol. 3 (July 19, 1991), p. 10.

27. Ed A. Hewett and Clifford G. Gaddy, *Open for Business: Russia's Return to the Global Economy* (Brookings, 1992), p. 13.

28. Ibid., p. 52.

29. Robert Campbell, "Resource Stringency and Civil-Military Resource Allocation," in Timothy J. Colton and Thane Gustafson, eds., *Soldiers and the Soviet State: Civil-Military Relations from Brezhnev to Gorbachev* (Princeton University Press, 1990), p. 151.

30. Marcus A. Kuiper, "From War Economy to De-Militarized Economy," *Journal of Soviet Military Studies*, vol. 4 (December 1991), pp. 649–73 [footnote 8].

31. "Rech' tovarishcha Gorbacheva M. S.," *Pravda*, October 2, 1987.

32. "Yashin on Future Military Reform, Conversion," Moscow Domestic Service, February 22, 1990, in Foreign Broadcast Information Service, *Daily Report: Soviet Union*, February 27, 1990, pp. 76–78.

33. "Ural: nadezhnost' i nadezhdy. Vystupleniye M.S. Gorbacheva na vstreche s trudyashchimisya Sverdlovskoy oblasti 26 aprelya 1990 goda [The Urals: Promise and hope. M. S. Gorbachev's speech at a meeting with working people of Sverdlovsk province, April 26, 1990]," *Pravda*, April 28, 1990, p. 1.

34. Ibid.

35. "Status—oboronke. Predsedatelyu Verkhovnogo Soveta SSSR A. Lyuk"yanovu, narodnym deputatam SSSR, Verkhovnym Sovetam soyuznykh respublik [Status for the defense complex: Letter to the chairman of the Supreme Soviet of the USSR, A. Luk"yanov, to the People's Deputies of the USSR, and to the Supreme Soviets of the Union Republics]," *Pravda,* September 6, 1990, p. 2.

36. Tedstrom, *"Glasnost'* and the Soviet Defense Budget," p. 8. Tedstrom's estimates are based on information on the Soviet defense budget published in the Soviet press. His conclusions are consistent with a more recent statement by Russian Deputy Defense Minister Andrei Kokoshin that hardware procurement in 1991 was 30 percent lower than in 1988 and R&D expenditures 75 percent lower. Kokoshin, "Defense Industry Conversion in the Russian Federation," p. 48.

37. See Cooper, *The Soviet Defence Industry,* pp. 75–88, for information on the political role of the Soviet military-industrial complex in 1989–91. In addition to Baklanov and Tizyakov, several of the other coup plotters were linked to the military and security apparatus, if not directly to defense industry: Dmitri Yazov, minister of defense; Vladimir Kryuchkov, head of the Committee on State Security (KGB); and Boris Pugo, minister of internal affairs.

Chapter 5

1. "Boris Yel'tsin: Obyazuyus' pered svoim narodom sformirovat' kabinet reformi rasschityvayu na ponimaniye i podderzhku deputatov, kazhdogo rossiyanina [Boris Yeltsin: I pledge before my people to form a reform cabinet and I count on the understanding and support of the deputies and every Russian citizen]," *Izvestiya,* October 28, 1991, pp. 1–2.

2. More details on the defense industries inherited by the various post-Soviet states are in Julian Cooper, "The Soviet Union and the Successor Republics: Defence Industries Coming to Terms with Disunion," in Herbert Wulf, ed., *Arms Industry Limited* (Oxford University Press/SIPRI, 1993), pp. 87–108.

3. "Status—oboronke. Predsedatelyu Verkhovnogo Soveta SSSR A. Luk"yanovu, narodnym deputatam SSSR, Verkhovnym Sovetam soyuznykh respublik [Status for the defense complex: Letter to the chairman of the Supreme Soviet of the USSR, A. Luk"yanov, to the People's Deputies of the USSR, and to the Supreme Soviets of the Union Republics]," *Pravda,* September 6, 1990, p. 2.

4. There was one concession to *glasnost'* in the new committee's internal workings. In contrast with the old ministries, which in some cases had innocuous and deliberately misleading names (for example, the ministry responsible for Soviet intercontinental ballistic missiles went by the name of the Ministry of General Machine-Building), the names of the *Roskomoboronprom* departments were fairly straightforward. The eight were the departments for Aviation Industry, Ammunition and Special Chemical Products, Armaments Industry, Communications Industry, Radio Industry, Missile and Space Technology, Shipbuilding Industry, and Electronics Industry.

5. Meanwhile, at least for a period, some of the radical reformers pursued the goal of downgrading, and even eliminating it. Mikhail Malei, a member of the

defense-industrial establishment, spoke of Yegor Gaidar's intention to wind up *Roskomoboronprom* and "create in its place a small directorate in the Ministry of Economy." Aleksandr Yegorov, "Dolgiye shagi na meste ili vse zhe start marafona? [Long strides in place or the start of a marathon after all?]," *Krasnaya zvezda,* December 21, 1993, p. 2.

6. The argument about the negative consequences of the continued special status of the defense-industrial complex has been made most notably by Yury Yaryemenko, director of the Institute of Economic Forecasting, and his colleagues. See, for example, Yu. V. Yaryemenko and V. N. Rassadin, "Ipostasi konversii [Hypostases of conversion]," *Ekonomika i organizatsiya promyshlennogo proizvodstva (EKO),* vol. 234 (December 1993), pp. 2–13.

7. "Osnovy voyennoy doktriny Rossii (Proyekt) [Foundations of the military doctrine of Russia (Draft)]," *Voyennaya mysl',* special issue (May 1992), pp. 3–9.

8. Mary E. Glantz, "The Origins and Development of Soviet and Russian Military Doctrine," *Journal of Slavic Military Studies,* vol. 7 (September 1994), pp. 443–80 [p. 473].

9. The actual document presenting the military doctrine is unavailable and presumably will remain secret. A "detailed account" of the doctrine was published in various Russian newspapers, including "Voyennaya doktrina Rossii [Russia's military doctrine]," *Rossiyskiye vesti,* November 18, 1993; and "Osnovnyye polozheniya voyennoy doktriny Rossiyskoy Federatsii [Fundamental tenets of the military doctrine of the Russian Federation]," *Krasnaya zvezda,* November 19, 1993, pp. 1–8. A Yeltsin decree (No. 1833) of November 2 confirmed the doctrine, but it is not clear that the edict contains the text of the doctrine.

10. Mary FitzGerald, "Russia's Military Reasserts Influence," *Defense News,* vol. 8, no. 46 (November 22–28, 1993), pp. 27, 28. Similarly, Michael R. Gordon wrote on November 29 that the doctrine was "everything the military would have liked." Michael R. Gordon, "As Its World View Narrows, Russia Seeks a New Mission," *New York Times,* November 29, 1993, pp. A1, A10. The main provisions of the doctrine such commentators were referring to were that Russia now proclaimed the right to use military force to protect its citizens and its military bases in other countries. Russia also reserved the right to be the first to use nuclear weapons in a conflict.

11. Anatoly Stasovsky, "Voyennaya doktrina Rossii: novoye ponimaniye bezopasnosti strany [Russia's military doctrine: a new conception of the country's security]," *Krasnaya zvezda,* November 4, 1993, pp. 1, 3.

12. "Zakon Rossiyskoy Federatsii: O konversii oboronnoy promyshlennosti v Rossiyskoy Federatsii [Russian Federation Law: On conversion of the defense industry in the Russian Federation]," *Rossiyskaya gazeta,* April 27, 1992, p. 6. The law went into effect on January 1, 1993. Viktor Glukhikh, "Mozhno li privatizirovat' tankoviyy zavod? [Is privatizing a tank plant allowed?]," *Rossiyskiye vesti,* June 17, 1993, p. 7.

13. "O konversii oboronnoy promyshlennosti v Rossiyskoy Federatsii," p. 6.

14. A. Shulunov, "Konversiya: novyye podkhody [Conversion: New approaches]," *Ekonomika i zhizn',* no. 15 (April 1994), p. 1.

15. Ibid. To take one (possibly self-serving) example, Aleksei Shulunov, the president of the League of Assistance to Defense Enterprises, claimed that it would

cost 4,400 billion rubles if enterprises in 1994 were to complete programs approved by the federal government in 1992 and 1993. Yet the government submitted a draft budget for 1994 that provided for only 900 billion rubles for conversion programs.

16. As time went on, the desired "nucleus" seemed to shrink. By the fall of 1993, there were statements that the nucleus should consist of about 200 enterprises. These are the ones that should be guaranteed a minimum of 30 percent of their output under defense orders. See Valentin Rudenko, "Oboronke nuzhny opredelennost' i vzveshennyye, produmannyye reformy [The defense complex needs certainty and balanced, well-thought-out reforms]," *Krasnaya zvezda,* October 27, 1993, p. 1.

17. The distinction between legal property rights and economic property rights is one emphasized by the economist Yoram Barzel. He defines the economic property rights of individuals over assets as "the rights, or the powers, to consume, obtain income from, and alienate these assets," regardless of legal rights to the asset. Yoram Barzel, *Economic Analysis of Property Rights* (Cambridge University Press, 1989), p. 2.

18. In a interesting switch, the person he replaced as head of the privatization ministry, Mikhail Malei, was moved to the defense industry bureaucracy as Yeltsin's special adviser on conversion issues. Malei had been chairman of the GKI, and a deputy prime minister, from November 1990 to November 1991. His background was in defense industry. *Kto est' kto v Rossii i v blizhem zarubezh'ye* [Who's who in Russia and the Near Abroad], (Moscow: Novoye vremya, 1993), pp. 400–401.

19. A blow-by-blow description of the overall privatization program is in Anders Åslund, *How Russia Became a Market Economy* (Brookings, 1995), pp. 223–71.

20. "Gosudarstvennaya programma privatizatsii gosudarstvennykh i munitsipal'nykh predpriyatiy Rossiyskoy Federatsii [State program for the privatization of state and municipal enterprises of the Russian Federation]," *Rossiyskaya gazeta,* July 9, 1992, p. 2. Section 2 of the program lists fifteen classes of enterprises and facilities that must obtain government permission in order to be privatized. Four of the fifteen are defense-related: enterprises and R&D facilities engaged in weapons development or production; civil defense and mobilization facilities; nuclear equipment manufacturers; and storage facilities for state reserves and mobilization stocks.

In addition, article 2.3.11 specified that enterprises' mobilization reserves [*mobilizatsionnyye zapasy*] would be dealt with separately from the rest of the plant. Any enterprise, defense or not, with mobilization reserves would have to relinquish those reserves when it privatized. Privatization of the reserves would be a matter for the GKI to decide.

21. The workers' additional 10 percent was at 70 percent of the shares' nominal price, which was fairly low to begin with, and declined rapidly in value as inflation raged. The price of the managers' 5 percent was 100 percent of book value or the nominal price.

22. Åslund, *How Russia Became a Market Economy*, p. 232. Clearly, privatization of large enterprises was always a thorny issue. Even in his speech on reform on October 28, 1991, Yeltsin had stated that privatization of "the giants of industry" would be "considerably more complicated" than the rest: "A significant portion

of them will remain under state ownership." "Boris Yel'tsin: Obyazuyus' pered svoim narodom," p. 2.

23. "On Industrial Policy in the Privatization of State Enterprises," Russian Federation Presidential Edict No. 1392, November 16, 1992, Paragraph 1. English translation mimeo from Ruslegisline.

24. Ibid., Paragraph 5.

25. Åslund, *How Russia Became a Market Economy,* p. 243.

26. See "On State Guarantees for Citizens of Russia to Participate in Privatization," Russian Federation Presidential Edict No. 640, May 8, 1993, Paragraph 2. English translation mimeo from Ruslegisline.

27. "Mekhanizm konversii: problemy i perspektivy [The conversion mechanism: Problems and prospects]," *Ekonomist,* no. 7 (July 1993), p. 54. This refers to so-called production associations and scientific production associations (known as POs and NPOs, respectively), which were made up of multiple organizations (often a dozen or more) including enterprises, research institutes, and design organizations.

28. Ibid., p. 55.

29. Ibid., p. 54.

30. "Ob osobennostyakh privatizatsii i dopolnitel'nykh merakh gosudarstvennogo regulirovaniya deyatel'nosti predpriyatiy oboronnykh otrasley promyshlennosti [On the special features of privatization and supplementary measures of state regulation of the activity of enterprises of the defense sectors of industry]," Russian Federation Presidential Edict No. 1267, August 19, 1993.

31. Ibid. The profits handed back to the enterprises were to be used to finance "conversion measures, retooling, reconstruction, and expansion of production facilities, implementation of environmental-protection measures, and maintenance of objects of the social sphere of these enterprises." The edict did not stipulate whether this meant that the earnings of all the enterprises would be handed back to the enterprises from which they derived or whether they were to be pooled and redistributed, but not in exactly the same proportion as their source—as a way of equalizing within the defense-industrial sector.

32. A statute on certification of defense enterprise directors was approved on February 28, 1995. For the text of the statute and a commentary, see Commentary by Sergei Ptichkin, "Statute on Administrative Certification of Weapons Producers," *Rossiyskaya gazeta,* March 18, 1995, p. 4, in Joint Publications Research Service, *Military Affairs,* April 11, 1995, pp. 6–8.

33. *Roskomoboronprom* was further elevated in status by a law signed on September 10, 1993, which declared it a "state committee," thus nearly equal in status to a ministry. "Body on Defense Sectors Industry Becomes State Committee," *Rossiyskiye vesti,* September 29, 1993 (first ed.), p. 2, in Foreign Broadcast Information Service, *Daily Report: Central Eurasia,* September 30, 1993, p. 18.

Chapter 6

1. The general director of the VPIK was Vitaly Doguzhiyev, who served from 1983 to 1989 as deputy minister, first deputy minister, and minister of the USSR

Ministry of General Machine-Building—the ministry responsible for the Soviet missile industry. From 1989 to 1991 he was deputy chairman of the USSR Council of Ministers, and then first deputy prime minister of the USSR. The chairman of the board of directors was Sergei Petrov, an associate of Borovoi who was in his thirties and who helped found and manage Borovoi's Russian Raw Materials and Commodity Exchange and the Russian National Commercial Bank. Petrov was also the CEO of another of Borovoi's joint ventures with defense industry, the "Military-Industrial Exchange." Information from the VPIK investment prospectus, "Aktsionernoye obshchestvo 'Voyenno-promyshlennaya Investitsionnaya Kompaniya' [Joint stock company, 'Military-Industrial Investment Company']," December 1991.

2. "Status—oboronke. Predsedatelyu Verkhovnogo Soveta SSSR A. Lyuk"yanovu, narodnym deputatam SSSR, Verkhovnym Sovetam soyuznykh respublik [Status for the defense complex: Letter to the chairman of the Supreme Soviet of the USSR, A. Luk"yanov, to the People's Deputies of the USSR, and to the Supreme Soviets of the Union Republics]," *Pravda,* September 6, 1990, p. 2.

3. VPIK, "Aktsionernoye obshchestvo 'Voyenno-promyshlennaya Investitsionnaya Kompaniya'."

4. Right before the August 1991 coup attempt, there had been an effort by conservatives to close some cities again. That, of course, was reversed after the coup. Andrei Kokoshin, "Defense Industry Conversion in the Russian Federation," in Teresa Pelton Johnson and Steven E. Miller, eds., *Russian Security after the Cold War: Seven Views from Moscow* (Washington: Brassey's, 1994), p. 66.

5. Ibid., p. 68.

6. This was, of course, not an experience unique to Russian defense industry. In 1991 and 1992, Russian government experts projected that the nation's economy needed and would be able to absorb $10 billion to $12 billion a year in foreign investment (some said as much as $40 billion to $50 billion). By the end of 1993, however, cumulative external investment came to only $2.7 billion, with the overwhelming majority of that in the fuels and metals sectors. See A. Kirin, "Inostrannyye investitsii v Rossii: reshat li novyye mery staryye problemy? [Foreign investments in Russia: Will new measures solve old problems?]," *Ekonomika i zhizn',* no. 9 (March 1995), p. 30.

7. Yeltsin's support for an active arms export policy dated back at least to the fall of 1991. For public statements by Yeltsin from October and November 1991, see Clifford G. Gaddy and Melanie L. Allen, "Russian Arms Sales Abroad: Policy, Practice, and Prospects," *Brookings Discussion Papers* (September 1993), p. 2. That report also details how radical reformers in the government overcame initial opposition to the policy and began echoing Yeltsin's stance by mid- or late 1992.

8. Interview with V. Gladyshev in "Oboronka mozhet pomoch' ekonomike strany [Defense industry can help the country's economy]," *Rossiyskaya gazeta,* June 26, 1992, p. 1.

9. Gaddy and Allen, "Russian Arms Sales Abroad," p. 39.

10. K. Samsonov, "Konversiya predpriyatiy oboronnogo kompleksa promyshlennosti v usloviyakh perekhoda k rynku [Conversion of the enterprises of the defense complex under conditions of transition to the market]," *Voprosy ekonomiki,* no. 9 (September 1993), pp. 89–99 [p. 96].

11. See Table A.2 in Abraham S. Becker, *Ogarkov's Complaint and Gorbachev's Dilemma: The Soviet Defense Budget and Party-Military Conflict*, RAND Publication R-3541-AF (Santa Monica, Calif.: RAND Corporation, December 1987), p. 45.

The point here is not that a large volume of exports is necessarily bad or that it was unique to the USSR. In fact, for at least some weapons systems, the United States appears to have had a ratio of export shipments to domestic procurement that was as high as the Soviet Union's in the 1970s and 1980s. According to Randall Forsberg, in 1973–92 the Soviet export-to-domestic procurement ratio for combat aircraft was 67 percent, whereas the U.S. ratio was 72 percent. Randall Forsberg and Jonathan Cohen, "The Global Arms Market: Prospects for the Coming Decade: A Study of Trends and Potential Future Developments in World Arms Production and Trade, with Special Attention to Tanks and Combat Aircraft," paper prepared for the Brookings Institution and International Fighter Study, an international consortium project coordinated by the Institute for Defense and Disarmament Studies, January 1994, table 4.9. The difference is that it may be presumed that the United States engaged in such a policy of high exports in substantial measure because it was profitable. Indeed, it is frequently argued in the arms control community that U.S. arms manufacturers reaped large profits from the additional markets provided by exports, and that their proliferation of weapons even put peace at risk for that motive. It is not at all clear that the Soviet Union reaped a net economic benefit from its exports.

12. Confidential communication, February 4, 1994.

13. The information on these debts varies. The figure of 870 billion rubles is as of December 25, 1993, and is from "A ved' byli ukazaniya i ves'ma strogiye [And they were quite strict]," *Krasnaya zvezda,* December 30, 1993, p. 1. "Despite orders by Yeltsin, Chernomyrdin, and repeated appeals of the Ministry of Defense, the Ministry of Defense has still not received funds to pay the enterprises." Valentin Rudenko, "Oboronke nuzhny opredelennost' i vzveshennyye, produmannyye reformy [Defense industry needs certainty and balanced, well-thought-out reforms]," *Krasnaya zvezda,* October 27, 1993, p. 1. Rudenko says that government debts to enterprises at that point were 400 billion rubles. In late December First Deputy Prime Minister Oleg Soskovets ordered the Ministry of Finance to pay off some 600 billion to 700 billion rubles in debts incurred by the Ministry of Defense for arms purchases. John Lepingwell, "Payment for Arms," *RFE/RL Daily Report,* December 27, 1993.

14. The GTU was reorganized in early 1992 as a new state-run arms trading company known as *Spetsvneshtekhnika.* See Gaddy and Allen, "Russian Arms Sales Abroad," p. 11.

15. Krasnov predicted 1992 sales of $7.5 billion. Interview with Deputy Minister of Foreign Economic Affairs Vladimir Shibayev, in Pavel Fel'gengauer, "Vse v Rossii khotyat torgovat' oruzhiyem [Everyone in Russia wants to sell weapons]," *Nezavisimaya gazeta,* September 30, 1992, p. 1.

16. Ibid.

17. Barry W. Ickes and Randi Ryterman, "Roadblock to Economic Reform: Inter-Enterprise Debt and the Transition to Markets," *Post-Soviet Affairs,* vol. 9 (July–September 1993), pp. 231–52 [p. 247].

18. *O razvitii ekonomicheskikh reform v Rossiyskoy Federatsii v 1992 g.* [On the development of economic reforms in the Russian Federation in 1992] (Moscow: Goskomstat, 1993), p. 10.

19. Ickes and Ryterman, "Roadblock to Economic Reform," pp. 239–50.

20. See interview with Mikhail Malei in "Dolgiye shagi na meste ili vse zhe start marafona? [Long strides in place, or the start of a marathon after all]," *Krasnaya zvezda,* December 21, 1993, p. 2.

21. *O razvitii ekonomicheskikh reform v Rossiyskoy Federatsii v 1992 g.,* p. 10.

22. Ibid.

23. Ibid., p. 11.

24. See, for example, the reports in late 1992 that of the total amounts of credits and subsidies received by defense enterprises in 1992, around 55 percent was reportedly used "to maintain employment" and for wages, 25 percent for social infrastructure, and only 20 percent for R&D and investments. V. Telnov, "Kredity na konversiyu poluchat ne vse [Not everyone is receiving credits for conversion]," *Finansovyye izvestiya,* November 26, 1992, p. 8, cited in Yevgeny Kuznetsov, "Adjustment of Russian Defense-Related Enterprises in 1992–94: Macro-economic Implications," *Communist Economies and Economic Transformation,* vol. 6, no. 4 (1994), pp. 473–513.

25. See, for example, Philip Hanson and Elizabeth Teague, "The Industrialists and Russian Economic Reform," *RFE/RL Research Report,* vol. 1 (May 8, 1992), pp. 1–7.

26. *O razvitii ekonomicheskikh reform v Rossiyskoy Federatsii v 1992 g.,* pp. 10–11.

27. Interview with Vladimir Salo, head of the Ministry of Economics' Department for Defense Industry Economy and Conversion, "Lack of Orders Depresses Defense Sector Wages," *Komsomolskaya pravda,* April 14, 1993, p. 1, in Foreign Broadcast Information Service, *Daily Report: Central Eurasia,* April 21, 1993, pp. 36–37.

28. Chart in Kenneth Gooding, "Scarcities May Return," *Financial Times,* October 28, 1992, p. 29.

29. Richard Mooney, "A Cold Wind Blows in from the East," *Financial Times,* October 23, 1991, p. 34.

30. Soviet statistics on most branches of industry had been available since the end of the Stalin era. But a 1956 decree stipulated that data for a number of strategic industries, including aluminum, would still be classified as state secrets. Theodore Shabad, *The Soviet Aluminum Industry* (New York: American Metal Market Co., 1958), p. 3.

31. *Statistical Yearbook,* 37th issue, 1988/89 (New York: United Nations, Department of Economic and Social Development Statistical Office, 1992), p. 651.

32. David Humphreys, "Mining and Metals in the CIS: Between Autarky and Integration," paper prepared for the Post-Soviet Business Forum, Royal Institute of International Affairs, November 23, 1993, draft version, p. 12.

33. Compare, for instance, the reports in the *Financial Times* in the fall of 1991 that the flood of aluminum from the former Soviet Union was "a temporary phenomenon" and that the entire industry was about to collapse. Mooney, "A Cold Wind Blows in from the East," p. 34; Kenneth Gooding, "Russia's Aluminium

Sector May Soon Grind to a Halt," *Financial Times,* April 2, 1992, p. 30. This underappreciation of the ability of Russian industry to endure under difficult circumstances was compounded by overoptimistic views of general recovery in Russia. The consulting group, Anthony Bird Associates, assured the Western aluminum industry that because of a "strong industrial recovery" in Russia that "could start in 1992," Russia would soon be using more aluminum at home. Mooney, "A Cold Wind Blows in from the East," p. 34.

34. Kenneth Gooding, "Giants with a Deadly Breath—Russia's Smelters," *Financial Times,* October 28, 1992, p. 30.

35. Ibid.

36. A similar honest effort to incorporate titanium into a civilian product was the case of a defense plant in Perm that had long been a major Russian manufacturer of bicycles. After elementary market research, the plant management realized there was an international market for bikes with titanium frames. Trying to solicit my assistance, the director told me that I could reassure any prospective American partner that he had "guaranteed" access to high-quality titanium. By my next visit a few months later, the factory had no titanium at all.

The ultimate example of titanium conversion projects, though, may be the case of the defense materials research institute in Perm that tried to produce toy rabbits made of titanium powder. When an incredulous Danish researcher, Tarja Cronberg, asked the institute director if the rabbits would not be extremely expensive, he admitted that the true cost would probably be around $1,000 each. But, he argued, they would be "very durable."

37. Personal communication, April 1993.

38. Gooding, "Giants with a Deadly Breath," p. 30.

39. Compare the annual review of Russian economic performance in "Sotsial'no-ekonomicheskoye polozheniye Rossii v 1994 g. [Socioeconomic position of Russia in 1994]," *Voprosy statistiki,* no. 3 (March 1995), p. 62, which names four such plants in which the increase in civilian output in 1994 was large enough to compensate for the drop in military production for that same year.

40. The prices of imported sewing machines and television sets in 1994 were reported by Ministry of Economics sources to be up to twice as high as for comparable Russian products. For radios the prices were three times higher, and for irons, more than ten times higher. N. E. Smetanin, "Potrebitel'skiy rynok: nyneshneye sostoyaniye i perspektivy [The consumer market: Current situation and prospects]" [interview with N. E. Smetanin, head of the Main Directorate of the Consumer Market and Light Industry of the Ministry of Economics], *Ekonomist,* no. 11 (November 1994), pp. 42-51 [p. 43].

41. Ibid.

42. Tsentr ekonomicheskoy kon"yunktury i prognozirovaniya, *Rossiya—1993. Ekonomicheskaya kon"yunktura* [Russia—1993: Economic situation], no. 3 (Moscow, August 1993), pp. 212-23.

43. "O razvitii ekonomicheskikh reform v Rossiyskoy Federatsii v 1992 godu (dopolnitel'nyye dannyye) [On the development of economic reform in Russia in 1992 (supplementary data)]," (Moscow: Goskomstat, 1993), p. 77. The figures cited represent the drop in square meters of cloth produced.

Chapter 7

1. This lack of information about workers is not a new problem, nor is it unique to defense industry. As one observer of the Soviet working class noted in the early 1980s, "Of all the secrets buried deep within the labyrinth of the Soviet Union, few are so closely guarded as those concerning the status of workers. . . . Valid information about general working conditions is perhaps second only to military information on the list of secrets maintained by the Soviet Union." Murray Seeger, "Eye-Witness to Failure," chapter 4 of *The Soviet Worker: From Lenin to Andropov*, Leonard Schapiro and Joseph Godson, eds. (St. Martin's Press, 1984), pp. 77, 78.

As of this writing (March 1996), the prospects for greater official openness about the defense labor force seem dim. An example of the pressure for even greater secrecy is in an article in the official newspaper, *Rossiyskaya gazeta,* in September 1994, which implied that even the number of employees in defense plants constitutes a state secret. Sergei Gorlenko, "Vmesto shifrogramm—ankety. Zachem shpionam shpionit', kogda rossiyane sami vsyo rasskazhut" [Instead of coded messages—questionnaires: Why should spies need to spy, when the Russians themselves are telling everything]," *Rossiyskaya gazeta,* September 3, 1994, p. 3. Gorlenko is not identified in his (signed) article, but it was later revealed by an American journalist that he is a colonel in the Federal Counterintelligence Service (formerly the KGB). Sonni Efron, "Russia Livid over Alleged Spying by U.S.," *Los Angeles Times,* September 7, 1994, p. A1.

2. The Russian term for turnover, *tekuchest'*, includes "departure [*vybytiye*] of one's own volition and dismissal [*uvol'neniye*] on account of (excessive) absenteeism [*progul*] and other violations of labor discipline." Goskomstat SSSR, *Narodnoye khozyaystvo SSSR v 1990 g. Statisticheskiy yezhegodnik* [The national economy of the USSR in 1990: Statistical yearbook] (hereafter *Narkhoz*) (Moscow: Finances and Statistics, 1992), p. 690. The relative proportions between employee-initiated and management-initiated turnover in Russian industry in the late 1980s was 5:1. This can be calculated from data on total turnover in *Narkhoz RSFSR 1988,* p. 362, and on the percentage of the labor force fired for disciplinary reasons in *Statistika sotsial'nykh anomaliy: Statisticheskiy sbornik* [Statistics on social anomalies: Statistical handbook] (Moscow: Goskomstat RSFSR, 1991), p. 139.

3. Sergei A. Belanovsky, *Faktory effektivnosti upravlencheskogo truda v promyshlennosti* [Factors of efficiency of managerial labor in industry] (Moscow: Science, 1988), pp. 83–94.

4. See statistics on industrial turnover in Goskomstat SSSR, *Trud v SSSR. Statisticheskiy sbornik* [Labor in the USSR: Statistical handbook] (Moscow: Finances and Statistics, 1988), p. 258.

5. Ibid., p. 259. Surveys revealed that in the early 1980s more Soviet workers left their jobs because of dissatisfaction with the social benefits offered by their enterprise than because of low wages.

6. Ibid. In the 1980s, 58 percent of workers who quit their jobs in Soviet industry in any given year were under age thirty.

7. The simple comparison of turnover rates in high and low defense oblasts begs the question of whether the observed difference in rates is due to defense industry presence or to other differences in the two groups, such as population size, degree of urbanization, and so on. In an earlier study, I found a positive association between lower rates of turnover and defense industry concentration even when those other variables were taken into consideration. Clifford Gaddy, "Economic Performance and Policies in the Defense Industrial Regions of Russia," in Michael McFaul and Tova Perlmutter, eds., *Privatization, Conversion, and Enterprise Reform in Russia* (Boulder, Colo.: Westview, 1995), pp. 103–136.

8. Goskomstat SSSR, *Trud v SSSR*, p. 258.

9. The figure of 5 million includes both defense- and nondefense-related employment in the defense-industrial complex, plus employees in other industries producing for defense industry. Total employment was an estimated 10 million to 12 million in the mid-1980s; see figure 2-3.

10. Labor market surveys revealed that 3.1 million Russians were subject to "involuntary part-time employment" in October 1993 and 4.8 million in October 1994. Z. Ryzhikova and M. Fidler, "O dinamike i strukture bezrabotitsy v Rossiyskoy Federatsii [On the dynamics and structure of unemployment in the Russian Federation]," *Voprosy statistiki*, no. 2 (1995), pp. 21–25.

11. In principle, these sorts of work-sharing arrangements are not uniquely Russian. Employers in most countries do not simply shed redundant labor as they please when business conditions are poor. One difference is that in other countries the employer is bound by legislation or explicit contractual obligations to have recourse to measures such as short-time work rather than layoffs; in Russia it is to a great extent an informal solution adopted without the support of law or contract. At present, when short-time arrangements are made without paying workers, they are illegal in Russia. The Labor Code [*Kodeks zakonov o trude Rossiyskoy Federatsii*] in its September 25, 1992, version explicitly requires enterprises to pay workers at least two-thirds of their normal pay whenever they are put on leave for work stoppages "for which the [workers are] not at fault" (Articles 91–94). Pravovaya Biblioteka Predprinimatelya, *Kodeks zakonov o trude Rossiyskoy Federatsii* [Labor Code of the Russian Federation] (Moscow: Brandes, 1992).

12. Clifford G. Gaddy, " 'Dead Souls': The Perverse Incentives of Russian Wage Tax Legislation," memorandum, Brookings, March 1994.

13. Of course, to compute true productivity, one would need an accurate measure of output. To the extent that labor is applied in producing goods for which there is no market demand, this too is "hidden unemployment," but of a different kind. This raises the question of whether there is more hidden unemployment in the Russian economy today than before reform.

14. Moreover, there are also cases of what might be called "hidden employment." I have encountered cases where workers may formally have left an enterprise but remain bound to it by an informal contract in which both the firm and the laid-off former employee retain rights and obligations of the employer-employee relationship. That is, the worker lets it be known that he or she is ready to accept reemployment at any time; the firm implicitly promises to rehire him or her if and when business conditions permit. This is similar to situations in the United States,

especially in large corporations that rely on the practice of (formal) fires and rehires to adjust to changes in the product market demand.

15. "Konversiya voyennogo proizvodstva [Conversion of military production]," *Vestnik statistiki*, no. 12 (December 1992), p. 46; Tsentr ekonomicheskoy kon"yunktury i prognozirovaniya, *Rossiya—1993. Ekonomicheskaya kon"yunktura* [Russia—1993: Economic situation], no. 1 (Moscow, 1993), p. 153. It was reported that "half" the workers who left military production in 1992 were reassigned to civilian production.

16. To attempt to infer the relative weight of military and civilian production by looking at output figures is also dangerous. Prices remained skewed, and a good bit of both military and civil output is recorded without having been sold.

17. Between 1979 and 1987, the size of the Russian population of legal working age (ages 16–59 for men and 16–54 for women, inclusive) grew by a minuscule rate of barely more than one-tenth of 1 percent a year. During the previous decade, the rate of growth had been 1.5 percent a year. Computed from data in Goskomstat SSSR, *Naseleniye SSSR, 1987, Statisticheskiy sbornik* [Population of the USSR, 1987: Statistical handbook] (Moscow: Finances and Statistics, 1988), pp. 50–51.

18. Goskomstat RSFSR, *Pokazateli sotsial'nogo razvitiya avtonomnykh respublik, krayev i oblastey RSFSR*, pp. 13–14, shows the age structure of the population of Russia's oblasts. These data can be combined with total population figures for 1980 (*Narkhoz RSFSR 1979*, pp. 7–9) and 1987 (*Narkhoz RSFSR 1988*, pp. 19–21). Perm, for example, shows an absolute drop in the working-age population.

19. Russia's total labor force dropped from 65.6 million in 1980 to 63.9 million in 1990. Industry's share declined from 34.7 percent to 32.9 percent in that same period. *Narkhoz RSFSR 1990*, p. 110.

20. The Russian for layoff is *sokrashcheniye chislennosti* or *shtata rabotnikov;* voluntary termination is *uvol'neniye po sobstvennomu zhelaniyu*.

21. The continuing existence of the labor booklets (in Russian, *trudovaya knizhka*) is one of the remnants of the old Soviet system that inhibit the current labor market. For those Russians who work in what used to be the state sector (though it now may be formally privatized), the labor booklet is still something to take very seriously. An example of how seriously it is taken was given in a newspaper story. Nikolai Maksimov, "Kak ya poluchil zarplatu [How I received my wage]," *Argumenty i fakty*, no. 16 (April 1995), p. 1. A man employed as a watchman at a private warehouse was so upset by the fact that his labor booklet was not properly filled in when he was fired (and that he was not receiving some of the back pay due him) that he barricaded himself in the warehouse and demanded negotiations with management. In the end, he got his pay and had the company record in his booklet that he had not been fired but released "in connection with reorganization of the enterprise."

22. See *Kodeks zakonov o trude Rossiyskoy Federatsii* [Russian Labor Code], article 34, September 25, 1992: "In the event of a layoff, the priority right to retain the job shall be granted to employees with the highest labor productivity and qualifications."

23. There are other ways of concealing layoffs as well: for example, workers can be granted early retirements or fictitious disability pensions. There are some incentives for workers to prefer layoffs to voluntary quits, because workers who are

laid off are entitled to severance pay and unemployment compensation. However, currently both these payments are quite low.

24. Consider, for instance, this statement in an authoritative report prepared in 1993 by an analytic unit of the Russian government: "Earlier, the level of wages in the defense complex was substantially higher than in other sectors, something that facilitated the recruitment of highly skilled labor into its enterprises." *Rossiya—1993. Ekonomicheskaya kon"yunktura*, p. 214.

25. *Sotsial'no-ekonomicheskoye polozheniye Rossii. 1994 g.* (Moscow: Goskomstat, 1995), p. 16.

26. See chapter 6.

27. L. V. Korel' and others, "Konversiya: Poisk optimal'nogo varianta [Conversion: The search for the optimal variant]," *EKO*, No. 12 (December 1993), pp. 14–28. The deputy directors represented seventeen separate enterprises.

28. The predominant use of unofficial job search channels has been reported consistently to me by officials of the oblast employment centers in Chelyabinsk, Perm, Saratov, and Udmurtia for the period 1991–95. Household labor market survey results from Perm in October 1993 showed the following proportions for leading job search methods by unemployed people in that oblast: direct application to enterprise/employer, 38 percent; personal contacts, 31 percent; state employment service, 29 percent. Labor Market Survey data, Perm Oblast Employment Center, October 1993.

29. Malei interviewed by German Lomanov, "Bogach-bednyak [Rich man, poor man]," *Moskovskiye novosti*, no. 8 (February 21, 1993), p. 13A.

30. German Lomanov, "Oboronka teryaet kadry" [Defense complex loses workers], *Moscow News*, business supplement "MN Business," no. 11 (March 14, 1993), p. B11.

31. Ye. Nekipelova, "Emigratsiya i 'utechka umov' v zerkale statistiki [Emigration and 'the brain drain' in the mirror of statistics]," *Voprosy statistiki*, no. 3, 1995, pp. 90–94, table 5 (p. 93). Nekipelova's estimates are based on data from Russian Ministry of the Interior.

Another authoritative set of statistics revealed that in 1993, only 13,000 Russian citizens with higher education emigrated from the country. Of those, about 4,200 were scientists, engineers, or university teachers. Departament nauki i obrazovaniya, "Kommentariy k postanovleniyu no 1261. 'O Mezhvedomstvennoy programme po regulirovaniyu migratsii kadrov iz nauchno-tekhnicheskoy sfery' [Commentary to Decree No. 1261: On the interagency program for regulation of migration of workers from the scientific and technical sphere]," *Ekonomika i zhizn'*, no. 52 (December 1994), p. 9 of the supplement, "Vash partnyer [Your partner]." This is from a nation that in the decade of the 1980s alone graduated almost 5 million people from universities, including more than 2 million engineers. *Narkhoz RSFSR 1988*, pp. 191–92.

Still, the problem was perceived to be so important that in late 1994 the Russian government issued a decree providing for an "interagency" program of measures assigning specific tasks to no fewer than two dozen different ministries, state committees, and other federal agencies to help "regulate" this emigration.

32. There has been a similar, though less pronounced, trend in specialized secondary education.

33. Women make up about 50 percent of the Russian civilian labor force. Their share of the total unemployed was also around 50 percent in 1992, but it has since declined. (It was less than 45 percent in the fall of 1994.) On the other hand, the female share of *registered* unemployed workers—a category that better reflects involuntary unemployment—remained at about 65 percent in 1994 (even though it too is declining). Z. Rukhkova and M. Fidler, "O dinamike i strukture bezrabotitsy v Rossiyskoy Federatsii [On the dynamics and structure of unemployment in the Russian Federation]," *Voprosy statistiki*, no. 2 (1992), pp. 21–25.

Registered unemployment is the number of individuals whose formal applications for unemployment status have been officially recognized by regional employment centers. This notion of unemployment was the only one recognized in Russia until 1993. In October 1993 and again in October 1994, the Russian state statistics office (*Goskomstat*) conducted labor market surveys using the methodology of the United Nations International Labour Office (ILO). These surveys give unemployment data that meet international standards.

34. *Kodeks zakonov o trude Rossiyskoy Federatsii* [Russian Labor Code], article 34, pp. 13–14.

35. Susanne Oxenstierna, *From Labour Shortage to Unemployment? The Soviet Labour Market in the 1980's* (Stockholm: Gotab, 1990), table 7-3, p. 194.

36. Vladimir G. Kostakov, "Labour Surplus and Labour Shortage in the USSR," in Guy Standing, ed., *In Search of Flexibility: The New Soviet Labour Market* (Geneva: International Labour Office, 1991), pp. 81–105.

37. Ibid.

38. The work week for teachers in Russia was 32.8 hours. In 1987, 36.2 percent of employees in education worked fewer than 33 hours a week. *Narkhoz RSFSR 1988*, p. 51. Out of the total female labor force of 34,928,000 in 1987, 4,272,000 worked in education. Thus, if one assumes female education employees' workweeks were distributed the same as the total (women made up 79 percent of all employed in education), that would imply $4,272,000 \div 0.362 = 1,546,000$ women working 33 hours or less. This is $1,546 \div 34,928 = 4.4$ percent of total female labor force.

In Soviet *industry*, 1.8 percent of all workers worked no more than 33 hours a week. Goskomstat SSSR, *Trud v SSSR*, p. 135.

39. Oxenstierna, *From Labour Shortage to Unemployment*, p. 192. Certain mechanisms may have been found to introduce more flexibility into the system. My own study of the Soviet labor market in the 1970s based on household data showed that the excessive rigidity of wages and hours in the Soviet labor market was not in the interest of either workers or managers. They therefore introduced informal mechanisms to make the labor market more flexible. One of those mechanisms was management-condoned "theft of hours," meaning that actual part-time employment was much more prevalent than official figures suggest. That study did not have separate data for defense industries. But it did show that the rate of stolen hours for the machine-building industries was substantially lower than for any other sector of either industry or the rest of the Soviet economy, with the sole exception of education (where the weekly hours are officially only 80 percent of the average across the economy). Clifford G. Gaddy, "The Labor Market and the Second Economy in the Soviet Union," *Berkeley-Duke Occasional Papers on the Second Economy in the USSR*, no. 24 (January 1991).

40. In 1989, Kostakov estimated that the total amount of labor devoted to housework by all members of the Soviet labor force was the equivalent of nearly 80 million full-time workers. Three-fourths of that household labor was by women. V. Kostakov, "Kak my stavim sotsial'nyye tseli [How we pose social goals]," *Kommunist,* November 1989, pp. 56–67 [p. 63]. This implies that women supplied household labor equivalent to (80 million × 0.75) = 60 million full-time workers. The female labor force employed outside the home (including collective farm workers) in the USSR in 1987 was 65.303 million; see Goskomstat SSSR, *Trud v SSSR,* p. 105.

Chapter 8

1. One of the others was Tantal (mentioned in chapter 7). The other, and the largest of the three, was the Saratov Aviation Plant (SAP).

2. Unless otherwise indicated, information on SEPO's history is from Vladimir I. Lifanov, *SEPO: Smelost', entuziazm, poisk, optimizm! K 50-letiyu Saratovskogo ordena Krasnoy Zvezdy elektroagregatnogo proizvodstvennogo ob"yedineniya* [SEPO: Boldness, enthusiasm, initiative, optimism; in honor of the 50-year anniversary of the Saratov Order of the Red Star Electromechanical Production Organization] (Saratov: Volga Book Publishers, 1989).

3. *Istoriya Velikoy Otechestvennoy Voyny Sovetskogo Soyuza 1941–1945* [History of the Great Patriotic War of the Soviet Union 1941–1945], vol. 2 (1963), pp. 148, 500. Cited by Aleksandr I. Pozharov, *Ekonomicheskiye osnovy oboronnogo mogushchestva sotsialisticheskogo gosudarstva* [The economic foundations of the military power of the socialist state] (Moscow: Military Publishing House, 1981), p. 49.

4. Work force percentage engaged in refrigerator production derived from interview material. Rank as third-largest refrigerator manufacturer: "Russian Federation Defense Conversion: Two Enterprises in Transition," case studies prepared by International Finance Corporation in conjunction with Company Assistance Ltd. (Washington, August 1992), p. 44. Total output of refrigerators in Russia in 1988 was about 3.5 million. See Goskomstat RSFSR, *Narodnoye khozyaystvo RSFSR v 1988 g. Statisticheskiy yezhegodnik* [The national economy of the RSFSR in 1988: Statistical yearbook] (Moscow: Finances and Statistics, 1989), p. 417 [hereafter *Narkhoz*].

5. Personal communication from SEPO management, April 1993.

6. Goskomstat Rossii, *Stolitsy respublik, krayevyye i oblastnyye tsentry Rossiyskoy Federatsii v 1992 g.* [Republic capitals, territorial and provincial centers of the Russian Federation in 1992] (Moscow: Republic Information Publishing Center, 1994), p. 86.

7. Ibid., p. 251 (thirty-nine per 1,000 population; family size assumed to be three persons).

8. Ibid., pp. 38, 142, and 144.

9. See Murray Yanowitch, "Schooling and Inequalities," in Leonard Schapiro and Joseph Godson, *The Soviet Worker: From Lenin to Andropov,* 2d ed. (St. Martin's Press, 1984), pp. 135–61. Figures on admissions to higher education are in table 6-2, p. 139.

10. The number of PTU-49 graduates to SEPO is from Lifanov, *SEPO*, p. 110. The number of graduates of all PTUs in the oblast is from Goskomstat Rossii, *Obrazovaniye i kultura v Rossiyskoy Federatsii, 1992* [Education and culture in the Russian Federation, 1992] (Moscow: Republic Information Publishing Center, 1992), p. 166. There were 84 PTUs in Saratov oblast in 1985 (p. 166) with 28,001 graduates (p. 170). Nationwide, 22 percent of PTU graduates were in MBMW (p. 172). If that percentage applies to Saratov, this implies 6,160 graduates in MBMW: $400–500 \div 6,160 = 6.5$ to 8 percent.

11. Goskomstat Rossii, *Stolitsy respublik*, p. 149.

12. Ibid., p. 180.

13. Besides the three big defense plants, only two other Saratov enterprises apparently had more than 10,000 employees, and another half-dozen had between 5,000 and 10,000.

14. Lifanov, *SEPO*, p. 114.

15. Andrei A. Neshchadin, "Zanyatost' i promyshlennaya politika v Rossii" [Employment and industrial policy in Russia], paper presented at the Workshop on the Design and Implementation of a Vocational Education, Training, and Retraining Strategy for Russia's Transition to a Market Economy, cosponsored by the Russian Ministry of Labor and the RAND Corporation, Moscow, March 9–11, 1994.

16. Lifanov, *SEPO*, p. 87.

17. See, for example, the entry for *posyelok* in Vladimir Dal', *Tolkovyy slovar' zhivogo Velikorusskogo yazyka* [The great Russian language explanatory dictionary], 3d ed. (St. Petersburg: M. O. Vol'f, 1903).

18. Janos Kornai, *Economics of Shortage,* vol. B (New York: North-Holland Publishing, 1980), pp. 561–71. Chapter 22 is entitled "Degrees of 'Paternalism'."

19. Paternalism is not a topic to which economists have devoted much attention. For a survey of some Western literature on the topic and discussion of possible parallels with the Soviet/Russian case, see Clifford G. Gaddy, "Notes for a Theory of the Paternalistic Russian Enterprise," paper presented at the conference of the American Association for the Advancement of Slavic Studies, Philadelphia, November 18, 1994.

20. Neshchadin, "Employment and Industrial Policy in Russia."

21. *Narkhoz RSFSR 1988,* p. 38. The category of "manager" [*rukovoditel'*] in Soviet/Russian terminology includes, from highest, director [*direktor*], chief engineer [*glavnyy inzhener*], deputy director [*zamestitel' direktora*], superintendent of a shop [*nachal'nik tsekha*], superintendent of a production section or shift [*nachal'nik uchastka ili smena*], and foreman [*master*]. See Sergei A. Belanovsky, *Faktory effecktivnosti upravlencheskogo truda v promyshlennosti* [Factors of efficiency of managerial labor in industry] (Moscow: Science, 1988), pp. 83, 99.

22. In a sample of fifty-nine enterprises that I tracked for the period 1991 to 1993, the general director was replaced in only eight enterprises. This included all reasons for such a personnel change, including death and retirement; yet it amounts to a rate of less than 7 percent a year. This rate is essentially what would be expected simply as a result of death or retirement, leaving no margin for turnover due to resignations or firings. (A mean tenure before retirement from the position of

general director—fifteen years—would imply an annual turnover rate of 6 to 7 percent for that reason alone.)

23. SEPO's current general director has served since 1980. Tantal's director has been in his position for thirty-four years. Indeed, by mid-1993, Tantal reported no turnover among its top managers at all—despite an overall decline in its work force of 33 percent. Tatyana Krylova, "In-Depth Study of SEPO and Tantal," unpublished manuscript prepared for the U.S. National Academy of Sciences (August 1993), p. 55.

24. *Narkhoz RSFSR 1988,* p. 146. In 1988, the share of all state-financed housing built by enterprises with their own funds rose to 44 percent, from 9.4 percent in 1987; 1988 also marked the beginning of an overall decline in housing construction in Russia that continued until 1993.

25. Lifanov, *SEPO,* p. 168.

26. Ibid.

27. Ed A. Hewett, *Reforming the Soviet Economy: Equality Versus Efficiency* (Brookings, 1988), pp. 340–42.

28. Lifanov, *SEPO,* p. 142.

29. Ibid., p. 169.

30. "Russian Federation Defense Conversion," p. 41.

31. Krylova, "In-Depth Study of SEPO and Tantal," p. 12.

32. Tarja Cronberg, "The Entrenchment of Military Technologies: Patriotism, Professional Pride and Everyday Life under Russian Military Conversion, 1992–1994," in Joseph Di Chiaro III, ed., *Conversion of the Defense Industry in Russia and Eastern Europe,* proceedings of the BICC/CISAC Workshop on Conversion, August 10–13, 1994 (Bonn: Bonn International Center for Conversion, April 1995), pp. 65–75 [p. 72].

33. To measure the true extent of employment in the social sector, we ought to add two other categories of labor to the social sector workers formally employed as such by SEPO. The first includes the numerous nonemployees who worked for SEPO—teachers, medical staff, and many others. The second is the labor supplied to the social sector by many workers who were formally listed as production employees. For instance, production line workers regularly helped build new housing or recreational facilities, even during working hours. Not unexpectedly, this diversion of labor away from manufacturing appears to have increased.

34. Personal communication from SEPO management, April 1993.

Chapter 9

1. A total of twenty-four regions were excluded. In addition to the oblasts in the areas mentioned in the text, I also excluded the cities of Moscow and St. Petersburg (but not their respective oblasts). The division of the remaining forty-nine oblasts into "defense" and "nondefense" is based on the same index as explained in chapter 2 (see endnote 46, pp. 202–203). The twenty-three defense oblasts had a score of 0.62 or higher (with Sverdlovsk as the highest, at 1.70, and

Ryazan as the lowest, with 0.62). The twenty-six nondefense oblasts had scores ranging from 0.55 (Tambov) to 0.05 (Ivanovo). Of the twenty-four excluded regions, only Moscow and St. Petersburg would have been classified as defense regions by this same criterion.

2. Here, we should not be too hasty in attributing the higher infant mortality in defense oblasts to deficiencies in the health care system. If, for instance, defense oblasts were relatively more burdened by other factors contributing to disease and illness—for instance, environmental pollution—even a superior health system might not have been able to compensate.

3. The only sources I have been able to obtain that provide comparable data on a large number of Russian cities give information only on oblast capitals. However, this is not as serious a limitation as it might appear. In contrast with the United States, where the largest cities are usually not state capitals, virtually all of Russia's largest cities are the capitals of their oblasts. Only five of the fifty most populous Russian cities are not capitals.

4. The order within the groups is approximate, as are the employment ranges themselves. The cutoff line for inclusion of cities in the bottom category is particularly arbitrary. Other provincial capitals (Kaluga, Penza) and even a couple of noncapitals (Nizhny Tagil, Kamensk-Ural'skiy) could arguably be included as well.

5. The available data seem to bear out this conclusion even when other analytical approaches are used. In a previous and more detailed statistical study based on oblast data, I used multiple regression methods that took into account the separate statistical effect of factors such as urbanization levels, geographical location, ethnicity, and so on, as well as defense-industry concentration. See Clifford Gaddy, "Economic Performance and Policies in the Defense Industrial Regions of Russia," in Michael McFaul and Tova Perlmutter, eds., *Privatization, Conversion, Enterprise Reform in Russia* (Westview Press, 1995), pp. 103–36.

6. In the sample of 69 Russian capital cities, the correlation between the total population of the city and the average size of the manufacturing enterprise in 1985 was + 0.33. It had dropped to + 0.20 in 1991. Average enterprise size was computed from data in Goskomstat Rossii, *Sotsial'no-ekonomicheskoye razvitiye stolits respublik, krayevykh i oblastnykh tsentrov Rossiyskoy Federatsii. 1992*, pp. 217–18, 231–34 (for total industrial labor force), 15–16 (for number of industrial enterprises). City population data from Tsentral'noy statisticheskoye upravleniye, *Narkhoz SSSR v 1984 godu. Statisticheskiy yezhegodnik* [The national economy of the USSR in 1984: Statistical handbook], pp. 20–25; and Goskomstat RSFSR, *Narkhoz RSFSR v 1990 g. Statisticheskiy yezhegodnik* [The economy of the RSFSR in 1990: Statistical yearbook] (Moscow: Republic Information Publishing Center, 1991), pp. 81–84.

In a sample of 315 U.S. metropolitan areas, the correlation between city size and manufacturing establishment size is − 0.15. This makes for a substantial gap between large and small cities: in the 94 metro areas with populations of more than 500,000, the average manufacturing firm employs 51.7 workers. In the 224 with populations under 500,000, the average establishment employs 61.1 workers. Data from Bureau of the Census, *State and Metropolitan Area Data Book, 1991* (Government Printing Office, August 1991), Table A, Metro Areas, pp. 1–72. The average establishment size is computed by dividing the number of manufacturing employees (total) by the number of establishments. Manufacturing establishment and employee figures are as of 1987; population figures are for 1990.

7. Data in this section on population of Russian cities are taken from Tsentral'noye statisticheskoye upravleniye, *Statisticheskiy spravochnik SSSR, 1927* [Statistical abstract of the USSR, 1927] (Moscow, 1928), pp. 2–3, 21–24; Tsentral'noye statisticheskoye upravleniye, *Narkhoz SSSR v 1965 g.* [The national economy of the USSR in 1965: Statistical yearbook] (Moscow: Statistics, 1966), pp. 30–39; *Narkhoz SSSR 1970*, pp. 37–45; *Narkhoz SSSR 1984*, pp. 20, 25; *Narkhoz RSFSR 1990*, pp. 81–85.

8. For the first four years of the industrialization campaign (from 1929 to 1932), the turnover rate in large-scale industry was well in excess of 100 percent a year—that is, the average worker moved to a new job each year. Alec Nove, *An Economic History of the U.S.S.R.* (London: Allen Lane/Penguin, 1969), p. 197.

9. From a question-and-answer session with Soviet President Mikhail Gorbachev following his speech to workers' representatives in Nizhny Tagil on April 27, 1990. See "[Gorbachev] Responds to Questions," Moscow Television Service, April 28, 1990, in Foreign Broadcast Information Service, *Daily Report: Soviet Union*, April 30, 1990, pp. 112–15. (This episode does not appear to have been covered in the Soviet print media.)

10. One of the most detailed accounts of life in a Soviet industrial city also happens to be about such a "second" city of a defense province. In *Steeltown, USSR: Soviet Society in the Gorbachev Era* (University of California Press, 1991), Stephen Kotkin described the city of Magnitogorsk in Chelyabinsk oblast. There, too, the goal was to get out: to Chelyabinsk or to Sverdlovsk. But that was a goal not often realized. "With rare exceptions," wrote Kotkin, "anyone born in Magnitogorsk could expect to be buried there" (p. 151).

11. "O prave grazhdan Rossiyskoy Federatsii na svobodu peredvizheniya, vybor mesta prebyvaniya i zhitel'stva v predelakh Rossiyskoy Federatsii [On the rights of Russian Federation citizens to freedom of movement and choice of place of residence in the boundaries of the Russian Federation]," *Rossiyskaya gazeta,* August 10, 1993, p. 5.

12. Kronid Lyubarsky, "Otmena krepostnogo prava [Serfdom abolished]," *Novoye vremya,* no. 35 (1993), pp. 8–12.

13. Russian labor market statistics consistently report higher levels of unemployment in rural areas and smaller cities than in the large urban areas. The situation reported for Perm oblast in the spring of 1995 seems to be typical: registered unemployment (see chapter 7 for the definition of that term) in the capital city of Perm was 2.1 percent; in the secondary towns of the oblast, it was 4.4 percent; and in the rural areas, it was 6.3 percent. "Informatsiya ob osnovykh itogakh raboty sluzhby zanyatosti Permskoy oblasti za I kvartal 1995 g." [Information on the basic results of the work of the Perm oblast employment service for the 1st quarter of 1995], Perm Oblast Employment Center, mimeo, no date.

14. Detroit is the U.S. central city with about 1 million population that historically had the image of a rust-belt manufacturing center. Nashville and Louisville, on the other hand, seemed to be suitable to illustrate two different kinds of cities identified by David Rusk as "elastic" and "inelastic" cities in his book, *Cities*

without Suburbs (Washington: Woodrow Wilson Center Press, 1993). Elastic cities are those that grew by filling in vacant land within their city limits and by annexing new land. Inelastic cities were those unable or unwilling to expand their city limits. Nashville (elastic) and Louisville (inelastic) formed one of Rusk's illustrative pairs of cities.

Chapter 10

1. The Russian government does not disclose how the aggregate data on defense production are computed. But Western estimates of Russian defense production bear out at least the general trend depicted in figure 10-1. The Ministry of Defence of the United Kingdom, for instance, estimates that between 1991 and 1994, the decline in production of several major weapons systems by Russian military industry was as follows:

Weapons system	1994 level (percent of 1991 level)
Main battle tanks	4.4
Infantry fighting vehicles	13.3
Bombers	< 17
Fighters/fighter ground attack	22.2
Strategic missiles	25.0

Source: U.K. Ministry of Defence estimates cited in International Institute for Strategic Studies, *The Military Balance 1995/96* (London: Oxford University Press, 1995), table 5, p. 110.

2. S. Burkov, V. Gusev, and V. Ilyukhin, "Defense Industry Privatization Results—Nothing to Write Home About," *Birzhevyye vedomosti*, no. 23 (1995), pp. 1, 7, cited in Raymond C. Sikorra, *Post–Cold War Defense Conversion in the U.S. and Russia: A Comparative Approach*, Ph.D. dissertation, Indiana University, March 1996, p. 53.

3. These are figures for actual deliveries of arms. Pavel Fel'gengauer, "Spetseksport: Nadezhdy na mnogomilliardnyye dokhody ot torgovli oruzhiyem sovershenno ne opravdalis' [Special exports: Hope for multibillions in revenue from arms sales proven completely false]," *Segodnya*, November 24, 1995, p. 2. Fel'gengauer, a veteran observer of Soviet and Russian military affairs, is skeptical about the Russian government officials' claims of $2.5 billion in exports (deliveries) in 1995. He points out that year after year, those officials make excessive forecasts.

4. Russia's leading exports in the first half of 1995, for instance, were oil and oil products ($8.4 billion), natural gas ($5.7 billion), iron and steel ($3.5 billion), aluminum ($1.9 billion), and timber ($1.0 billion). V. Chernyshev, "Vneshnyaya torgovlya Rossii v I polugodii 1995 goda [Russia's foreign trade in the first half of 1995]," *Ekonomika i zhizn'*, no. 40 (October 1995), p. 28.

5. "Pridut li investitsii v Rossiyu? [Will investment come to Russia?]," interview with Yury V. Petrov, chairman of the State Investment Corporation, in *Ekonomika i zhizn'*, no. 41 (October 1995), p. 37.

6. This motive for joining with a Russian partner is generally expressed more euphemistically. A recent article aimed at American companies looking to do business in Russia lists as the first reason why a joint venture would be desirable the possibility that a Russian partner can provide "valuable help in navigating through Russian bureaucracy." Carl F. Fey, "Success Strategies for Russian-Foreign Joint Ventures," *Business Horizons*, vol. 38 (November–December 1995), pp. 49–54.

7. Alexei Shulunov, "Strukturnaya perestroyka v oboronnykh otraslyakh. Yest' li ona? [Structural transformation in defense branches: Does it exist?]," *Ekonomika i zhizn'*, no. 32 (August 1995), p. 1.

8. Burkov and others, "Defense Industry Privatization Results," pp. 1, 7, in Sikorra, "Post–Cold War Defense Conversion."

The percentage of defense enterprises that have been fully privatized is roughly the same as for nondefense enterprises. The former acting head of the State Property Committee (GKI), Al'fred Kokh, has estimated that by the beginning of 1996 approximately 38 percent of Russia's 33,000 medium-size and large former state enterprises would have no state ownership at all. N. Mitrofanova, "Sud'ba Privatizatsii-95 reshayetsya na finishe goda [The fate of Privatization-95 will be decided at year-end]," *Ekonomika i zhizn'*, no. 44 (November 1995), p. 1.

9. This requirement was stipulated in the August 1993 decree on defense industry privatization (see chapter 5).

10. One example is a law, effective April 1995, which stipulates that defense enterprises (and other establishments dealing with state secrets), regardless of ownership status, will have to have special security officers approved by the FSB—Federal Security Service—to serve that function. This has been interpreted as a revival of the old "First Departments" of the KGB at enterprises. "Chekisty vozvrashchayutsya k zavodam [Chekists come back to plants]," *Moskovsky komsomolets*, April 21, 1995, p. 1.

11. A decree of November 1993 had promised that the current management would vote for the state shares (see chapter 5).

12. A particularly clear example of *Goskomoboronprom*'s bias is its role in the privatization fight at the giant aircraft engine manufacturer, Rybinsk Motors, in Yaroslavl oblast. Voting the state's 37 percent share, the *Goskomoboronprom* representative on the company's board allied with management to prevent sale of shares to outsiders. He argued that such a sale would jeopardize national security. See Andrei Serov, " 'Rybinskiye Motory' as the Engine of the Defense Industry's Privatization," *Kommersant-Daily*, August 19, 1995, pp. 1, 2, translated in *EVP Press Digest*, August 19, 1995 (electronic version, part 2), and numerous later articles in the Russian press.

13. At least one major industrial city, Chelyabinsk in the Urals, has already acted to prevent enterprises from abandoning their social responsibility. In the fall of 1995, the mayor of that city issued a decree banning the sale of social assets from any enterprise without permission from the mayor's office. "Chelyabinskim predpriyatiyam zapreshcheno prodavat' sotsial'no znachinyye ob"yekty [Chelyabinsk enterprises prohibited from selling socially significant facilities]," *Finansovyye izvestiya*, November 3, 1995, p. 2.

14. The programs are named for the principal sponsors of the legislation, Senators Sam Nunn (D-Ga.) and Richard Lugar (R.-Ind.). A summary and as-

sessment of the Nunn-Lugar programs and other Western aid related to Russia's defense sector may be found in Kevin P. O'Prey, *A Farewell to Arms: Russia's Struggles with Defense Conversion* (New York: Twentieth Century Fund Press, 1995), pp. 84–92.

15. Although funded by the U.S. government, TUSRIF is chartered to operate as a private investment firm that can provide capital (both equity and loans) and technical assistance to Russian and Western companies in Russia. TUSRIF was established in May 1985 through a merger of two previously existing institutions, the Fund for Large Enterprises in Russia and the Russian-American Enterprise Fund.

Glossary of Russian Terms

barshchina In old Russia, the labor that had to be performed by Russian peasants for their lord; similarly, the Soviet military-industrial complex could appropriate anything produced (including scientific and technical discoveries) by the civilian sector if it was perceived to have any potential military value.

brak Junk, substandard items. Under the Soviet system large quantities of a good would be produced, and the military would choose only a small amount of the item that met its quality standards; the rejected *brak* would then be passed to the civilian producer goods sector and finally to the civilian consumer goods sector.

fakul'tet Department in a university or other academic institution.

glasnost' Term given to Mikhail Gorbachev's policy in the late 1980s of increasing freedoms of speech, expression, and the press; usually translated "openness" in English, the term also means "publicity." *Glasnost'* allowed, among other things, unprecedented criticism of defense policy and the defense industry.

Glavnoye tekhnicheskoye upravleniye (GTU) Main Technical Administration of the Ministry of Foreign Economic Relations. One of three departments of the MFER responsible for arms exports in the Soviet era. Transformed into the Russian arms trading firm *Spetsvneshtekhnika* in early 1992.

Goskomimushchestvo (GKI) State Committee for the Management of State Property; the ministry-level state privatization agency.

229

Goskomoboronprom   State Committee for the Defense Sectors of Industry, the successor of the old Soviet VPK; upgraded to a state committee from *Roskomoboronprom* in September 1993.

Goskomstat   State Committee on Statistics.

Gosplan   Soviet-era State Planning Committee.

gospriyemka   Literally, "state acceptance"; term for the quality control system instituted by Gorbachev and Lev Zaikov in 1987; *gospriyemka* attempted to transfer the quality control techniques that had been used by the defense industry (see *voyennyy predstavitel'* and *brak*) to the civilian sector.

gosudarstvennyye strategicheskiye rezervy   Literally, "state strategic reserves"; stockpiles of major raw materials and finished goods maintained by the Soviet government in peacetime; included minerals and oil products, food, rails, rolling stock, and so on.

investitsionnaya tekhnika   Literally, "investment goods"; roughly equivalent to capital or producer goods.

konstruktorskoye byuro (KB)   Design bureau.

kray   One of several types of administrative-territorial units in the Russian Federation; usually contain within their borders one or more autonomous *okrugs* and have traditionally had relatively more autonomy than an *oblast,* but less than a republic.

mobilizatsionnyye zapasy   Mobilization stockpiles; the production capacity that defense plants are required to have available on site for quick mobilization in an emergency.

nalazhivat'   Set up; arrange; adjust; *nalazhivat' proizvodstvo* is to organize production. Suggests the process of adjusting a machine so that it can turn out the products for which it was designed.

nauchno-issledovatel'skiy institut (NII)   Scientific research institute.

nauchno-proizvodstvennoye ob"yedineniye (NPO)   Literally, "scientific production association"; amalgamation of manufacturing enterprises, research institutes, and design bureaus in a single organization.

nomenklatura   The Communist party elite.

oblast   The main type of administrative territorial division in the Russian Federation; traditionally, oblasts have had less autonomy than republics or krays.

perestroika   Restructuring; term for Mikhail Gorbachev's policies of economic reform. Was also the term used by military economists such as Andrei Lagovsky to describe the transfer of the economy to a wartime footing. Verb, *perestroit'*.

po ostatochnom printsipe   Literally, "according to the residual principle"; a reference to the process whereby the defense industry had first choice of raw materials, capital goods, and labor resources—the remaining sectors of the economy were then allocated whatever was left, "according to the residual principle."

posyelok   In Soviet usage, a housing area surrounding a major factory, mine, or the like, with a population of 3,000 or more, of which at least 85 percent are manual or office workers or members of their families. Historically referred to a group of peasants, usually related by blood, who had left the main village and founded a new community on nearby communal land. Plural, *posyelki*.

professional'no-tekhnicheskoye uchilishche (PTU)   Professional-technical school; a trade school in which the emphasis is on learning a trade and significant time is spent in apprenticeship.

promyshlenno-proizvodstvennyy personal (PPP)   Literally, "industrial production employees"; includes manual workers, apprentices, engineering and technical personnel, office employees (including management), junior service personnel, and guards. Not included: employees of the enterprise's nonindustrial activities—for example, farms, kindergartens, and hospitals.

propiska   Residence permit; established in 1932 (reviving a Tsarist-era system), mandatory registration of residence of all Soviet citizens; used to control and steer labor to priority regions.

rayon   District or borough; administrative-territorial region within an oblast or large city. Plural, *rayony*.

Roskomoboronprom   Russian Committee for the Defense Sectors of Industry, one of several committees for industrial branches created in early 1992 from a short-lived Ministry of Industry; *Roskomoboronprom* replaced the former Military-Industrial Commission (VPK), with eight departments that exactly duplicated the structure of the old VPK. In September 1993, it was elevated to a state committee, *Goskomoboronprom*—essentially equivalent to a ministry.

smezhnik   Manufacturer of subcomponents to a main assembly plant; "subcontractor." Plural, *smezhniki.*

tekuchest'   Labor turnover; includes "departure [*vybytiye*] of one's own volition" and dismissal [*uvol'neniye*] for absenteeism or other misconduct.

trudoustroystvo   Job placement.

trudovaya knizhka   Passport-like document containing record of an individual's job history; used as a mechanism to control labor.

ukaz   Edict.

uskoreniye   Acceleration; Gorbachev used the term to mean "accelerated economic development."

voyennyy predstavitel'   Literally, "military representative" (also called *voyenpred*); military officer who served as a quality control inspector in a defense plant. Plural, *voyennyye predstaviteli.*

Voyenno-promyshlennaya komissiya (VPK)   Military-Industrial Commission (see figure 2-2, p. 17); VPK may also stand for *voyenno-promyshlennyy kompleks* (military-industrial complex).

Voyenno-promyshlennaya investitsionnaya kompaniya (VPIK) Military-Industrial Investment Company.

zavod-unikum   Literally, "one-of-a-kind plant"; a single plant responsible for the nation's entire output of a given product. Plural, *zavody-unikumy.*

Acronyms

GDP   Gross domestic product

GKI   State Committee for the Management of State Property (also *Goskomimushchestvo*); Russia's "privatization ministry"

GRU   Main Intelligence Directorate (*glavnoye razvedyvatel'noye upravleniye*) of the General Staff; military intelligence

GTU   Main Technical Administration (*glavnoye tekhnicheskoye upravleniye*)

ILO   International Labor Organization

KB   Design bureau (*konstruktorskoye byuro*)

LKEI   Lockheed-Khrunichev-Energiya International

MBMW   Machine-building and metalworking (industrial sector)

MFER   Ministry of Foreign Economic Relations

NII   Scientific research institute (*nauchno-issledvatel'skiy institut*)

NPO   Scientific production association *(nauchno-proizvodstvennoye ob''yedineniye)*

PPP   Industrial production employees (*promyshlenno-proizvodstvennyy personal*)

PTU   Trade school (*professional'no-tekhnicheskoye uchilishche*)

SAP   Saratov Aviation Plant

SEPO   Saratov Electromechanical Production Organization
         (*Saratovskoye elektroagregatnoye proizvodstvennoye ob"yedineniye*)

VPIK   Military-Industrial Investment Company (*Voyenno-
         promyshlennaya investitsionnaya kompaniya*)

VPK   Military-Industrial Commission (*Voyenno-promyshlennaya
         komissiya*)

Who's Who

Akhromeyev, Sergei   Marshal of the Soviet Union, chief of the Soviet General Staff, 1984–88; advisor to Mikhail Gorbachev, December 1988–August 1991. Committed suicide in August 1991 after being implicated in the August 19 attempted coup against Gorbachev.

Baklanov, Oleg   Leading Soviet defense-industry official. Deputy minister, first deputy minister, and minister of general machine-building (missile and space industry) of the USSR (1976–88); secretary of the Communist Party Central Committee for the military-industrial complex (1988–91); deputy chairman of the Defense Council (1991); one of the conspirators in the attempted coup against Mikhail Gorbachev.

Borovoi, Konstantin   Leading Russian capitalist; president of the Russian Raw Materials and Commodities Exchange. Cofounded the Military-Industrial Investment Company (VPIK) in the fall of 1991.

Chernomyrdin, Viktor   Prime minister of the Russian Federation since December 1992; formerly Soviet minister of the gas industry (1985–89) and chairman of state concern *Gazprom* (1989–92); deputy prime minister for the fuel and energy complex (May–December 1992).

Chubais, Anatoly   Leading Russian reformer; chairman of the State Committee for the Management of State Property (GKI) (November 1991–November 1994); deputy prime minister (June 1992–November 1994); first deputy prime minister (November 1994–January 1996).

Gaidar, Yegor   Leading Russian reformer; minister of economics and finance, 1991–92; acting prime minister of the Russian Federation (June–December 1992); first deputy prime minister (September 1993–January 1994).

Glukhikh, Viktor   Chairman of the Russian Committee for the Defense Sectors of Industry (*Roskomoboronprom/Goskomoboronprom*) from October

235

1992 to January 1996; previously, first deputy minister of industry of the Russian Federation (1990–92). Replaced in January 1996 as director of *Goskomoboronprom* by Zinovy Pak.

Grachev, Pavel   Russian defense minister since May 1992; formerly commander of Soviet airborne troops (December 1990–August 1991).

Kokoshin, Andrei   First deputy defense minister of the Russian Federation (since 1992), dealing with procurement, conversion, and military-technical issues. The first civilian to serve as a deputy defense minister. Formerly deputy director of the Institute for USA and Canada (1984–92).

Lagovsky, Andrei   Military economist; author of *Strategy and Economics* (1957), key work that stressed the need to prepare in peacetime for the rapid mobilization of defense production during wartime.

Malei, Mikhail   Leading defense-industry official; advisor to President Boris Yeltsin on conversion questions, 1991–93. In September 1993 named chairman of the Security Council's Interdepartmental Commission for Scientific and Technical Issues of the Defense Industry. Previous career in defense industry. Formerly head of the GKI and deputy prime minister, 1990–91.

Ogarkov, Nikolai   Marshal of the Soviet Union; chief of the Soviet General Staff, 1977–84. Strongly emphasized technological development as a factor in modern war and advocated reorganizing the structure and management of the Soviet economy to ensure rapid transition to wartime production. Removed from office in September 1984.

Pozharov, Aleksandr   Military economist and author of *The Economic Foundations of the Military Power of the Soviet State* (1981). Stressed the "mobility" of the economy—that is, its ability to adapt rapidly to changing needs.

Romanov, Grigory   Rival to Gorbachev for leadership of the USSR in the mid-1980s. First secretary of Leningrad City Communist Party organization, 1970–83; secretary of the Communist Party Central Committee, 1983–85; member of the Politburo, 1973–85; forced into retirement after Gorbachev became general secretary.

Ryzhkov, Nikolai   Gorbachev's senior economic policymaker; career in defense-related industry in Sverdlovsk (Yekaterinburg), culminating in directorship of the giant *Uralmash* enterprise. Formerly secretary of the Communist Party Central Committee (1982–85) and prime minister of the Soviet Union (1985–91); ran unsuccessfully for president of the Russian Soviet Federated Socialist Republic against Yeltsin in 1991. Advisor to Military-Industrial Investment Company (VPIK).

Shlykov, Vitaly   In the Soviet era, official of military intelligence (GRU).

Shulunov, Aleksei   President of the League of Assistance to Defense Enterprises (the main lobbying organization of the defense industry) since 1992; general director of Pleshkova Scientific and Production Group.

Silayev, Ivan   A leader in Gorbachev's government, head of the Machine-Building Bureau; career in defense industry in Gorky (Nizhny Novgorod), culminating in general directorship of an aviation plant; USSR deputy prime minister, 1985–90; RSFSR prime minister, June 1990–September 1991.

Sokolov, Sergei   Soviet defense minister, 1984–87. An opponent of Gorbachev's policy to tighten military spending. Forced to resign in May 1987.

Tizyakov, Aleksandr   Defense industry manager; general director of the Kalinin Machine-Building Plant in Sverdlovsk (Yekaterinburg) and president of the USSR Association of State Enterprises and Industrial, Construction and Communications facilities until 1991. One of the members of the emergency committee in the attempted coup against Mikhail Gorbachev.

Yablokov, Aleksei   Advisor to President Yeltsin on questions of ecology and health (1991–93); since 1993, chairman of the Security Council's Interdepartmental Commission for Ecological Security.

Zaikov, Lev   A leading advocate of Gorbachev's policy of *uskoreniye* and of the *gospriyemka* quality control campaign. Appointed secretary of the Central Committee of the CPSU for the military-industrial complex in 1985, replacing Grigory Romanov; career in defense industry in Leningrad (St. Petersburg).

Index

Accelerated development. *See Uskoreniye*

Aeroflot (Soviet airline), proposal to purchase foreign aircraft, 41

Aerospace industry: use of titanium, 102; role in establishing VPIK, 87–88. *See also* Aviation industry; Missile industry

Afghanistan: Soviet war in, 52

Agriculture: artificial development to serve defense industry, 168; defense enterprise (SEPO) involvement in, 131, 132, 134, 144. *See also* Food; Rural areas

Agricultural lobby, as rival of defense industry for budget funds, 97

Aircraft. *See* Aviation industry

Akhromeyev, Sergei: succeeds N. Ogarkov as Soviet chief of general staff, 55; in Who's Who, 235

Aluminum: as leading Russian export, 174; and military quality control, 42–43; accusations of dumping on world markets, 100; consumption and production in West and Soviet Union, 99–100; exports from Russia/Soviet Union, 100–104; industry response to market reform, 99–104. *See also* Nonferrous metallurgy

Andropov, Yuri: on importance of economic strength, 49; head of Soviet Communist Party, 53, 56

Arms control agreements, in Brezhnev era, 50

Arms exports. *See* Exports, military

Åslund, Anders, on *gospriyemka* campaign, 59

Austro-Prussian War (of *1866*), lessons for military economy, 34–35

Aviation industry: defense-complex ministry, 17; wartime production rate, 35; military standards for civilian equipment, 41; mobilization reserves, 38; quality control of aluminum, 42–43; military output levels in *1994*, 226n

Backup manufacturing systems. *See* Duplication of manufacturing

Baklanov, Oleg: role in August 1991 coup attempt, 66; in Who's Who, 235

Baltic republics, role in Soviet defense industry, 68

Bankruptcy, and defense enterprises, 170–71

Barshchina (labor-service duty): as metaphor for defense-industry demands on civilian science, 44; in Glossary of Russian Terms, 229

Barter, and Soviet military exports, 91–92

Bashkortostan, as leading defense-industry region, 149, 151. *See also* Ufa

Belarus, Soviet defense industry in, 18–19

Belkin, Viktor, on Soviet practice of designing civilian products for military use, 41

Benefits. *See* Social services; Paternalism

Bolsheviks, and military industry, 32

Borovoi, Konstantin: role in VPIK, 87; in Who's Who, 235

Brain drain: from Russia, 125; from defense industry, 125–26, 181

Brak (junk): items rejected by military quality control, 42–43, 58, 60; in Glossary of Russian Terms, 229. *See also* Gospriyemka; Quality control